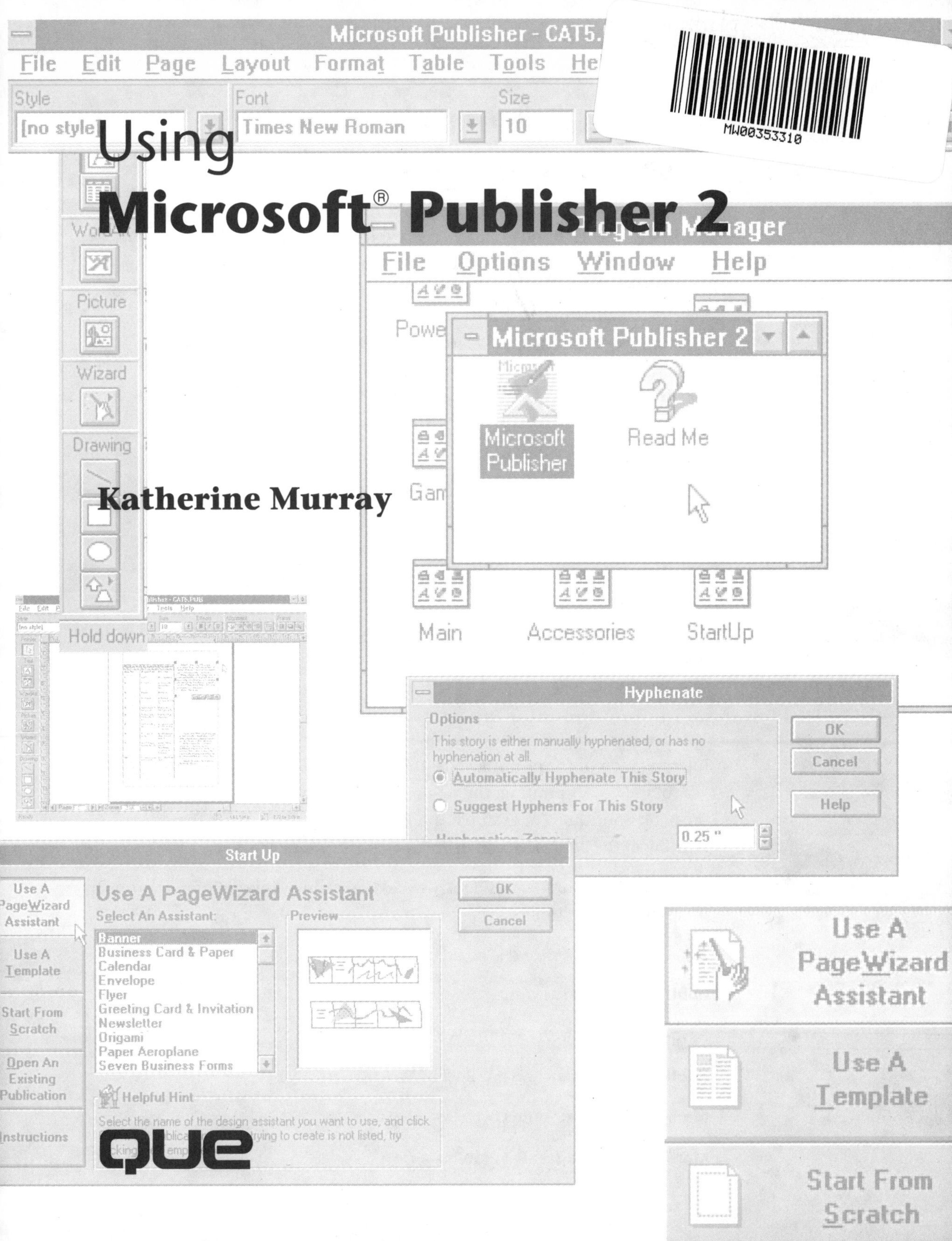

Using
Microsoft® Publisher 2
Katherine Murray
que
MW00353310
Microsoft Publisher - CAT5.
File Edit Page Layout Format Table Tools He
Style
[no style]
Font
Times New Roman
Size
10
Program Manager
File Options Window Help
Microsoft Publisher 2
Microsoft Publisher
Read Me
Main
Accessories
StartUp
Hyphenate
Options
This story is either manually hyphenated, or has no hyphenation at all.
Automatically Hyphenate This Story
Suggest Hyphens For This Story
0.25 "
OK
Cancel
Help
Start Up
Use A PageWizard Assistant
Select An Assistant:
Preview
Banner
Business Card & Paper
Calendar
Envelope
Flyer
Greeting Card & Invitation
Newsletter
Origami
Paper Aeroplane
Seven Business Forms
Helpful Hint
Use A Template
Start From Scratch
Open An Existing Publication
Instructions
Use A PageWizard Assistant
Use A Template
Start From Scratch

Using Microsoft Publisher 2

Library of Congress Catalog No.: 94-65329

ISBN: 1-56529-284-7

96 95 5 4

Interpretation of the printing code: the rightmost double-digit number is the year of the book's printing; the rightmost single-digit number, the number of the book's printing. For example, a printing code of 94-1 shows that the first printing of the book occurred in 1994.

Screen reproductions in this book were created using Collage Complete from Inner Media, Inc., Hollis, NH.

Using Microsoft Publisher 2 is based on Version 2.0.

Publisher: David P. Ewing

Associate Publisher: Corinne Walls

Publishing Director: Lisa A. Bucki

Managing Editor: Anne Owen

Marketing Manager: Ray Robinson

Dedication

To TLW.

Credits

Publishing Manager
Thomas H. Bennett

Acquisitions Editor
Thomas F. Godfrey III

Product Director
Kathie-Jo Arnoff

Product Development Specialist
Ella Davis

Production Editor
Lori A. Lyons

Editors
Michael Cunningham
Noelle Gasco
Lynn Northrup

Technical Editor
Todd Knowlton

Book Designer
Amy Peppler-Adams

Cover Designer
Dan Armstrong

Acquisitions Assistant
Lisa Dickinson

Editorial Assistants
Theresa Mathias
Jill Stanley
Michelle Williams

Production Team
Gary Adair, Brad Chinn, Kim Cofer, Meshell Dinn, Mark Enochs, Stephanie Gregory, Jenny Kucera, Beth Rago, Marc Shecter, Kris Simmons, Greg Simsic, Carol Stamile, Robert Wolf

Indexer
Greg Eldred

Composed in *Stone Serif* and *MCPdigital* by Que Corporation

About the Author

Katherine Murray is the president of reVisions Plus, Inc., a writing and desktop publishing company that deals primarily with the development and production of computer-related materials. She is the author of over 30 computer books, including Que's *Introduction to Personal Computers* and *Using PFS: First Publisher*.

Acknowledgments

Thanks to Tom Godfrey, Lisa Bucki, Lori Lyons, Noelle Gasco, and Todd Knowlton for their help in putting together a timely, effective, and accurate book. And thanks, as usual, to Doug, Kelly, Christopher, and Cameron, who know what life is like when "Mom's got a deadline" and all chip in to get things done.

Trademarks

Contents at a Glance

Contents

II Working with Text 93

IV Finishing the Publication 229

10 Finishing the Layout 231

11 Printing the Publication 255

V Professional Techniques 271

12 Publisher Design Tips 273

Introduction

Today's Microsoft Publisher—Version 2.0—marks the arrival of a new software philosophy: "Let us do it for you." Yesterday's programs may have included good help systems, easy-to-use features, and a variety of flexible tools, but today's programs automate as much of our tasks as possible. Microsoft knows that we don't have hours and hours to spend at our desks, working a single flyer or business card. Time is at a premium, and we need our programs friendly, flexible, and *fast*.

Even though Publisher was a good program in its premiere version, Publisher 2.0 goes beyond making publishing *easy*—now the program will create your documents for you, if that's what you want. And then, after you add a few tricks of your own, Publisher will go back through and check your layout to make sure that you haven't missed something. And *then*, when you print, Publisher helps you solve any printing problems.

If you prefer the up-to-your-elbows approach to publishing, Publisher helps you get in there and do the task by providing a number of on-line help features. Cue Cards and Quick Demos show you the steps for often-used procedures before you try them yourself. Automated tools, like BorderArt, the Clip Art Gallery, and the Shape tool, with its palette of choices, help make adding art easier than ever before.

Publisher is the desktop publishing program for you if you don't know what desktop publishing is all about, don't really care, and just need to get this brochure printed fast. Publisher is also for the creatively inclined—people responsible for the corporate newsletter, business owners wanting to design a new business card or logo, staff members with little or no design experience who need to design and create a cool company newsletter.

What Is Microsoft Publisher?

Microsoft Publisher is a desktop publishing program that enables you to create short publications such as newsletters, booklets, brochures, flyers, business cards, invitations—and almost any other document you can dream up.

Unlike most other desktop publishing programs, Microsoft Publisher comes with everything you need to produce a finished publication. Need artwork? Publisher includes a set of art images—known as *clip art*—that you can use in your own publications. Want to produce a high-quality printout? Publisher supports your PostScript printer and includes a variety of fonts. Feel a little insecure about designing your own publication? Microsoft Publisher includes *PageWizards*—interactive page-design utilities—that can do everything for you.

What Are the Advantages of Microsoft Publisher?

If you are new to desktop publishing, you'll be amazed at the number of steps automating the process will save you. In that respect, *any* desktop publishing program has advantages. Microsoft Publisher, however, has some special advantages to help you produce your publications:

- A built-in word processor that enables you to add and edit text easily
- A 120,000-word spelling checker
- The capability to easily link columns and pages of text
- Support for a wide variety of graphics files
- Support for most popular word processing file formats
- A library of fonts
- Measurements in inches, picas, or centimeters
- Over 100 pieces of clip art

- Support for all Windows-supported printers
- Capability to import charts and data from Microsoft Works

Right off the bat, Microsoft Publisher proves wrong the old adage "There are no new ideas." In addition to including all the basic desktop publishing features—text and graphics layout, spacing options, font support, pull-down menus, mouse capabilities, and more—Microsoft Corporation added some terrific new features that significantly reduce the time and trouble users spend on their publications:

- A *PageWizard* is a kind of interactive publication generator. Microsoft Publisher comes equipped with 17 different PageWizards, which assemble your publication for you as you answer a series of questions. Whether you want to create newsletters, public relations materials, greeting cards, business forms, or a variety of other publications, a PageWizard can help you design and create the publication with a minimum of effort. PageWizards are explained fully in Chapter 3.
- *WordArt* is a feature that enables you to use text as graphics in your Publisher document. Want to curve letters? Do you need to create a special effect using your company's logo? WordArt gives you the special boost you need to turn text into a graphic element. See Chapter 7 for more about WordArt.
- *Publisher templates* help you create publications from pre-built samples. Use the layout already designed for you, plug in your own text and art, and print. You also can create and save your own templates using Microsoft Publisher. For more information, see Chapter 3.
- *BorderArt* is a special set of art with more than 100 border styles. If you are fond of bordering your publications, you won't have to go out of your way to create eye-catching borders; they are already in the program for you. Chapter 9 explains more about BorderArt.

- Logo Creator Plus is a special logo-design PageWizard that helps you create a logo with a unique look for your company or department. For more information on Logo Creator Plus, see Chapter 8.
- The new Layout Checker goes through the publication you have created and makes sure that there are no design problems—empty frames, overflowing text boxes, overlapping information. Chapter 10 tells you how to use the Layout Checker.
- The new Print Troubleshooter asks "Did your publication print as expected?" If you answer No, the Troubleshooter leads you through series of steps aimed at helping you resolve the problem. For more information about the Print Troubleshooter, see Chapter 11.

Why Do You Need a Book on Microsoft Publisher?

Wouldn't it be nice if knowledge just came to us as we were sitting at our desks looking out the window? Unfortunately, it doesn't happen like that. We have to investigate things. We have to try—and sometimes fail. We have to load programs, fiddle around with the mouse, open menus, click options, and feel our way around a program before any of it starts sinking in. In fact, research shows that most of us refuse to look in the program documentation—even when we're stuck—because we want to discover our own answers.

Even though Microsoft Publisher is far from the most complicated desktop publishing program on the market, it does involve a learning curve. Yes, the entire slant of the product—in fact, all Windows-type programs—is friendly and easy to use; but there still will be times when you want to do something you can't quite figure out or have questions you need to answer. *Using Microsoft Publisher 2* is meant to be a friendly, example-oriented text that will accompany your Publisher experience.

Who Should Read This Book?

If you are involved in desktop publishing projects, if you suspect you may someday wind up with publishing on your list of priorities, or if you simply want to find out what all the desktop publishing fuss is about, you'll find basic publishing information in this book that will give you insight into the advantages of electronic publishing. Specifically, if you have purchased or are considering the purchase of Microsoft Publisher, this book will be invaluable in helping you find your way through this simple but feature-laden program. This book speaks to readers of varying skill and experience levels, including

- Professionals who need to publish high-quality documents quickly
- Support staff personnel who are responsible for doing corporate reports
- Public relations people who need snazzy, attention-getting press releases
- Business owners who want to produce creative business cards and letterhead
- Corporate personnel who publish newsletters and other documents
- Home or business users interested in producing other publications such as calendars, cards, invitations, and so on

Whether you're new to computers or you've used a computer for years, you'll find that the features in Microsoft Publisher—and the examples in this book—enable you to produce effective documents quickly. With just a small time investment, you'll find yourself cranking out high-quality, professional-looking publications.

What Is in This Book?

This section shows where you can find what is in *Using Microsoft Publisher 2*.

Part I

Part I, "Getting Started," starts at the beginning and gives you some background on the mysterious workings of desktop publishing software. You also learn how to start and exit Publisher and create an instant publication—(See? You're being productive already!)—with a PageWizard or template file. Finally, you learn the basics of working with the Publisher files you create.

Chapter 1, "What Can You Do with Microsoft Publisher?" explains what desktop publishing software can do, what specifically Microsoft Publisher does, and how Publisher compares with other desktop publishing programs. It also provides an overview of Publisher features.

Chapter 2, "Starting Out with Publisher," explains many of the features you will use often in your Publisher experiences. Topics include understanding the work area, using various tools, opening menus and selecting options, and learning to use a mouse and keyboard. Additionally, you learn how to work with dialog boxes and find out about new Version 2.0 items like Cue Cards, first-time help, and Quick Demos.

Chapter 3, "Instant Publications: PageWizards and Templates," shows you the fast way to produce a published piece. With a PageWizard or a tempate, you can rely on the expertise of Microsoft to design the document for you. Add a few phrases (or paragraphs), and print.

Chapter 4, "Working with Publisher Files," teaches you how to open new files, retrieve existing files, save files, make backup copies, and save files under a different name. This chapter also gives you an overview of different types of text and graphics you can import and export with Publisher.

Part II

Part II, "Working with Text," helps you concentrate on the text aspect of your publication. You learn to enter text and import text from other applications. You are introduced to editing basics and utilities like the Spelling Checker. You also learn to enhance and fine-tune the text in your publication.

Chapter 5, "Entering Text," explains the basic procedures for getting text into the publication. This chapter shows the basics of typing text (including all necessary keys) and highlights the importation process for popular word-processing files.

Chapter 6, "Editing and Formatting Text," includes basic editing techniques, including using the spelling checker, linking frames, and editing frame content (keys and commands to use).

Chapter 7, "Enhancing Text," covers the tasks you might use to enhance the text you've entered: changing text attributes, fonts, and alignment. Additionally, you learn about setting leading and kerning, using tabs, and using indents (also bulleted lists). Also in this chapter, you're introduced to Publishers WordArt feature.

Part III

Part III, "Working with Pictures," lets you concentrate on adding special visual impact with clip art or imported art images. You also learn to edit the art pieces you add to your publications.

Chapter 8, "Adding Pictures," introduces the concepts of bit-mapped and object-oriented art, explains the clip art packaged with the program, and covers graphics files imported into Publisher. You also learn how to create frames, place graphics, and use the graphics tools. Additionally, you experiment with Logo Creator Plus and Microsoft Draw.

Chapter 9, "Modifying Pictures," covers resizing, moving, copying, pasting, and deleting graphics. You also learn about cropping graphics, controlling spacing, and BorderArt (the set of more than 100 predrawn borders for use in publication graphics).

Part IV

Part IV, "Finishing the Publication," helps you focus on the overall effect of your publication. Is the layout what you expected? How can you make it better? Finally, you can print the publication to see the final result.

Chapter 10, "Finishing the Layout," helps you evaluate the publication you've created thus far. You learn to use the Layout Checker to fix any potential layout problems. Reviewing for text and graphics placement, alignment, and effectiveness helps you determine whether your publication meets its goal.

Chapter 11, "Printing the Publication," includes basic printing techniques, such as setting up the printer, making sure you're ready to print, and going through the basic print routine. Additionally, you learn to use the automated Print Troubleshooter to help you decipher any unexpected printer hangups.

Part V

Part V, "Professional Techniques," brings up a library of design and support issues. What should you keep in mind as you create a newsletter? What will you do with the publication after you print it? These and other issues are dealt with in this final part of the book.

Chapter 12, "Publisher Design Tips," includes some basic design issues you may want to consider as you begin creating your own newsletters, brochures, flyers, or other publications.

Chapter 13, "Turning Your Publication into a Finished Product," tells you about various items that will come in handy when you have your publication professionally printed. How can you find a good printer? Should you have the publication professionally printed or photocopied? This chapter provides guidelines for finishing things off.

Chapter 14, "Publisher Troubleshooting Tips," gives some advice for various problems you may run into while working in the trenches with Publisher. Are frames giving you fits? Is layout layering a problem? You may find your answer here.

Chapter 15, "Publication Ideas," is a visual chapter showing a variety of publications based on PageWizards, templates, and original ideas. Callouts are placed to call your attention to specific design items.

Finally, this book concludes with an appendix that tells you how to install Publisher, if you haven't already done so. A glossary at the back of the book is your resource for looking up unfamiliar words and phrases.

Now that you're through with the warm up, you're ready to get down to the business of publishing.

Conventions Used in This Book

The conventions used in this book have been initiated to help you learn to use Microsoft Publisher quickly and easily.

Information that you are to type (generally found in examples with numbered steps) is indicated by boldface type. For example: Type **win** at the C:> prompt to start the Windows program.

Names of menu items are shown with the initial letters capitalized. Options and buttons also appear with initial capital letters. For example:

> File Print

Underlined letters in menu, option, or button names that are shortcut key letters are displayed in boldface type. For example:

> Choose **F**ile, **P**rint. The Print dialog box appears.

Messages and prompts that appear on-screen are printed in a `monospace` font.

This book contains special project tips that provide advice and information to help save you time and make your publications look more professional.

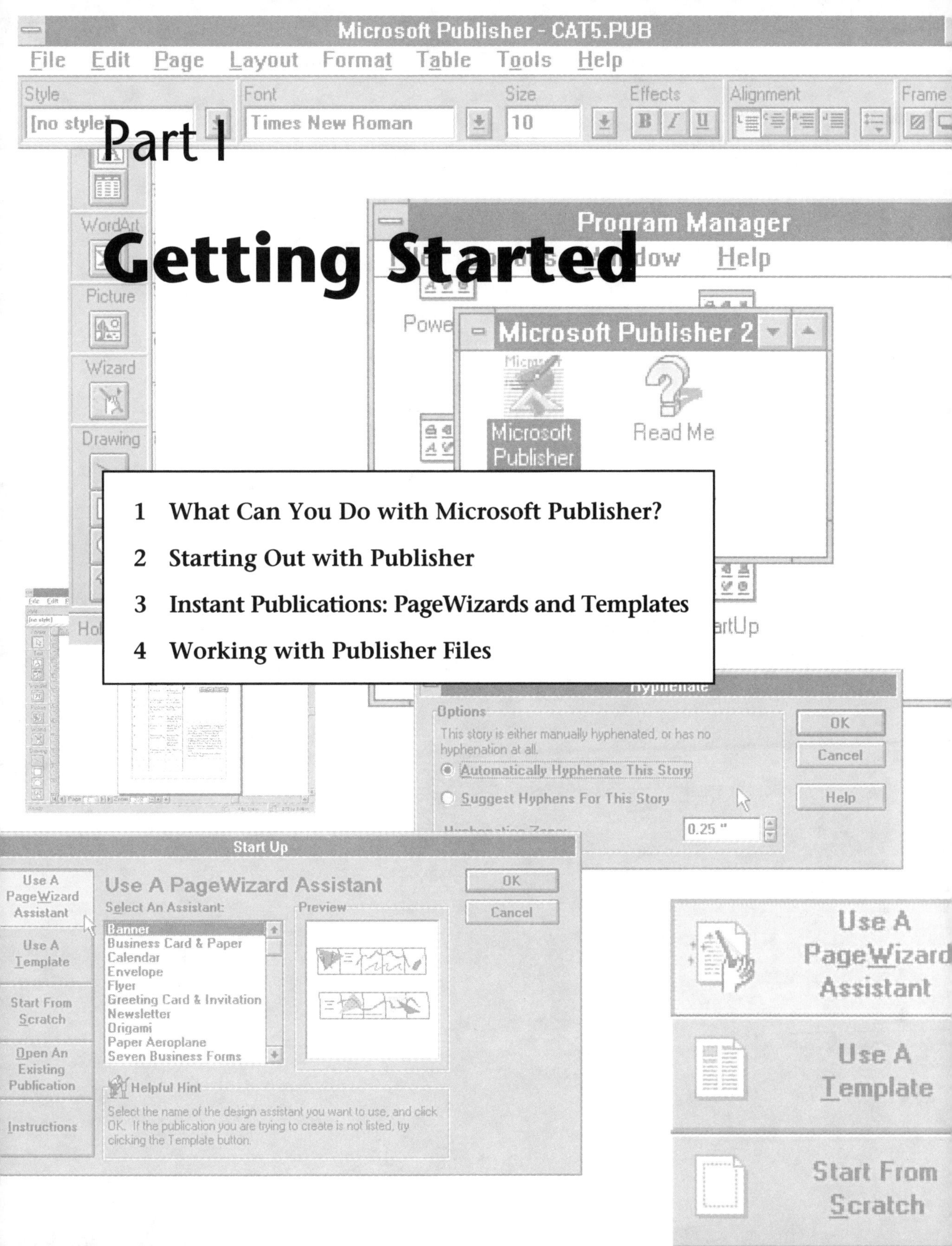

Part I

Getting Started

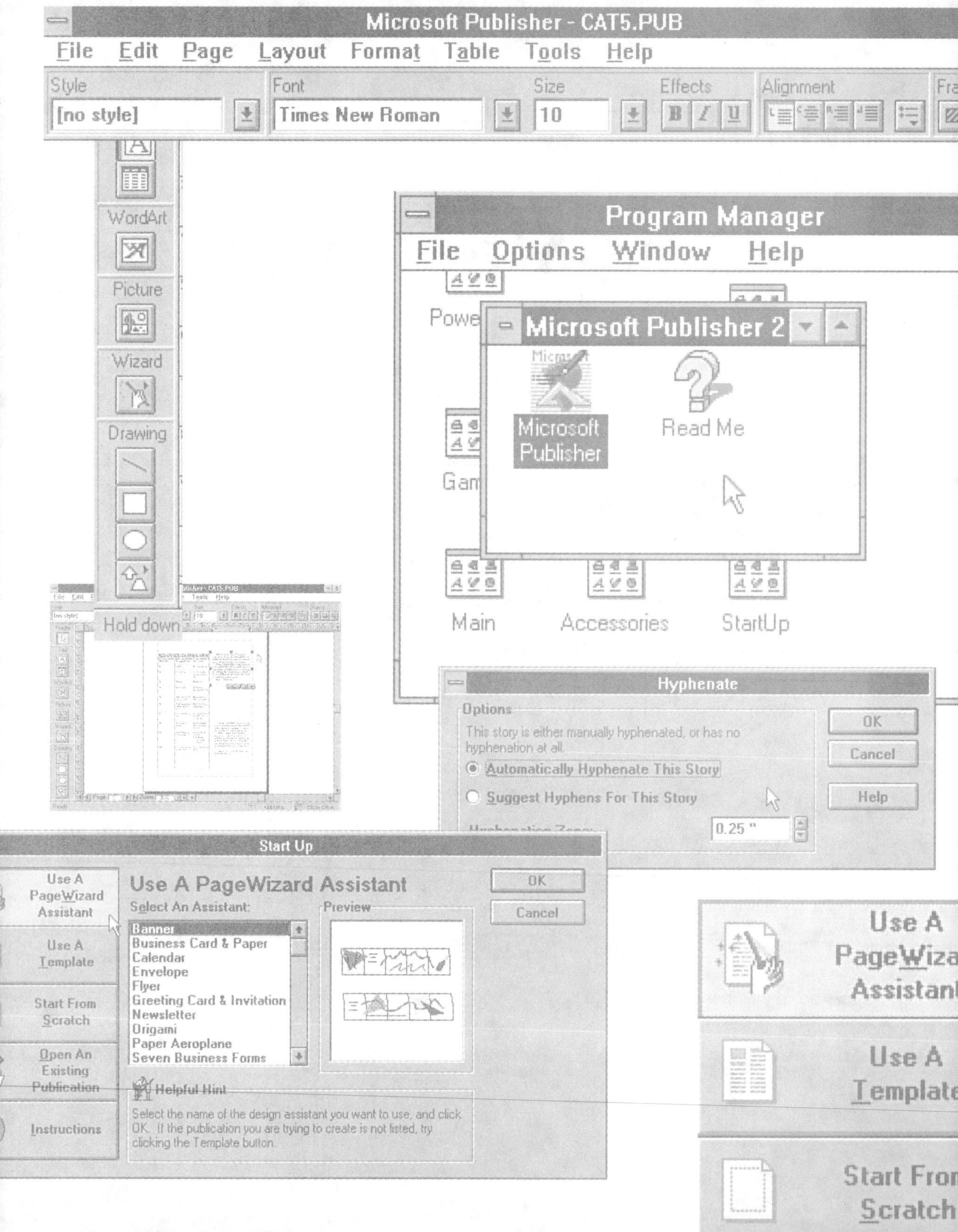

Microsoft Publisher - CAT5.PUB
File Edit Page Layout Format Table Tools Help
Style
[no style]
Font
Times New Roman
Size
10
Effects
Alignment
WordArt
Picture
Wizard
Drawing
Hold down
Program Manager
File Options Window Help
Microsoft Publisher 2
Microsoft Publisher
Read Me
Main
Accessories
StartUp
Hyphenate
Options
This story is either manually hyphenated, or has no hyphenation at all.
Automatically Hyphenate This Story
Suggest Hyphens For This Story
0.25 "
OK
Cancel
Help
Start Up
Use A PageWizard Assistant
Use A Template
Start From Scratch
Open An Existing Publication
Instructions
Use A PageWizard Assistant
Select An Assistant:
Preview
Banner
Business Card & Paper
Calendar
Envelope
Flyer
Greeting Card & Invitation
Newsletter
Origami
Paper Aeroplane
Seven Business Forms
OK
Cancel
Helpful Hint
Select the name of the design assistant you want to use, and click OK. If the publication you are trying to create is not listed, try clicking the Template button.
Use A PageWiza
Assistan
Use A Template
Start From Scratch

Chapter 1

What Can You Do with Microsoft Publisher?

Hey—welcome aboard. Whether this is your first experience with Microsoft Publisher or you've been a Version 1.0 enthusiast for a while, you'll find that the new features in Version 2.0 make Microsoft Publisher easier to use than ever. Let's add some punch to those publications.

In this chapter, you explore the following topics:

- The basics of desktop publishing
- Publisher steps for creating a publication
- Publisher highlights

The smell of rubber cement is one of those things you can file away as a past memory—Microsoft Publisher lets you mix and match all the elements you need, right there on-screen. With a little help from the pros and a little ingenuity, you can create your first publication just minutes after starting the program for the first time.

If you're anxious to get started, you might want to skip ahead to Chapter 2, where you begin your hands-on work with Microsoft Publisher. The next section slows down the pace a little and takes you on a leisurely tour of desktop publishing basics.

Tip
Using a desktop publishing program—specifically, Microsoft Publisher 2.0—can keep too many cooks from spoiling the broth. You can do everything yourself and have fun in the process.

A Desktop Publishing Primer

Sue's company was a small, four-person operation that dealt with the corporate communications of larger companies. She and her staff met with various clients, proposed, and wrote quarterly and annual reports, public relations materials, and press releases. Part of Sue's responsibility was to make sure that the materials were produced professionally—with clear, high-quality text and stunning graphics.

Depending on the work flow, Sue relied on the help of two or three typesetting companies to help her get the final product done in time for delivery to her client's office. She prepared the materials, sent everything to the typesetter, and then waited—sometimes as long as one or two weeks—to see the first draft of pages. Then, after her approval, she had to wait again while the materials were sent to the commercial printing company. The entire process—done conventionally—required Sue to give up the control of the project and keep her fingers crossed that the typesetting companies could deliver the publications in the time promised. If the typesetters or the printers missed their deadlines, Sue missed her deadlines.

Tip
Time is a precious commodity—especially when you need to have something printed commercially. By creating your own publications, you free yourself from having to rely on other peoples' deadlines.

With desktop publishing capabilities, Sue can do all of her publishing tasks in-house. She can lay out the publication, add graphics, modify text and art, and print page proofs. When she is ready to send the publication to the printer, she simply sends it (some printers even have the capability to receive publication files over the phone). No more extended delays—no more waiting for page proofs. Desktop publishing helps Sue maintain ultimate control of her projects and ensures that they are finished on time.

What Is Desktop Publishing?

Tip
Desktop publishing lets you mix text and artwork—whether it's original or clip art—to create publications on your personal computer.

When you get down to the nuts and bolts of it, what exactly is desktop publishing? Put simply, *desktop publishing* is the process of putting together publications—from simple fliers to complex annual reports—on your computer. Right on your desktop, you can create text and graphics and control special design elements, such as the number of columns, amount of white space, and size and placement of headlines. Without waiting for anyone else or relying on outside contractors (such as typesetters) to finish your work, you retain the ultimate control of your project.

The Publishing Process with Microsoft Publisher

In the last section, you learned about desktop publishing in general. This section gives you a bird's-eye view of the publishing process you will experience as you use Microsoft Publisher. Basically, the process involves the following steps:

1. Designing the publication
2. Choosing the layout
3. Adding text
4. Adding graphics
5. Finishing the layout
6. Printing the publication

Depending on the complexity of your project, these steps may take you an hour or a week. One of the benefits Publisher can offer you is in drastically reducing the time from concept to creation. You can envision the project this morning and have it in your hands this afternoon.

For simple projects, you can write the text, create simple art (or use Publisher's clip art), and lay out the publication quickly. For longer projects, you may have to spend more time on the creation of text and graphics, but the layout process should go relatively quickly. And if you're not too keen on the idea of designing the publication yourself, you can use a PageWizard or use one of the 35 professionally designed templates for the basis of your project.

The following sections explain each of the steps in the publishing process and some of Publisher's special features that help you in each stage.

Designing the Publication

Before you begin creating the publication, you need to spend some time thinking about your publication. Whether you plan in your head, on paper, or on-screen, ask yourself these kinds of questions:

- What type of document am I producing?
- How many columns do I want?
- Will I use photos?

- Do I need to create my own art?
- Who will read this publication?
- What type of look will my readers expect?

Tip
Out of time? PageWizards can design your document for you, right before your eyes. Just answer a few simple questions and you're in business.

Or, if you don't have time to spend on the design stage, you can rely on the expertise of Publisher's experts to design publications for you. PageWizards create the documents you select, right before your eyes. Templates give you the basic publication, and all you do is plug in the text and art.

If you're doing your own design from scratch, at least initially, you may find it helpful to sketch out the design for the publication. Suppose that you are doing a newsletter for a study group. You're not sure how many columns you want or where the art would look best. You could sketch out two or three designs (one with two columns, one with three columns, and one with three on top and two on the bottom) and then choose the one that looks best.

If you're letting Publisher help you with the design, simply choose a PageWizard. Figure 1.1 shows the Start Up PageWizard Assistant screen (this appears when you first start Publisher). If you want to choose a PageWizard after working with the program for a while, click the Wizard button on the left side of the screen (see fig. 1.2).

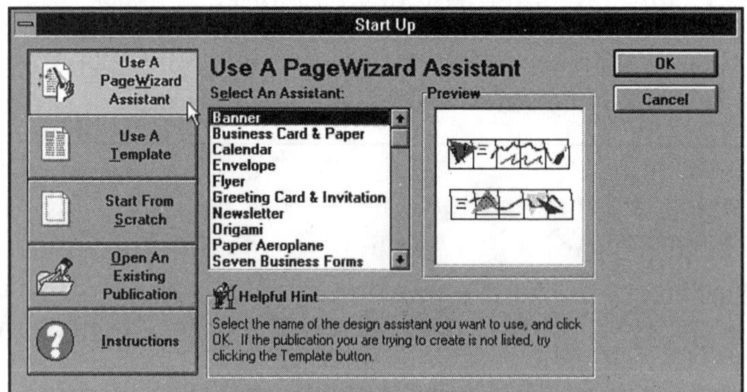

Fig. 1.1
You can let a PageWizard do the design work for you.

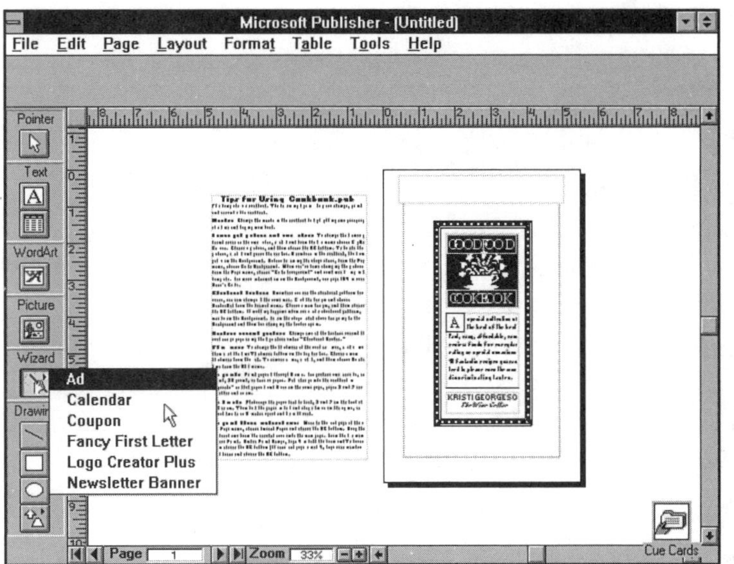

Fig. 1.2
You can select a PageWizard even after working with Publisher for a while.

Building the Layout

After you decide on the basic design of the publication, you need to choose a layout type. First, however, you choose the unit of measure you want to use (picas, inches, points, or centimeters) and select the printer you will use to print the publication later.

You then can choose the basic layout type for your publication. You use the Page Setup dialog box (choose Page Setup from the Page menu to display it) to choose a publication layout, select paper size, and choose orientation.

Publisher makes it simple for you to create a variety of publications easily. For example, you can create

- Newsletters
- Brochures
- Fliers
- Greeting cards
- Books and manuals

- Posters
- Banners
- Business cards
- Index cards

In some publications, you may want certain design elements to appear on every page. Microsoft Publisher gives you the option of placing repeating elements on the background page of the publication. The background page is like a page-behind-the-page, storing any design elements—such as a logo, company name, or page number—that you want to appear on every page of your publication.

Adding Text

After you choose the layout type and answer any necessary questions, you're ready to add text. With Publisher, you have the option of typing text directly into the document or importing text you create outside the program. As you know, Publisher accepts files from many popular word processing programs. This means that you can create the text (or have someone else create it) and then use the text in your Publisher document. Microsoft Publisher accepts files from the following word processing programs:

Plain Text
Plain Text (DOS)
RTF
Microsoft Word 6.0
WordPerfect 5.x for Windows
Windows Write 3.0 and 3.1
Word for Windows 1.x and 2.x
Word for DOS
WordPerfect 5.x
Works for DOS
Works for Windows 2.0 and 3.0

The first step in adding text involves creating a *text frame* (see fig. 1.3). You use frames to store all the elements in your Publisher documents—whether you're working with text, graphics, headlines,

lines, or anything else. Everything you put on your Publisher publication goes in a frame. After you create the frame, you can add text or graphics.

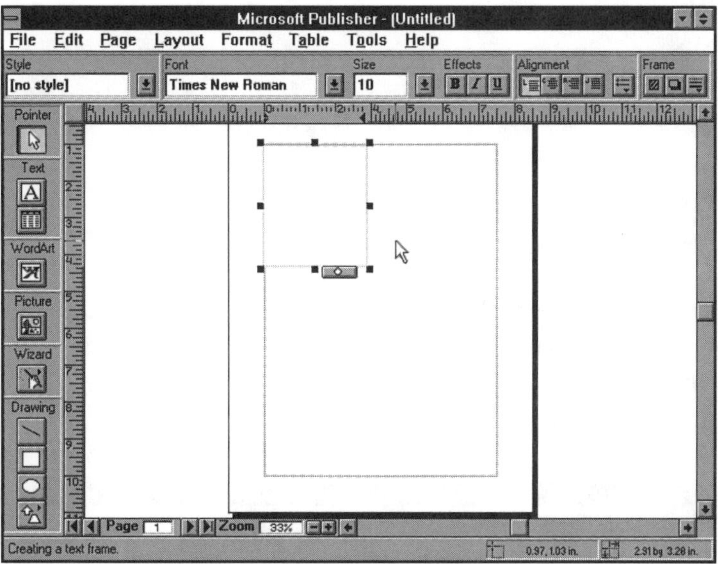

Fig. 1.3
All text goes in a text frame.

Publisher refers to the text blocks you enter or import as *stories*. You can connect, move, resize, duplicate, or delete text frames. You can change the *margin* (amount of white space around text) within the frame. These are just a few of the text-manipulation options: you also can edit the text, use the 120,000-word spelling checker, change the spacing of words and letters, change the font, use WordArt to add special effects to text, and much more. Figure 1.4 shows an example of text in a WordArt graphic.

Adding Graphics

After you place the text, you can add the artwork. Publisher comes with over 100 pieces of clip art that you can use in your own publications. Figure 1.5 shows a piece of clip art that appears on-screen in full color. You then can resize and work with the art to fit your publication. Additionally, Publisher has a set of art tools you can use to create your own graphics. If neither of those options meets your needs, you can create graphics in another program and use the files in your Publisher document.

Publisher accepts graphics files in the following formats:

BMP
CGM
DRW
EPS
PCD
PCX
TIFF
WMF
WPG

Similar to placing text, you place graphics (known as *pictures* in Microsoft Publisher) into picture frames. You also have the option of using different options to resize, move, duplicate, or delete picture frames.

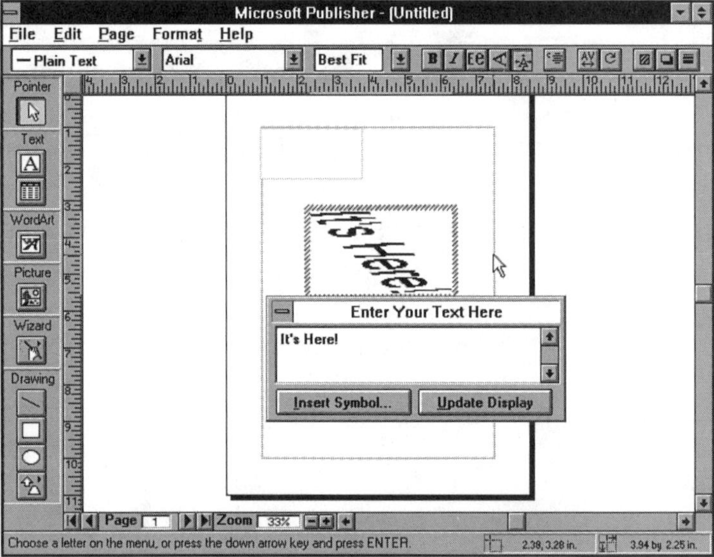

Fig. 1.4
Text skewed by using WordArt.

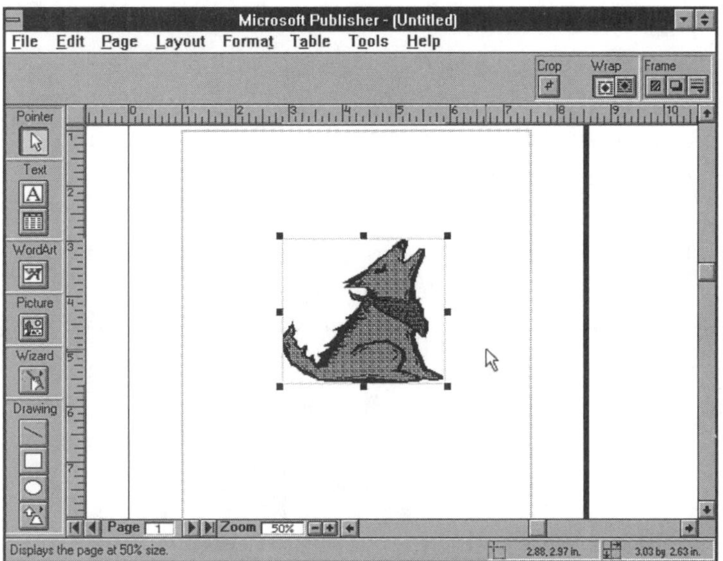

Fig. 1.5
An example of Publisher clip art.

Finishing the Layout

After you have the text and graphics set in the basic layout, you have some fine-tuning to do. Are you happy with the amount of white space around the text and graphics? Do you need to move the pictures or change the placement of a headline? Are the fonts appropriate? As you finish the layout, you consider the big picture: how the publication looks as a whole.

Publisher even includes a special layout checker you can use to make sure that you have things where you want them. You start the layout checker by choosing Check Layout from the Tools menu. When Publisher completes the check, a message box appears (see fig. 1.6).

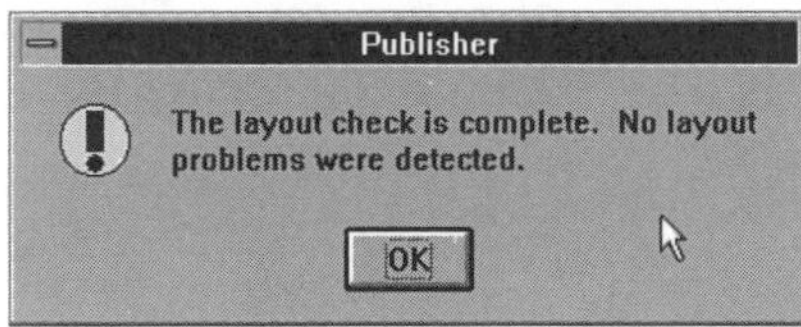

Fig. 1.6
Publisher can check the layout for you.

Printing the Publication

The final step in the Publisher process is printing the publication. By simply choosing the **P**rint command from the **F**ile menu, and then selecting a few options in the Print dialog box, you can have Publisher send your creation to the printer (see fig. 1.7). You can choose from a variety of options, such as the number of pages you want to print, the quality you want (low or high resolution), the number of copies, whether you want to collate the printed copies, and whether you want to include *crop marks* on the printed pages. (Crop marks are small marks in the outer margin of the page that the printer uses to align and trim the finished publication.)

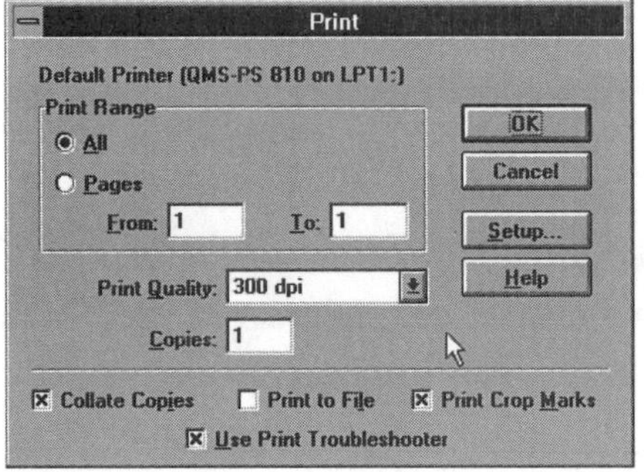

Fig. 1.7
Printing is easy in Publisher.

Version 2.0 includes the Print Troubleshooter, which helps you determine what happened (or what to do) if printing goes awry.

Now What?

After you have the publication in hand—edited, proofed, and printed—you have only one decision to make: what will you do with it? You may want to take the publication to a commercial printer for duplication, or you may want to copy it and send copies yourself. As another option, you could print copies yourself—on your own printer—but this can be time-consuming for large printings.

After everything is done, take a minute to congratulate yourself. You are a desktop publisher.

Publisher Highlights

Now that you know the basic process of desktop publishing with Microsoft Publisher, you can learn why Publisher is so popular for small business and home publishing. Besides the fact that Publisher is simple to learn and use, it also includes a number of special features other programs cannot claim:

- PageWizards
- Templates for creating Publisher documents
- WordArt
- BorderArt
- Publisher tutorial
- Microsoft Draw
- Logo Creator Plus
- Cue Cards
- Quick Demos
- Layout checker
- Print Troubleshooter

PageWizards walk you through the process of designing a publication, and all you have to do is answer a few simple questions. Publisher then assembles the document right before your eyes and displays it so that you can add text and graphics.

Templates are predesigned publications of many different kinds that let you benefit from the expertise of other Publisher designers. Version 2.0 includes over 35 templates that you can use for your own publications.

WordArt lets you do tricks with your text—turn it sideways vertically, curve it, display it upside-down, or even wrap it in a circle. By creating a WordArt frame and choosing the font and format you want for the text, you have flexibility with letters not possible in comparable programs.

BorderArt is a set of borders that the makers of Publisher have already created for you. With over 100 different predesigned borders, you can bring additional creative touches to your documents (see fig. 1.8).

Fig. 1.8
A border from Publisher's BorderArt.

Another Publisher perk is the colorful Introduction to Publisher—an interactive tutorial that leads you through the basics of publishing with Microsoft Publisher.

Microsoft Draw is a new addition with Version 2.0 of Publisher. Now you can create that piece of art—whether it's a border, a chart, or some other graphic element—and then bring the art directly into your publication without ever leaving Publisher. When you choose Insert O**b**ject from the **E**dit menu and Microsoft Draw, Publisher takes you right into the drawing program (see fig. 1.9).

Logo Creator Plus is actually a special PageWizard that helps you create your own logo (see fig. 1.10). Whether you want a classic, modern, or jazzy logo, Publisher can do it for you—fast.

Cue Cards are special on-screen help items you can display to help you learn procedures your first time out. When you start Publisher for the first time, the Cue Cards appear automatically on the right side of the screen (see fig. 1.11). You can choose to leave Cue Cards on, turn them off for this publication, or turn them off entirely.

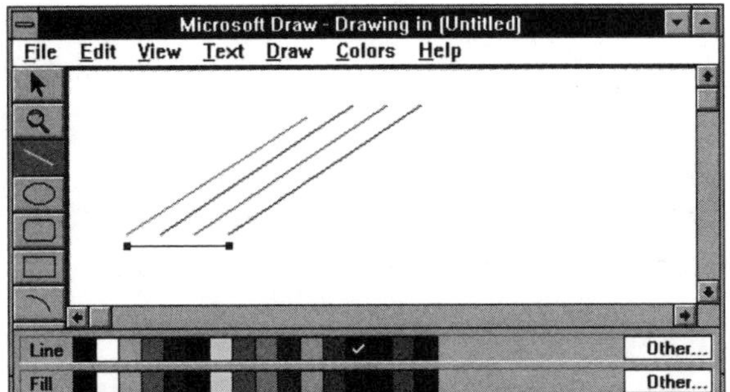

Fig. 1.9
Microsoft Draw in Publisher.

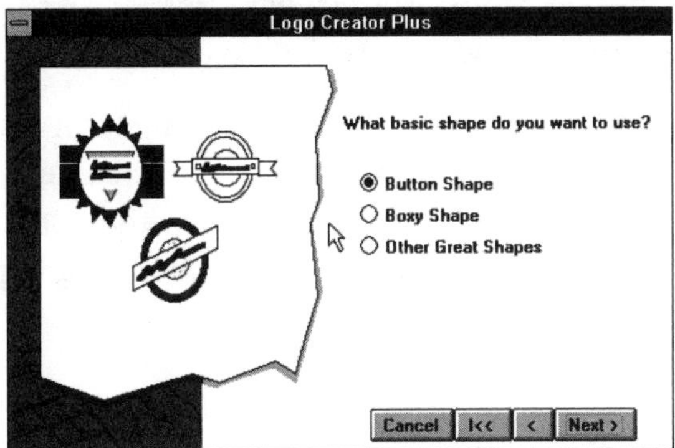

Fig. 1.10
Create your own logo by using a PageWizard.

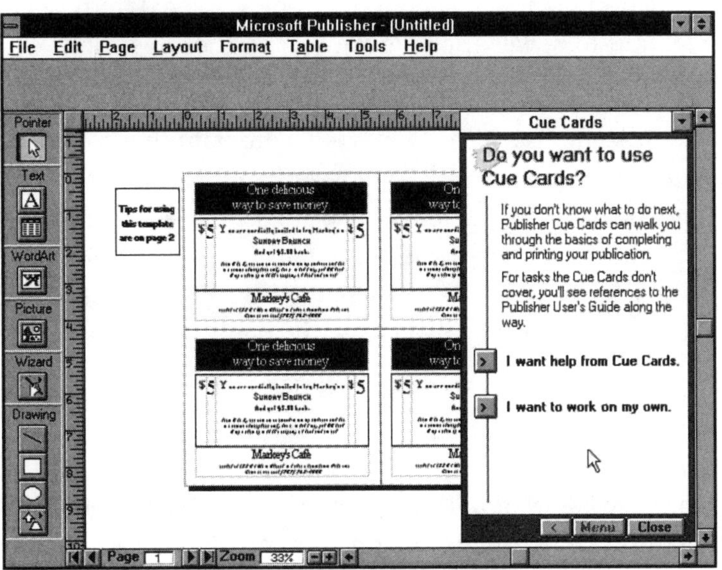

Fig. 1.11
Publisher Cue Cards.

Quick Demos are short, introductory lessons to a variety of often-performed tasks. Publisher asks you whether you want a Quick Demo the first time you try a new procedure, and you can choose whether to go ahead with the demo now or wait for another time. If you choose to wait, you can select the demo you want by choosing Quick **D**emos from the **H**elp menu at a later time.

The Layout checker is a feature new with Version 2.0. After you get everything in place just the way you want it, you can open the T**o**ols menu and choose Check **L**ayout. Publisher then goes through the publication and checks for various layout errors; if a problem is found, Publisher makes suggestions for correcting it.

The Print Troubleshooter keeps you from getting hung up on the printing part of the process. Before you print a document, make sure that the Use Print Troubleshooter checkbox (in the Print dialog box) is selected. When Publisher prints your document, the Troubleshooter helps you identify the cause of any problems.

From Here...

For information directly related to the topics covered in this chapter, you may want to review the following sections of this book:

- Chapter 3, "Instant Publications: PageWizards and Templates." In today's do-it-fast world, having a program that creates publications for you is a great benefit. By using Publisher's PageWizards, you can let Publisher assemble a project from the elements you choose yourself. If you choose a Publisher template, you benefit from the design talents of graphics arts experts. Either way, you can create the publication fast.

- Chapter 8, "Adding Pictures." No publication is complete without some kind of graphics—whether the art appears in the banner, the headline, the photos, or the page number backgrounds. Learn the basics of putting together your own artwork with Microsoft Draw and find out how to modify clip art included with Publisher.

- Chapter 12, "Publisher Design Tips." Facing a blank page is pretty scary, at first. If you've never designed a publication before, how do you know where to start? PageWizards and templates will help, but what do you do when you're on your own? This chapter lists design considerations for different types of common publications.

Chapter 2

Starting Out with Publisher

Anxious to get started? This chapter gives you a whirlwind tour of Windows basics and shows you the ins and outs of Microsoft Publisher.

In this chapter, you learn to do the following tasks:

- Get around in Microsoft Windows
- Start a Publisher work session
- Work with Cue Cards
- Explore the screen area
- Use Undo and get help

This chapter assumes that you have Microsoft Windows installed on your computer. If you haven't already done this, consult the user's manual that was packaged with your Windows program for complete installation instructions. The next section takes you through many of the basic operations you will use as you work with Microsoft Windows and Publisher.

Windows Basics

If you have never used Microsoft Windows and you have just purchased Microsoft Publisher, you have two programs to learn at once. But don't panic; it's not going to be as difficult as it sounds.

Microsoft has designed all its programs that run under Windows to have the same look and feel so that once you learn the basic Windows techniques, you can apply that knowledge to all programs that run in Windows. Publisher is one of those programs.

After you learn the simple techniques for working with the mouse, menus, and windows, you will never have to learn those techniques again; the techniques are the same in Publisher. In this section, you find step-by-step instructions for Windows basics—tasks that you will find yourself repeating often as you create your Publisher documents.

What Is Windows?

First, what is Microsoft Windows? Windows is a program that helps you organize and work with different programs. Each program runs in a different section of the screen, graphically shown as a *window*.

Depending on the amount of memory available in your computer, you can have several programs running at once, which enables you to switch between applications without exiting one and starting another. Moving between programs is simple, working with files is simple, and the menus and basic operations (such as printing, selecting files, choosing options, and so on) are the same from program to program.

Windows also has several built-in applications that help you organize your daily tasks: a calendar helps you plan more effectively, and a calculator and notepad give you electronic access to traditional desktop items. In addition to these accessories, Windows includes several other programs, such as a word processor (Windows Write), a graphics program (Windows Paintbrush), and a communication utility (Windows Terminal).

Microsoft Windows was instrumental in bringing mouse operations to PC users. Before the advent of Windows, few programs for IBM (or IBM-compatibles) used the mouse interface. Today, you can open menus, select options, move items on-screen, and execute commands by using the mouse. Before Windows, almost all programs required the exclusive use of the keyboard, which resulted in time-consuming and elaborate series of keystrokes necessary for carrying out operations. Now you can complete those operations simply by positioning the mouse pointer and clicking the mouse button.

Learning Mouse Basics

If you have never used a mouse before, you're in for a treat. What once took many key presses to accomplish, you can do in a simple point-and-click movement with a mouse. A *mouse* is a pointing device that works like an extension of your hand. You move the mouse so that the on-screen pointer is positioned on the object you want, and then you click the mouse button to make a choice. You will see the following terms used in all materials that discuss using a mouse:

Term	Definition
Point	To move the mouse so that the mouse pointer on-screen is positioned on the item you want to select
Click	To press and release the mouse button
Double-click	To quickly press and release the mouse button twice
Drag	To press and hold the mouse button while moving the mouse in the direction desired

Learning Keyboard Basics

Of course, you also can use the keyboard with Windows programs. In many cases, you may opt to use the mouse (this will seem easier), but as you become more familiar with Windows, you may find that certain operations are more comfortable from the keyboard. When you want to close a particular window, for example, you can do so by pressing the quick-key combination Ctrl+F4.

Windows Primer

This section takes you quickly through the Windows features you will use most often.

Starting Windows

Starting Microsoft Windows is simple. Here's how:

1. Move to the root directory of your computer by typing **cd** and pressing Enter.
2. If Windows is installed on another drive in your computer, type the name of the drive (such as **c:** or **d:**) and press Enter.
3. Type **win** and press Enter.

The Microsoft Windows title screen appears. After a brief moment, the Program Manager window appears (see fig. 2.1). Your screen may appear differently, depending on the programs you have set up to run with your version of Windows.

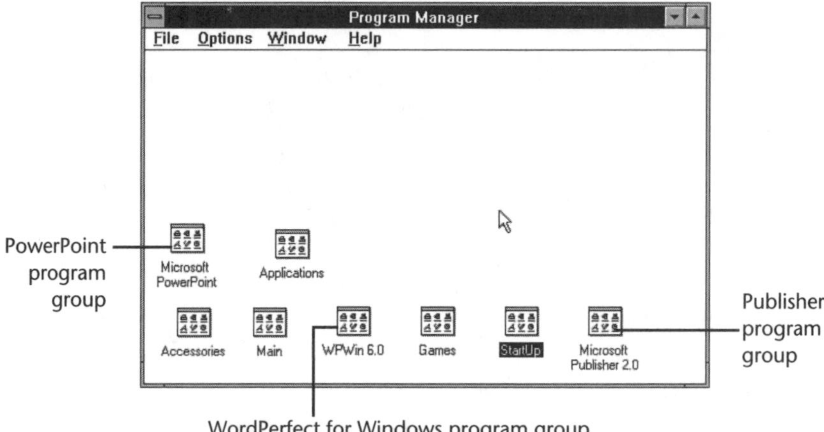

Fig. 2.1
The Program Manager window.

Opening a Window

Windows programs are shown in the Program Manager as *icons*, or small pictures that represent the programs on your hard disk. In figure 2.1, you see icons for three different program groups—Microsoft PowerPoint, WordPerfect for Windows, and Microsoft Publisher.

Before you can start a program, you have to open the program's group window. To do that, follow these simple steps:

1. Place the mouse pointer on the icon you want to select.

2. Double-click the mouse button.

The window opens and you can see the various files associated with the program. Figure 2.2 shows the Publisher group window after it's been opened.

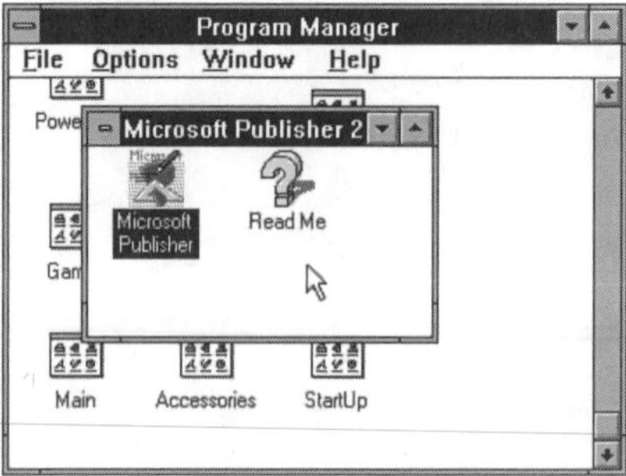

Fig. 2.2
The open Microsoft Publisher group window.

Closing a Window

When you finish using a program, you return to the group window. You can close the group window you were working with in one of two ways:

- You can click once on the gray box in the upper left corner of the window (called the control menu box) and then choose **C**lose from the displayed menu.
- You can double-click the control menu box.

Tip
You can close a window quickly with the keyboard method: press Ctrl+F4.

Minimizing Windows

Sometimes you may want to get rid of a window for a moment, but keep it nearby. Suppose that you're working with one program and need to look something up in another. You can shrink the first program's window to an icon while you work with the second program, and then restore the first window back to its original size when you're ready.

Reducing a window to an icon is known as *minimizing* the window. To minimize a window, follow these steps:

1. Position the mouse pointer on the button with the triangle pointing down, in the upper right corner of the window.
2. Click the mouse button.

The window shrinks to an icon.

Redisplaying the Window

But then you want the thing back, right? You've got to restore the window to its earlier size. Here's how:

1. Position the mouse pointer on the icon.
2. Double-click the Publisher icon.

The window returns to its original size.

Maximizing Windows

You may not have noticed it, but the default size for most open windows is not full-screen size. Although the window fills most of the screen, you still see a border of Windows (it may be the Program

Manager or the desktop) beyond the edges of your window. When you maximize a window, the window grows to fill the entire screen, giving you the most workspace available.

You can maximize a window in two ways:

- Click on the Maximize button—the upward pointing triangle—in the upper right corner of the title bar.
- Open the control menu box and choose the Ma**x**imize command.

Resizing Windows

You can use additional options to change the size of the windows. Although you will use the Minimize and Maximize buttons frequently, at times you may want to make a window smaller—not completely reduced as an icon—but small enough to enable you to open another application window on-screen.

To resize a window by using the mouse, follow these steps:

1. Place the mouse on the corner of the window you want to resize. The mouse pointer changes to a double-headed arrow, indicating that Windows is ready to resize the window in the direction you specify (see fig. 2.3).

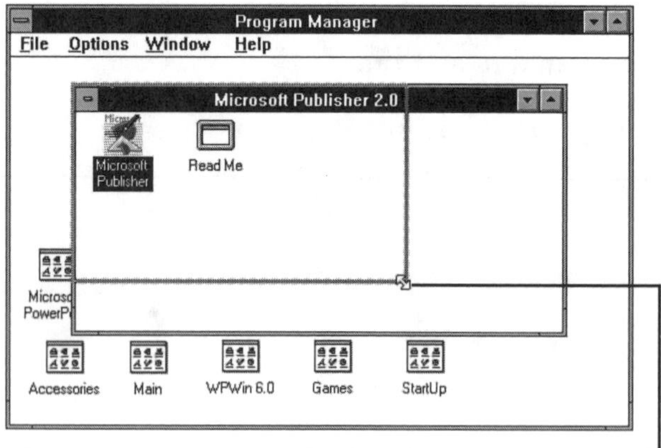

Fig. 2.3 Resizing a window.

2. Press and hold the mouse button and move (drag) the mouse in the direction you want to resize the window. You can make a window smaller or larger by using this procedure.

3. When the window is the size you want, release the mouse button.

Tip

If you want to change only the height or width of the window, position the mouse pointer along the edge of the window you want to move. Press the mouse button and drag the edge of the window.

Exiting Windows

As mentioned earlier, Windows runs in the background while you work with Microsoft Publisher. After you complete your Publisher work session (or your work with another Windows application) and you are ready to exit Windows, follow these steps:

1. Make sure that all files are saved and application windows are closed.

2. When the Program Manager is displayed, double-click on the control menu box or press Alt+F4. A dialog box appears, telling you that you're about to end your Windows session. Click OK to exit.

   You also can leave Windows by opening the File menu (by clicking on the **F**ile menu name in the menu bar) and choosing the Exit Windows option (see fig. 2.4).

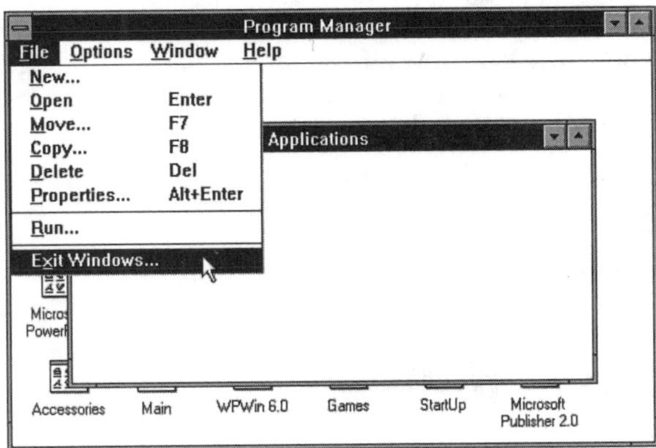

Fig. 2.4
Bye-bye Windows.

3. Make your selection and press Enter.

You return to the DOS prompt.

> **Note**
>
> For more information about using Windows, see Que's *Using Windows 3.1, Special Edition.*

Starting Microsoft Publisher

Now that you understand the fundamentals of Microsoft Windows, you're ready to tackle Publisher. As you know, Publisher runs within Windows, which means you need to start Windows before you start Microsoft Publisher.

> **Note**
>
> The rest of this chapter involves working with Publisher on your system, so if you haven't already installed Publisher, now is the time to do it. The installation process is so easy that it takes nothing more than a few keystrokes from you (although there is some waiting time involved while the program is copied to your hard disk). For detailed instructions on installing Publisher, see Appendix A.

To start Microsoft Publisher, follow these steps:

1. Start Microsoft Windows if it is not already running.
2. Open the Microsoft Publisher 2.0 group window.
3. Double-click the Microsoft Publisher icon.

After a moment, the opening Microsoft Publisher screen is displayed.

Tip
If you choose not to work through the tutorial at first, don't worry: it's not a one-time offer. You can return to the tutorial and review at your leisure by selecting the **I**ntroduction to Publisher command from the **H**elp menu.

First-Time Publisher

Another automated process happens only the first time you start the program: you are invited to take part in the Publisher tutorial already installed on your system. You can choose to continue through the tutorial by clicking on the Next> button, or you can cancel the tutorial by clicking Done and begin exploring Publisher on your own.

You may want to take a few minutes to work through the Publisher tutorial before you begin creating your own documents. This interactive class in the basic elements of desktop publishing in general—and Publisher in particular—will help give you an overview of the procedures and philosophies of this program.

Getting Down To Business: Publisher Basics

After you start Publisher by double-clicking the Publisher icon (in the Publisher group window, remember?), the first screen to meet your eager eye is the Start Up screen (see fig. 2.5). This screen lets you make some preliminary decisions about what type of help you want from Publisher.

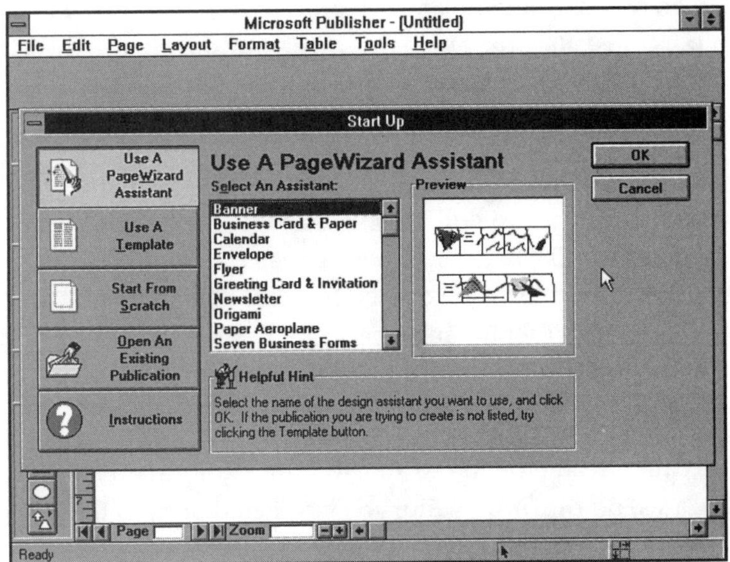

Fig. 2.5
The Start Up screen.

The Start Up screen gives you these choices:

- Do you want to let one of Publisher's PageWizards do the design for you? (You choose the style and add your own text and graphics; Publisher lays things out.)
- Do you want to create your publication based on one of the professionally designed templates?

- Do you want to create your publication from scratch, with no help from PageWizards or templates?
- Do you want to work on a publication you've saved in the past?
- Do you want help deciding what to do?

When you decide what your next step should be, click the button on the left side of the Start Up box that best reflects your choice. (Notice that the PageWizard button is selected by default.)

Choosing a PageWizard

If you want to choose a PageWizard, click on the name of a file in the Select An Assistant box (Preview shows you what you've selected). When you have the one you want, click OK.

Choosing a Template

If you plan on using a template, the process is the same as for a PageWizard. Just click the Use A Template button, choose the file name (watch Preview to see what you've selected), and then click OK when you've selected the right one.

A *template* is a professionally designed publication that you can alter to include your own text and graphics. Templates are great because all major decisions—like text font, style, and size; column layouts; border selection, and so on—are chosen for you. You know that all the elements work together because the templates were designed by professional designers. You can just plug in your text and art and print.

Templates are different from PageWizards in that they are already complete files, ready for you to add your own information. PageWizards, on the other hand, are automated utilities that create your publication for you after asking you a series of questions.

Doing It the Hard Way

For our purposes here (and because I'm a glutton for punishment), we're going to Start From Scratch. Actually, it helps to explain the different screen elements if everything else is blank. To start from scratch, just click the Start From Scratch button.

Oh, no! Not more choices! (And you thought this was going to be simple.)

After you click Start From **S**cratch, Publisher shows you that you need to select the type of layout you want. Do you want Full Page, Book, Tent Card, Side-Fold Card, Top-Fold Card, Index Card, Business Card, or Banner? When you decide, click it and click OK.

We're getting there. I promise.

Deal the Cue Cards, Will Ya?

One more stop. Just before Publisher displays that blank page, you see this cool little pop-up window that asks whether you want to use Cue Cards (see fig. 2.6).

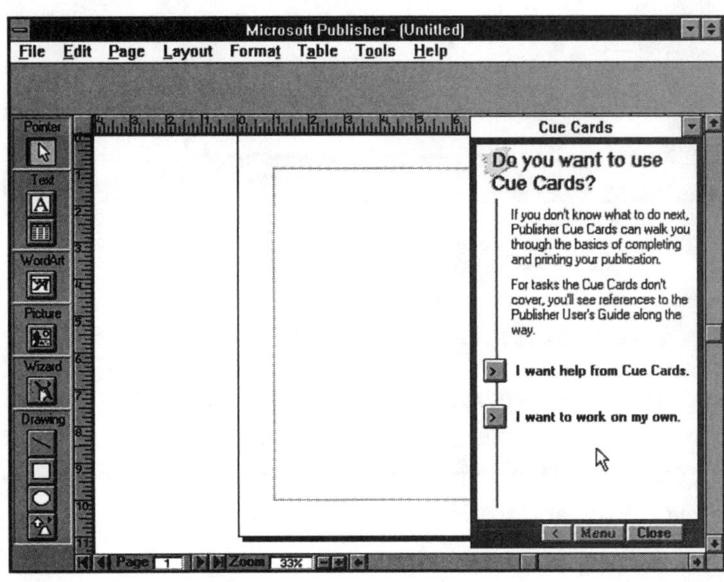

Fig. 2.6
Choosing Cue Cards...or not.

What are Cue Cards? These are enhancements added with Version 2.0 that are like hints—you use them when you need them. If you click I Want Help From Cue Cards, another screen appears asking what you want help with.

Tip
Yes, there's a lot more to know about Publisher's Cue Cards. If you're just dying to know all the ins and outs, see "The Cue's on You," later in this chapter.

Yes, we're abandoning you here. Choose the Cue Cards you want, if any, and click Close when you finish. When Publisher asks you whether you want to close the Cue Cards for this publication only or for all future publications as well, click the button of your choice. Finally, the blank page appears (see fig. 2.7).

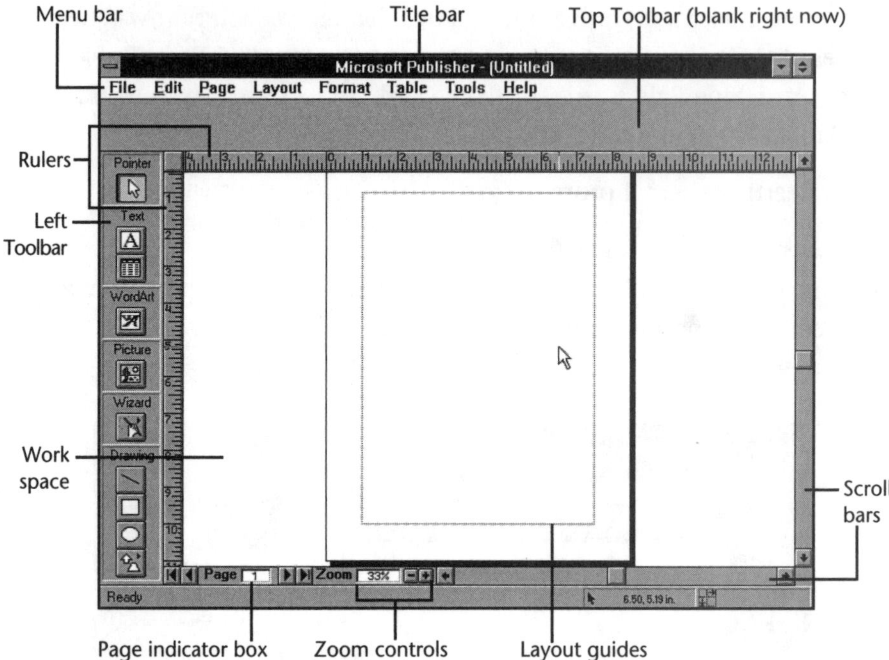

Fig. 2.7
Ahhh. The blank screen.

Understanding the Publisher Screen

As you can see, there are many different parts of the Publisher screen. Looking at figure 2.7, you can see menu names, tools, ruler lines, and all sorts of things. That's one of the benefits of Microsoft Publisher—as you're creating and working on a publication, everything you need is right in front of you.

The Work Space

The largest part of your Publisher screen is invested in the work space. You can think of this work space as a desktop; the publication is placed vertically in front of you, and the white space around the publication is the top of the desk. As you place frames of text and graphics, you can use the desktop as you would use a conventional desktop: you can use the space to place things temporarily as you readjust the layout of your publication.

Note

From the Full Page view, you cannot see the details of your publication. In order to place frames accurately and type text without typos, you need to display a closer view of your publication. The Page menu contains a number of options you can use to change the view of your document. You learn more about the Page menu in the later section, "The View Controls."

The Scroll Bars

Along the right and bottom edges of the work space you see two long bars with arrows at each end. These are known as *scroll bars*.

If you've ever worked with a Windows application, you should be familiar with scrolling. By scrolling through the display of your publication, you can see different parts of your publication that cannot be seen in the current view. (This is unnecessary in the default Full Page view, but when you are using closer views, you need to scroll the publication in order to see the parts of the publication that cannot be displayed on-screen at once.)

You can scroll the publication in several ways:

- By clicking on the arrows at either end of the scroll bars.
- By dragging the scroll box (the small square box in the center of both vertical and horizontal scroll bars) to the position in the scroll bar relative to the part of the publication you want to see.
- By clicking in the scroll bar, you scroll the window one screen in the direction of the place you click. To scroll up or down one screen, click the scroll bar above or below the scroll box. To scroll to any position, drag the scroll box to the position you want. For example, if you position the scroll box halfway down the scroll bar, the text halfway through the document appears.

The Rulers

Rulers also border the work space. The rulers are located on the top and left edge of the screen. You can choose the unit of measurement that is shown on the rulers; you have the option of inches (the default setting), centimeters, points, or picas. Table 2.1 describes these units of measurement.

Table 2.1. Publisher Units of Measurement

Measurement	Description	Comment
Inches		Publisher's default; used as a standard unit of measure.
Centimeters	2.5 per inch	Not often used in publications; in some engineering and architectural work, centimeters is preferred.
Picas	6 per inch	Used as a standard unit of measurement in the publishing and typesetting fields; used with points (12 points equal one pica).
Points	72 per inch	Used as a standard unit of measurement in publishing and typesetting fields; you see type size referred to in points (such as 12-point type).

As mentioned earlier, the default setting for your publication is inches. You can easily change this setting by using the **O**ptions command in the T**o**ols menu.

The Page Indicator Box

At the far left end of the horizontal scroll bar line, you see the page status information. Publisher gives you several options for moving among pages in your publication. First, in the center of the page status area, you see the word Page beside a white rectangle. In the rectangle is a number. This is the number of the page you're currently working on. On either side of the page number, you see two triangles. The following list explains each of these items:

Symbol	Click Here To Go To
	First page of publication
	Preceding page
	Next page
	Last page of publication

You also can move directly to another page (provided you know which page you want) by clicking in the Page box on the left side of the page status line and typing the number of the page you want to see. Publisher then displays the new page that you specify.

The Zoom Controls

In earlier versions of Publisher, in order to change the way your document was displayed—is it up close or full page?—you had to open the Page menu and choose a view command. Now with Version 2.0, you can simply point and click in the Zoom controls at the bottom of the screen.

You can adjust the display view in two ways:

- You can click the plus sign (+) to increase the display percentage or click the minus (–) to decrease the display one size.
- You can click in the Zoom box (the white rectangle that displays the current view) to display a pop-up list of available views (see fig. 2.8). Then simply click on the view you want.

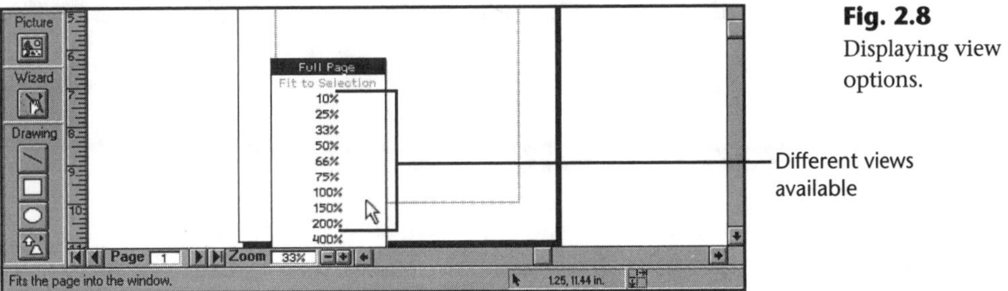

Fig. 2.8 Displaying view options.

The Status Line

At the bottom of the screen, a line displays information about the operation you're performing. When you complete a command and you're ready to move on, the status line displays `Ready`. When you select the Text tool, the status line displays the following message:

```
Hold down the mouse button and drag to create a text frame.
```

The status line gives you cues as to what to do next in certain operations. If you try to do something that Publisher will not enable you to do—such as selecting a command that is unavailable during that particular task (perhaps you need to select a different tool before the command is available)—the status line gives you information about what is wrong and what you can do to correct it.

Look at the status line when you are in doubt about a task or are wondering what to do next. For additional help, you can press F1 to access the help system.

With Publisher 2.0, some new important-looking bits of information were added to the status line. Now two different boxes—a position box and a size box—reflect position and size when you move the cursor and create boxes for your Publisher objects. Figure 2.9 shows the position and size box settings. The first value (Position) shows the placement of the pointer; the second value (Size) shows the size of the currently selected text box.

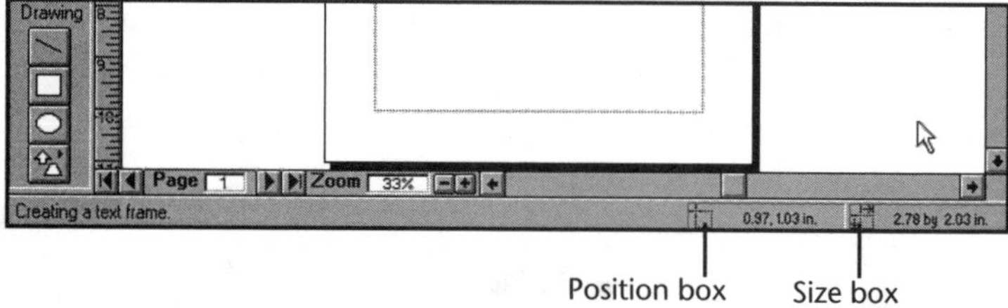

Fig. 2.9
Checking out the position and size boxes.

Working with Menus

In the last section, you explored some of the elements that always appear on your Publisher screen. This section introduces you to the menus that house all the commands you will use in your publishing endeavors.

Consistent with all Windows programs, the menus in Publisher remain hidden until you open a menu. This feature keeps the maximum work space available to you on-screen at all times and enables you to get to the menus only when you need them.

Before you learn about the individual menus and the commands they contain, you need to understand how to use Publisher menus.

Opening and Closing Menus

Earlier examples referred to opening menus in a rather cavalier way. What if you aren't sure how to open a menu? The process is simple. You can open a menu in one of two ways:

- Move the mouse pointer to position it on the menu name you want to open and click the mouse button.
- Press Alt and the underlined letter in the menu name (such as F for the **F**ile menu or T for the Forma**t** menu).

After you select a command, the menu closes automatically. If you want to close a menu without selecting a command, you can do one of two things:

- Move the mouse pointer off the open menu and click the mouse button.
- Press Esc.

Try these procedures by opening the File menu. Position the mouse pointer on the word **F**ile in the menu bar and click the mouse button. The File menu appears, as shown in figure 2.10.

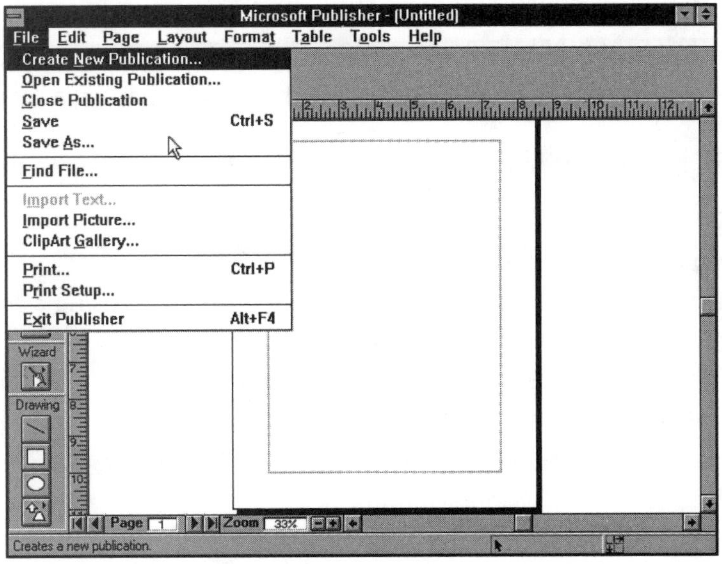

Fig. 2.10
The File menu.

There are several interesting things about the commands in this menu. First, you see that most of the commands appear in black type, while one—I**m**port Text—appears dimmed. You can select all the commands in black, but the Import Text command is unavailable.

Additionally, the commands that have an ellipsis (three dots) after them will display dialog boxes when selected. A dialog box is a pop-up box that displays additional options.

At the far right side of the menu, some commands have additional keys or key combinations (such as Ctrl+S for the Save command), indicating that you can bypass the menu selections by pressing that key or combination of keys.

Selecting Options

Now that you have the menu open, you can select a command in several ways:

- Point the mouse to the command you want to select and click the mouse button.
- Press the underlined letter in the command you want.
- Use the arrow keys to move the highlight to the command you want to select and press Enter.
- If a quick key is available, you can press the key or key combination. (Note: You use quick keys without first opening a menu.)

Again, if you want to close the menu without selecting a command, press Esc.

Using Dialog Boxes

A dialog box provides you with additional options for using a command. Using the steps described earlier, for example, open the **F**ile menu (if it's not already open). Choose the P**r**int Setup command. The dialog box shown in figure 2.11 appears.

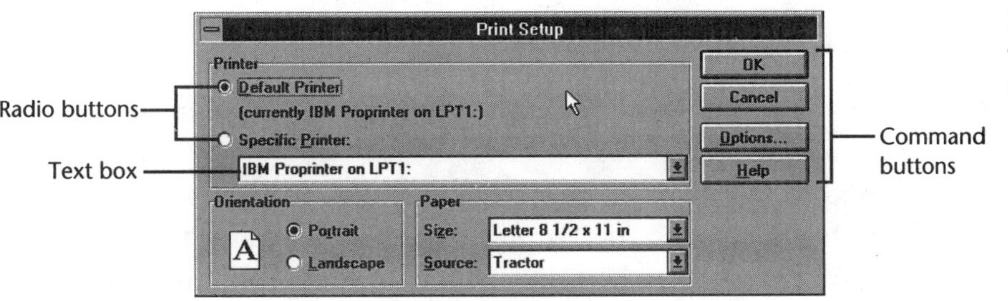

Fig. 2.11 The Print Setup dialog box.

This dialog box has several types of options. The Printer and Orientation boxes contain radio buttons. To select and deselect radio buttons, point the mouse to the option you want and click the mouse button. In the text boxes, position the mouse pointer in the box and click; then type the information you need. The buttons in the upper right corner are additional command buttons. To use these buttons, position the mouse and click, like pushing a real button. If you're using the keyboard, different techniques are required for selecting items in a dialog box. Table 2.2 explains the keys you can use to move around in a dialog box.

Table 2.2 Keys Used in Dialog Boxes

Key	Description
Tab key	Moves from one option or group of options to another (such as moving from the Printer group to the Orientation group in the Print Setup example).
↓ key	Moves to the next option in a group.
↑ key	Moves to the preceding option in a group.
Space bar	Selects or deselects a radio button or checkbox option.
Alt key	Chooses an option when pressed with the underlined letter of an option.

Working with Tools

Now that you've learned how to work with menus on the Microsoft Publisher screen, you're ready to tackle the last set of important items on the screen. As you've learned, Publisher offers you a wealth of support when it comes to publishing: from the easy-to-use screen area with its scroll bars, rulers, and status line to the comprehensive menus with context-sensitive help, Publisher doesn't leave a whole lot to chance. The tools included with Publisher are no exception.

Publisher 2.0 brings with it a tool renovation. Instead of the single toolbar, Publisher 2.0 has two toolbars—one along the left side of the work space (known as the Left Toolbar) and one along the top of the work space (called—you don't really need to hear it, do you?—the Top Toolbar).

When you first fire up Publisher, the Pointer tool is the selected tool (at the top of the Left Toolbar). Nothing is displayed in the Top Toolbar (see fig. 2.12). Why? The tools appear in the Top Toolbar only when you select a text or graphics frame on the page. Also, if you click on the Text tool, the tools appear in the Top Toolbar area (see fig. 2.13).

The Left Toolbar

The Left Toolbar in Publisher contains the major tools you'll use as you work with your publications. The big stuff. When you want to add text, you use the Text tool. When you want to add art, you use the Picture tool. Here are the tools and what they do:

Use This Tool	To Do This
Pointer	Select, resize, and move objects on-screen
Text	Add a text frame
Table	Add a table frame
WordArt	Create a WordArt frame and activate the WordArt feature
Picture	Add a picture frame
Wizard	Apply a PageWizard to your publication
Drawing	Add custom drawings to your page

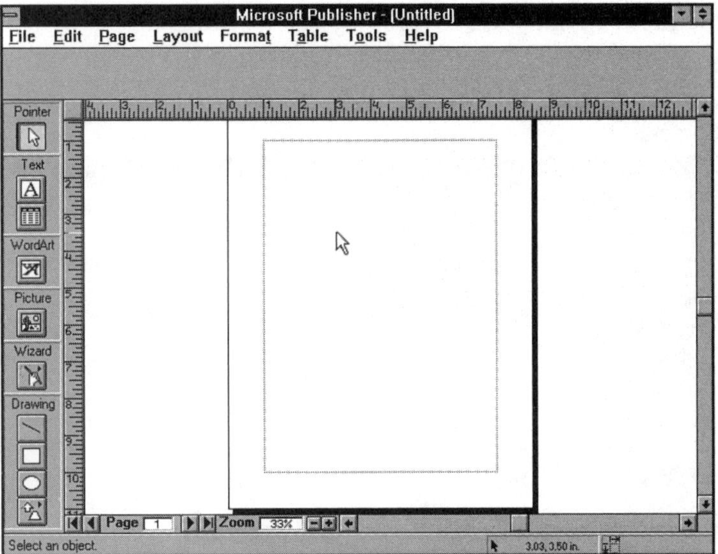

Fig. 2.12
The Left Toolbar is blank on top.

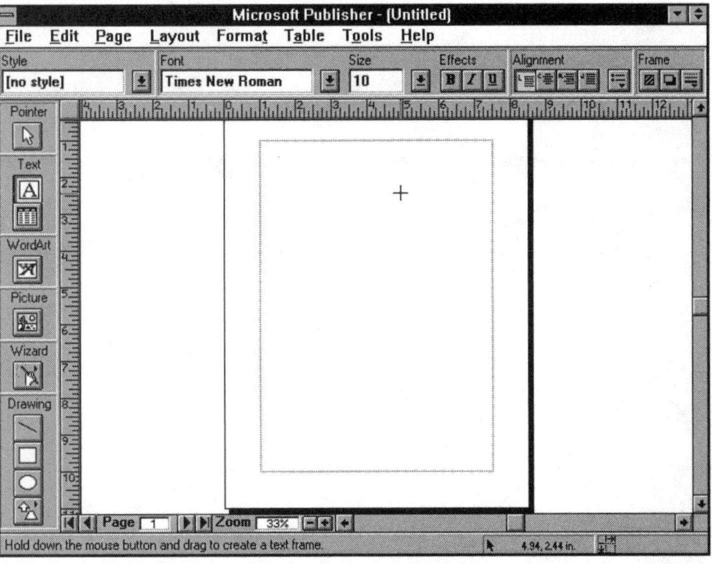

Fig. 2.13
When you click a tool other than Pointer, tools appear in the Top Toolbar.

What Happens When You Select a Tool? What you see on-screen after you select one of the tools in the Left Toolbar depends on the tool you've selected. If you choose Pointer, for example, nothing happens (except it looks like you pressed the Pointer button). If you click Text, WordArt, or Picture, the Top Toolbar changes.

If you click Wizard, a pop-up menu of PageWizards appears, as shown in figure 2.14. If you click the bottom drawing tool (called the Shape tool), a pop-up palette of various shapes appears (see fig. 2.15).

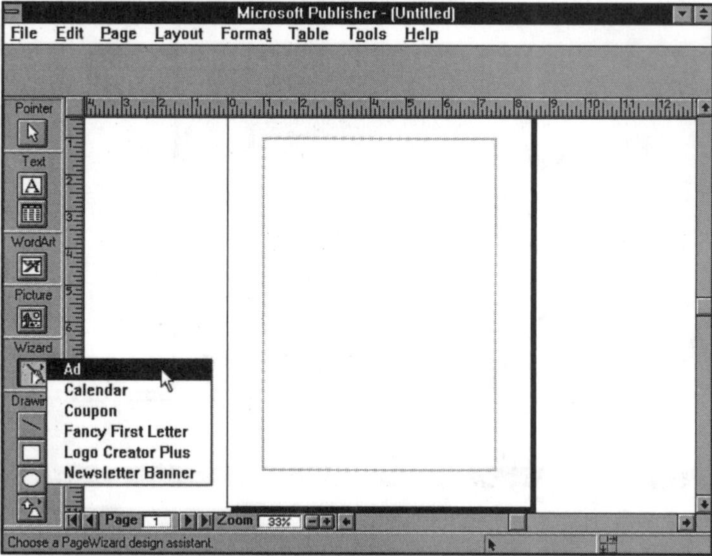

Fig. 2.14
Pop-up PageWizards.

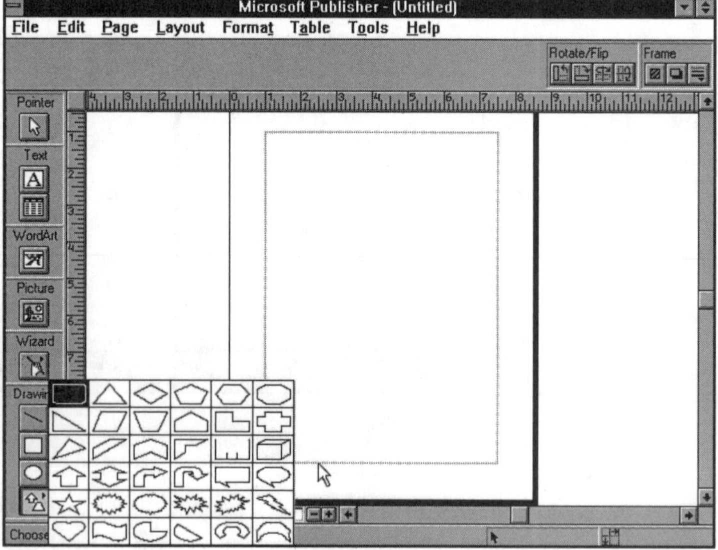

Fig. 2.15
Pretty shapely, eh?

The Top Toolbar

So you already know what to expect from the Top Toolbar, right? The Top Toolbar shows you those smaller choices you have when you're working with a specific tool. For example, when you click the Text tool, the Top Toolbar gives you the following choices:

- Style
- Font
- Size
- Effects
- Alignment
- Frame

That's just about everything you need to worry about when it comes to text. To display your choices for Style, Font, and Size, click the down-arrow symbol at the end of the text boxes. To choose an Effect, Alignment, or Frame style, click the button that represents the style you want.

It's almost too easy.

When you click the WordArt or Picture tools, only the Frame buttons appear in the Top Toolbar.

When you use the Drawing tools, you get another set of options in the Top Toolbar. Figure 2.16 shows the Top Toolbar when the Line tool is selected. Three sets of buttons give you your choices: Arrows (for the ends of the lines), Rotate/Flip controls, and Line style. Again, you just click on the button(s) you want and Publisher does the rest.

The Cue's on You

One other element you might want to display on-screen, especially while you're first learning Publisher, is the set of Cue Cards Microsoft has included with the program.

When you first start Publisher, Cue Cards pop up unbidden. You are given a set of options so that you can choose whether you want them displayed or not.

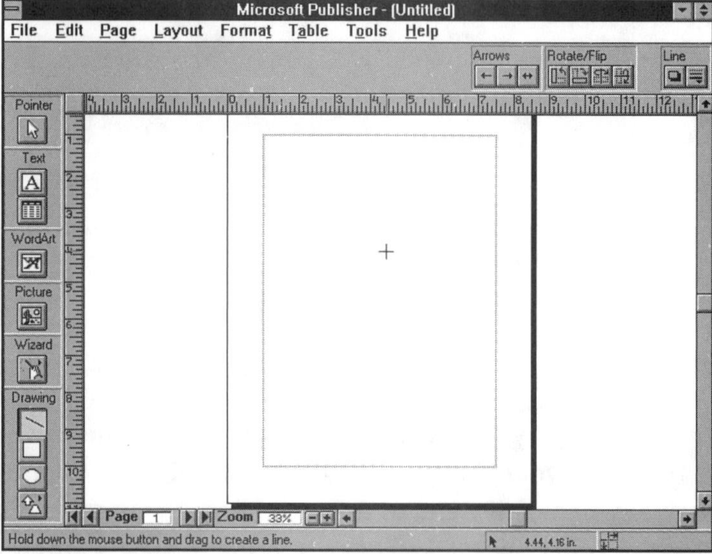

Fig. 2.16
Other stuff in the Top Toolbar.

But suppose that you turned Cue Cards off and now you regret it. Can you turn them back on? Sure. Just follow these steps:

1. Open the **H**elp menu.
2. Choose C**u**e Cards. A pop-up dialog box appears, as shown in figure 2.17.

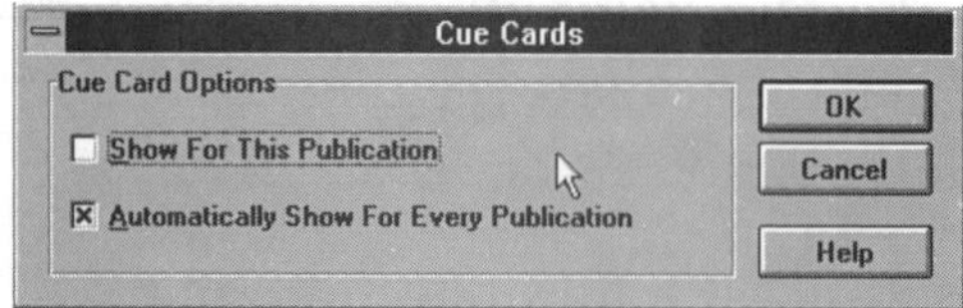

Fig. 2.17
The Cue Cards dialog box.

3. You can choose whether you want to display the Cue Cards for every publication or just this one. Click the box in front of the setting you want.
4. Click OK.

If you chose **S**how For This Publication in the Cue Cards dialog box, the Cue Cards Main Menu appears, asking you what you want help with (see fig. 2.18). Find the task you're having trouble with and click the corresponding button. A second screen of options appears, helping you narrow down the operation you're looking for. Follow the on-screen instructions to get to the topic you need.

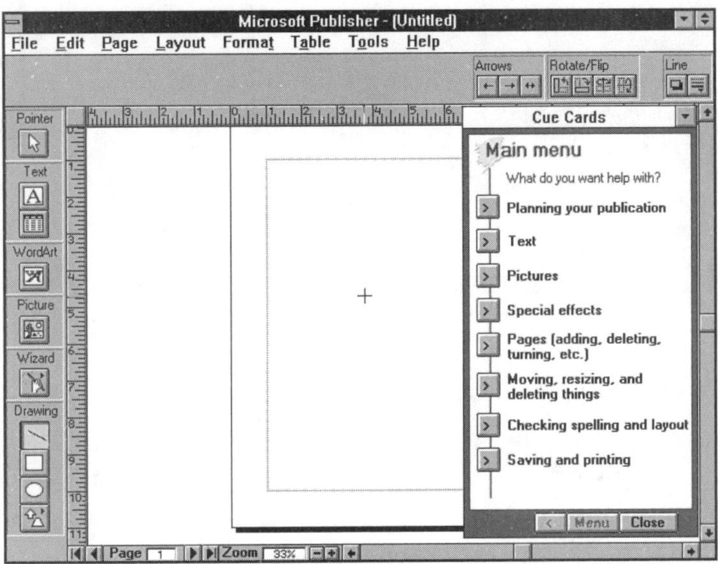

Fig. 2.18
Choosing help with Cue Cards.

Figure 2.19 shows an example of a Cue Card help screen. You can follow through the card set as far as you want to; at any time you can click the Close button or return to the Main Menu by clicking the buttons at the bottom of the Cue Card box.

When you click Close, Publisher asks whether you want to close Cue Cards just for this publication or for all future publications. Make your choice by clicking the appropriate button; Publisher returns you to the work area.

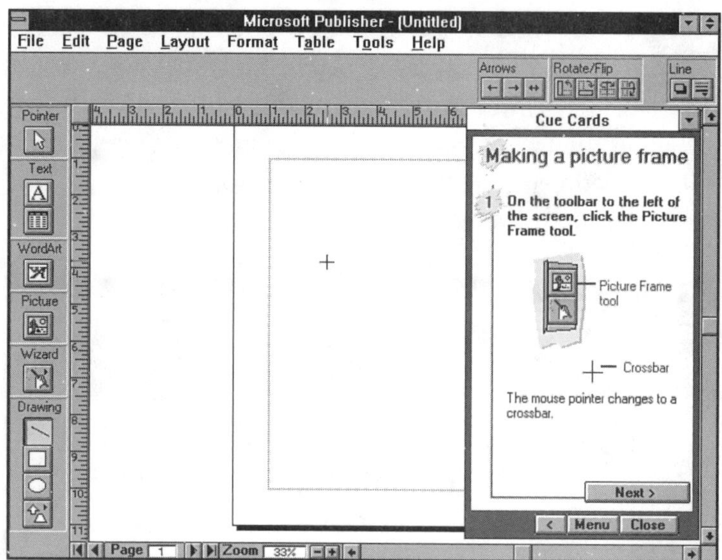

Fig. 2.19
A screen in Cue Card help.

Using Undo

Publisher has a built-in safety net that can save you quite a few headaches. Everyone needs an "oops" button that they can push when they do something they wish they hadn't done. At least in desktop publishing, this feature is available to you. You can use Undo in the following cases (among others):

- You accidentally delete a picture you need.
- You resize a frame and don't like the way it looks.
- You move an element and decide that you don't like where you placed it.
- You change the text style of a paragraph and liked the original better.
- You add something to a publication that you aren't happy with.

Undo is a quick way to erase your last operation. To use Undo, simply open the Edit menu and choose the Undo command. Remember, however, that Undo undoes only your last operation; so if you deleted a headline three steps ago, Undo won't help you now.

Yelling Help

At several places in this chapter, you have heard about Publisher's help system, although not in any great detail. Publisher's help system is *context-sensitive,* which means that at any time you can get help that is related to the actual tasks you are performing. It's almost as if Publisher is watching over your shoulder so that it can be ready if you get stuck in a certain operation.

Context-sensitive help brings you information you need on a specific operation you are performing whenever you press F1. Suppose that you are getting ready to use WordArt, but you're not exactly sure how to proceed. You can select the WordArt tool in the Toolbar and then press F1. Publisher displays a screen telling you how to continue with the WordArt operation (see fig. 2.20).

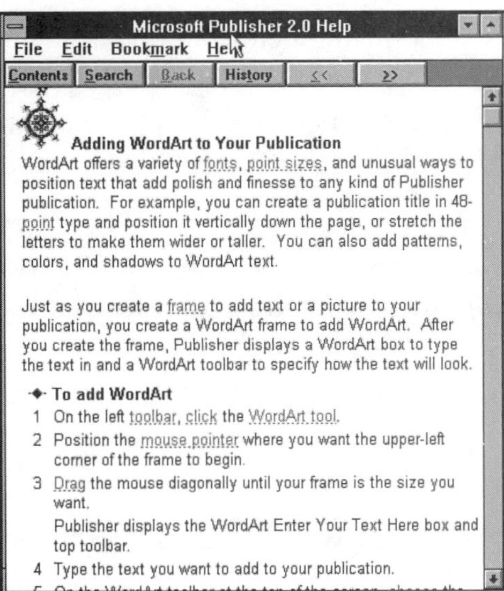

Fig. 2.20 Help using WordArt.

The help system has a look all its own. At the top of the window, you see the name of the program, the familiar control menu box, and the Minimize/Maximize buttons common to all Windows applications. The next line shows the menu bar, with four new menus: **F**ile, **E**dit, Book**m**ark, and **H**elp. Beneath the menu bar, you find a series of buttons that help you navigate through the Help system:

Button	Description
Contents	Takes you to an index of help topics
Search	Searches for a specific help subject
Back	Takes you back to the last help topic
History	Shows you what help you've asked for in the past
<<	Scrolls back through help topics
>>	Scrolls forward through help topics

Certain words in the help entry are underlined and appear in a different color than the rest of the text. You can position the mouse pointer on one of these words, and press and hold the mouse button to see a small window with related information.

After you spend some time wandering around in the help system, you can return to your publication, and close the Help window by double-clicking on the control menu box in the upper left corner of the window.

Remember that help is available by pressing F1 at any time during your Publisher work session. Additionally, you can use the Publisher tutorial at any point by opening the **H**elp menu and selecting **I**ntroduction to Publisher. Also, in many places in the program, you can find Help buttons that help you learn more about the procedure you are performing.

Quitting Microsoft Publisher

After you have spent some time finding your way around Microsoft Publisher, you'll be ready to find your way out. Like all Windows programs, quitting Publisher is easy. Just follow these steps:

1. Be sure to save the publication you've been working on. (Chapter 4 explains different aspects of saving files.)

2. Open the **F**ile menu.

3. Choose the Exit Publisher command by clicking the mouse button or by pressing X. You also can press Ctrl+F4 to quit the program (without opening the File menu). If you haven't saved your most recent changes to a file, Publisher prompts you to do so.

The Microsoft Publisher application is reduced to an icon within the Microsoft Publisher 2.0 group window. You can close that window by double-clicking on the control menu box or by pressing Alt+F4. You then are free to work in other Windows applications or to exit Windows altogether.

From Here...

For information directly related to the topics covered in this chapter, you may want to review the following sections of this book:

- Chapter 3, "Instant Publications: PageWizards and Templates." This chapter shows you how you can start running out those publications right away—no need waiting for the muse to strike. PageWizards and templates let you design your publication based on the expert designs of professional graphics artists.

- Chapter 5, "Entering Text." Learn how simple it is to create a text box and enter the text for your publication. And if you've already got the text in another file you created in some other program, don't despair—Publisher lets you import text from a variety of sources.

- Chapter 15, "Publication Ideas." Not sure where to start? Don't know what kind of publication you need? Take a look at Chapter 15 to get some possible ideas.

Chapter 3

Instant Publications: PageWizards and Templates

In this chapter, you learn to do the following tasks:

- Use a PageWizard to design a publication
- Use PageWizard portions
- Select and work with a template
- Replace existing template text and graphics
- Save a file as a template

Some things in life we like to do the hard way. For the trip to Grandma's house, we take the back roads (it's the more scenic route). Chocolate chip cookies made from scratch—the hard way—are much better than their store-bought counterparts.

Work, we usually don't like to do the hard way.

Recognizing this, the makers of Publisher streamlined the process of publishing so that you can sit right down, type in some text, pick a picture or two, and have a publication, ready to print. It really can be that simple.

This chapter shows you how to create those publications—fast—by relying on the expertise built right into Microsoft Publisher. You tackle PageWizards first.

What Are PageWizards and How Will They Help Me?

Publisher PageWizards are automatic publication-generation utilities. (Whew!) In other words, they make your publication for you. Sound good?

Publisher includes a total of 12 different PageWizards (that's twice as many as in Version 1.0) that will help you create pretty much any project you're facing. Publisher has PageWizards for the following types of publications:

- Banner
- Business Card & Paper
- Calendar
- Envelope
- Flyer
- Greeting Card & Invitation
- Newsletter
- Origami
- Paper Aeroplane
- Seven Business Forms
- Tape Cassette Cover
- Three-Panel Brochure

As you can imagine, some of these PageWizards are more functional than others. (Some are more fun than functional.)

Basically, all there is to using a PageWizard is selecting the one you want and following the Wizard's instructions on the screen. In the sections that follow, we'll walk you through the process.

Choosing a PageWizard

Your first step is to select a PageWizard for the publication you're tackling. Open the **F**ile menu and choose Create **N**ew Publication (or you may be just firing up Publisher, in which case you'll see the Start Up box automatically).

The Use A PageWizard Assistant button is highlighted by default (see fig. 3.1). A list of PageWizards is displayed in the Select An Assistant list box. Click on the PageWizard you want and Publisher displays a smaller version of the file in the Preview window. Figure 3.2 shows the PageWizard Preview when the Flyer PageWizard is selected.

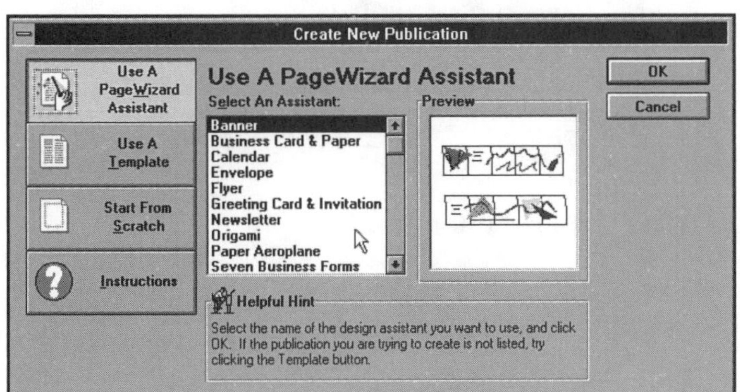

Fig. 3.1
Starting the PageWizard process.

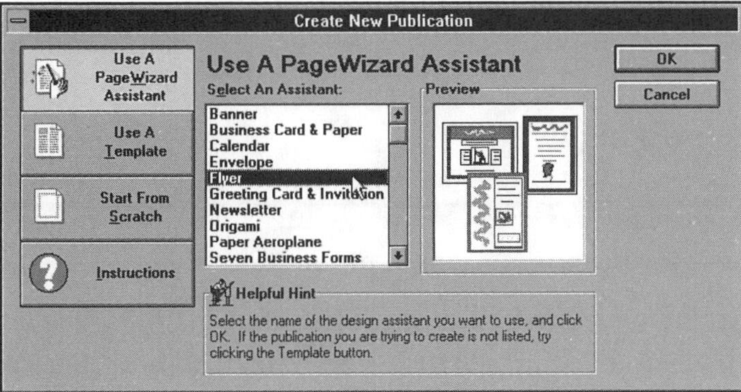

Fig. 3.2
Selecting the Flyer PageWizard.

Getting through PageWizard Screens

After you click OK to choose the Flyer PageWizard, Publisher displays the opening PageWizard Design Assistant screen (see fig. 3.3). At the bottom of the screen you see four buttons you use to navigate your way through the PageWizard system.

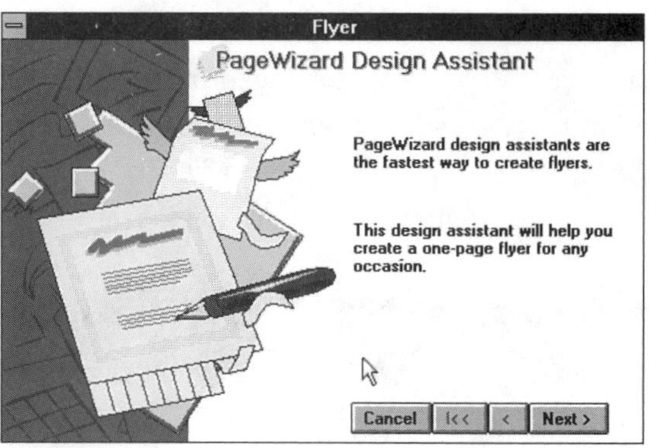

Fig. 3.3
The Flyer Assistant screen.

Project Tip
Just because a certain PageWizard says Banner or Newsletter doesn't mean you can't use it for other purposes. Use your imagination. Turn that calendar into a party invitation designed as a scavenger hunt. Use the newsletter layout to build a flyer. Feel free to try different things and see what works—and what doesn't.

The PageWizard Design buttons work like this:

Cancel	Gets you out of the PageWizard
I<<	Moves you back to the beginning
<	Moves you back one screen
Next>	Moves you to the next PageWizard screen

Click Next> to go on. You're ready to tackle this puppy.

PageWizard Inquisition

You'll soon find that these PageWizards are inquisitive little fellows. By asking you a series of questions, the PageWizard you've chosen narrows down exactly how you want the publication.

The first stop on the Flyer Assistant tour is the question of orientation. Do you want your flyer to be horizontal (Landscape) or vertical (Portrait)? You can click either button and the PageWizard will show you what it means (see fig. 3.4).

The next question involves the overall tone. What's your choice—traditional, classic, modern, or jazzy? Figure 3.5 shows a modern example.

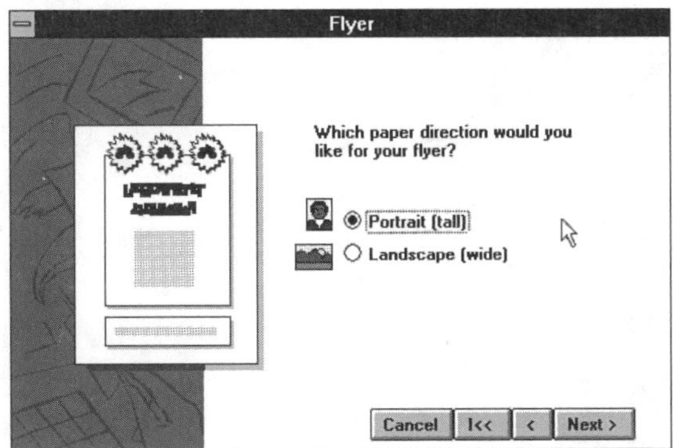

Fig. 3.4
Choosing orientation.

Roll-Your-Own Text

The next screen in the Flyer PageWizard asks you to enter the main headline for the flyer. Type the following phrase:

Work smarter, not harder.

Do you have to specify what font? Style? Color? Size? No, no, no. Publisher does it all for you. Nice to have a program that works for a living.

Project Tip
When you're making selections in the PageWizard screens, remember to keep a consistent tone in your publication. If something doesn't look right, click << to go back a screen and fix the problem.

Preparing for Art

Next, Publisher wants to know whether you plan to insert a picture. Make your choice, click Next, and the PageWizard asks you to choose a border. Figure 3.6 shows the Pyramids border.

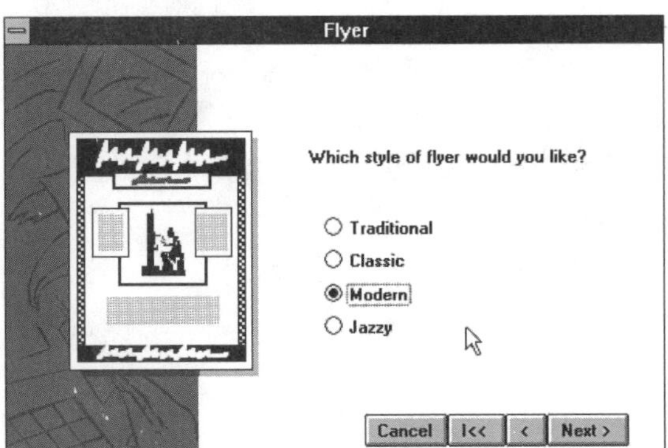

Fig. 3.5
Thoroughly modern Publisher.

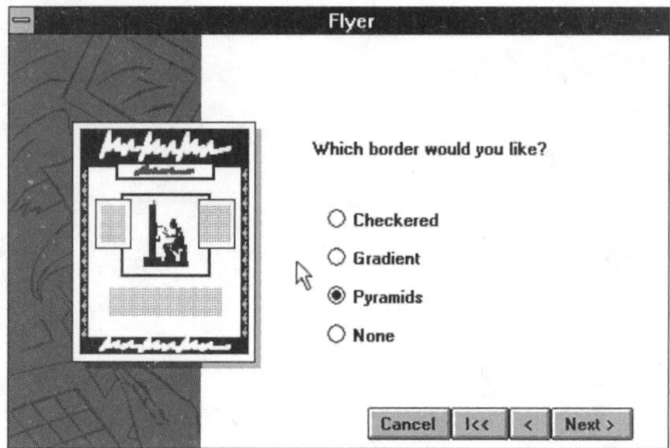

Fig. 3.6
Bordering on simplicity.

Finishing Things Off

Tip
One screen in the PageWizard asks about phone number tear-off coupons. Not interested? Just leave the default set to No and move on.

When you come up against the last of all the questions, Publisher tells you that you've answered everything and now all you have to do is sit back and let Publisher create the flyer based on your choices.

Just click the Create It button in the bottom right corner of the last PageWizard screen. A small pop-up box appears at the bottom of the screen, telling you what's going on as the PageWizard builds your publication (see fig. 3.7). First the border is added, then the headline text boxes, then the picture box, and finally, any additional text boxes.

Note

While you're watching the PageWizard assemble your document, you can speed up the process or slow it down by clicking the arrows in the Flyer box at the bottom of the screen. You might want to have the PageWizard work slowly—so you can easily see what's going on—until you learn the ropes. Then, after you figure out the basic process, you can speed up the assembly process and get on with your work.

Tip
Here come those Cue Cards again. If you want to get rid of them, click I Want To Work On My Own when the Cue Cards screen appears.

Figure 3.8 shows the publication the PageWizard created. Before sending this out as a real advertisement, however, you will want to enter your own text and substitute a picture that fits better with the overall theme. For more about adding text and graphics, see Chapters 5, "Entering Text," and 8, "Adding Art."

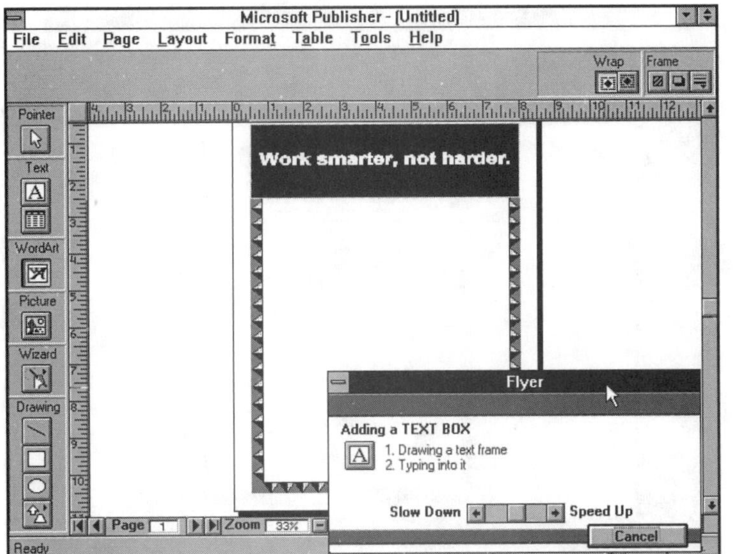

Fig. 3.7
A finishing screen appears. Click OK and Publisher displays the new publication in the work area.

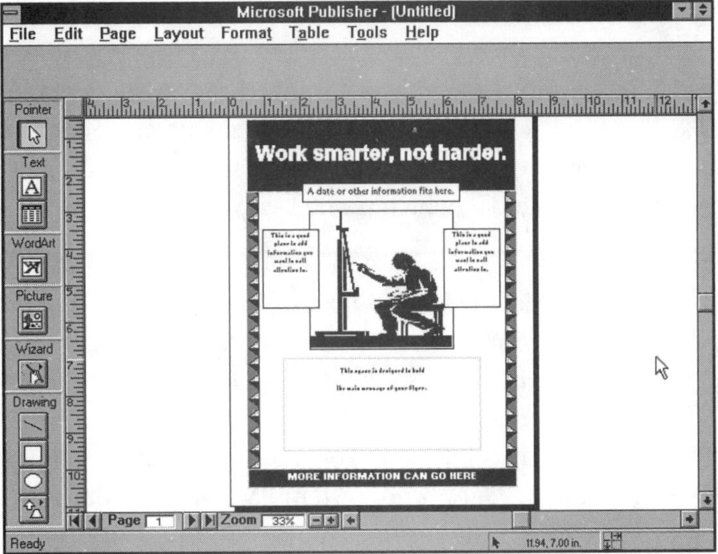

Fig. 3.8
The publication created by the Flyer PageWizard.

Figure 3.9 shows the PageWizard-created flyer after a few alterations have been made.

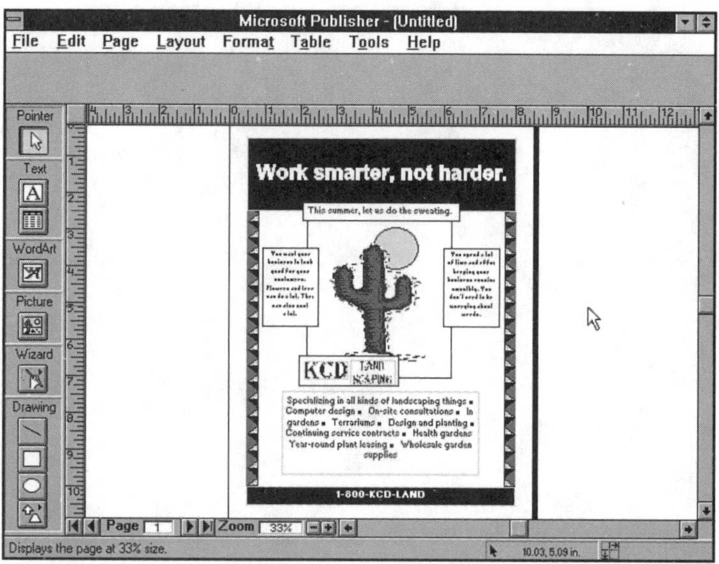

Fig. 3.9
The finished PageWizard-created flyer.

Using PageWizard Parts

Tip
After the PageWizard sets you loose, you're on your own. You still need to save the publication and add your own special touches to the document.

There may be times when you don't want to use a PageWizard to create your entire publication; you may just want to borrow some of the ideas in an existing PageWizard to use in your own document. For example, in this section, you're going to modify the flyer created in the last section to include a Calendar, which is one PageWizard offering.

You can add a PageWizard feature to part of your publication by using the Wizard tool in the Left Toolbar of the Publisher screen. In the following example, you use the Wizard tool to add another element to the flyer created earlier. First, make room for the item you want to add, if necessary. In figure 3.10, the paragraph at the bottom of the flyer was highlighted and deleted. For more information about deleting existing text on a PageWizard or template publication, see "Replacing Existing Text," later in this chapter.

Tip
You can choose from several predesigned PageWizard items to add to your publication. Simply click on the Wizard tool, create the frame, and choose the item you want.

The following steps explain how you can add a PageWizard feature (in this case, a calendar) to your own publication (the flyer):

1. Open the publication you want to work on.
2. Click on the Wizard tool (the last tool in the Left Toolbar, before the Drawing tools). A small pop-up list of PageWizard choices appears beside the tool.

3. Move the pointer to the area to which you want to add the PageWizard item—in this case, Calendar.

4. Press and hold the mouse button while drawing a frame for the item.

5. Release the mouse button. The Calendar PageWizard dialog box appears (see fig. 3.11).

6. Follow the prompts and answer questions about the feature. When you finish, click OK.

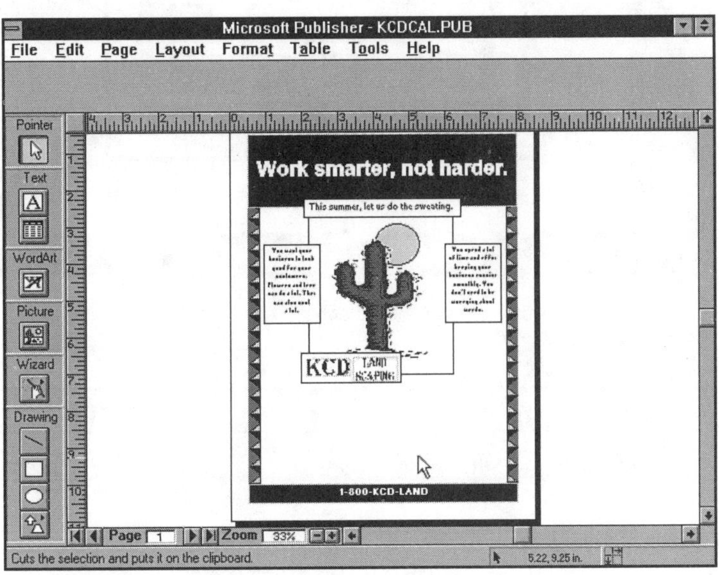

Fig. 3.10
Preparing to add the PageWizard feature.

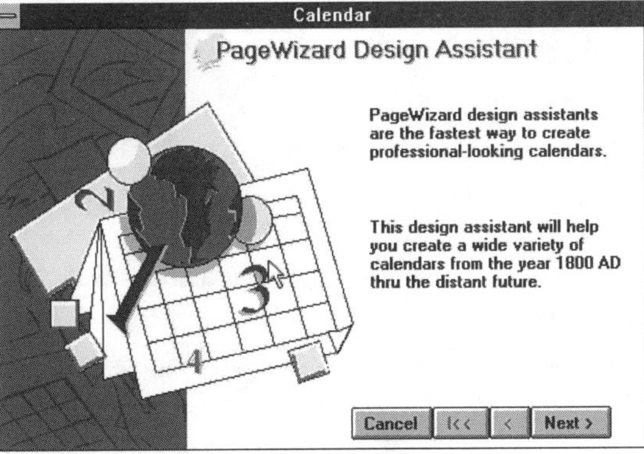

Fig. 3.11
The Calendar PageWizard screen.

Figure 3.12 shows the publication after the PageWizard calendar has been added.

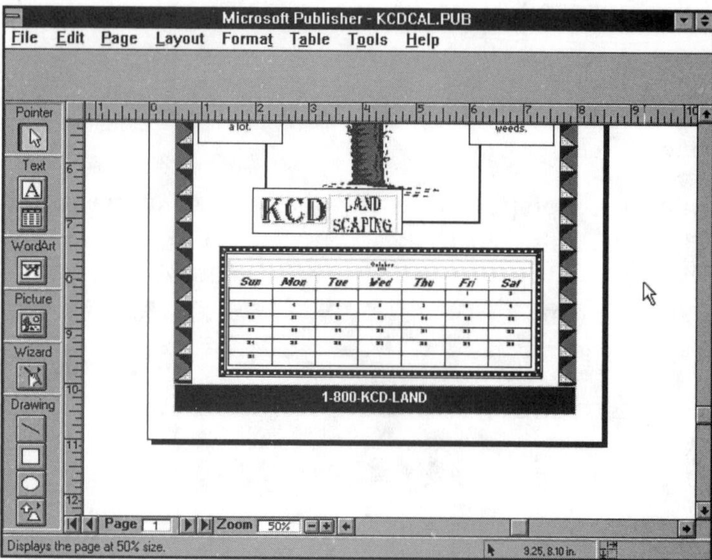

Fig. 3.12
The publication with the added PageWizard.

Troubleshooting

I used a PageWizard part in my publication, but the text is so small I can hardly read it.

If possible, resize the text box containing the small text. Enlarge the text size as much as you can. If that doesn't help, try a different PageWizard part or create something different.

I tried to add my own text, but it jumped over to the right and half of it disappeared.

One thing about PageWizards is that you can't see all the settings used to create the layout you're presented with. Look at the Top Toolbar to see whether the text is wrapping around a picture or is supposed to run right up to it. You should also check the line spacing and the alignment settings. (For more about text settings, see Chapters 5 and 6.)

Templates for Perfection

Now, don't feel bad about using templates. Yes, they are the design brainchildren of other people. Professionals. Yes, using a template means you didn't come up with everything—from the headline to the border to the text style—yourself. But so what?

Templates make things easier and they take the guesswork out of creating a cool publication. Not sure what works together and what doesn't? The designers who created the templates for you make it their mission to know. Rely on the built-in expertise. You paid for it.

At first glance, the difference between PageWizards and templates isn't too obvious. A *template* is a completed file—designed by experts—that you can modify for your own publications. A PageWizard, on the other hand, asks for your input before assembling the document. PageWizards produce a kind of customized template on which you can create your own publication.

What Templates Are in There?

Publisher includes a set of 36 templates, ranging from business cards to catalogs to resumés. They come with the basic layout already set—that includes the border, text boxes, pictures, and headline—and you just plug in your own text and graphics.

In addition to using the templates packaged with Publisher, you have the option of creating templates from your own publication files. Suppose that you have been given the responsibility of creating the company newsletter. Rather than recreating the same layout month after month, you can create the first issue and then make a template out of the file.

Project Tip
Publisher includes templates in a variety of flavors. Consider the tone and the expectations of your audience before you choose something too wild or too conservative.

The template stores the layout type, column format, text frames, picture frames, banner, and headline styles for the publication. In subsequent months, you can simply open the template file, add the text and pictures for the current month, and print the publication. Creating a template file can cut quite a bit of time off your initial page-design stage.

Choosing a Template

To display the list of templates available within Publisher, you can do one of two things:

- If you are just starting your Publisher work session, you can click on the Use A **T**emplate button in the Start Up box. A list of templates appears in the Select A Template box (see fig. 3.13).
- If you have been working in Publisher and now want to start working with a template file, open the **F**ile menu and choose Create **N**ew Publication. Then click the Use A **T**emplate button. A list of template files is displayed.

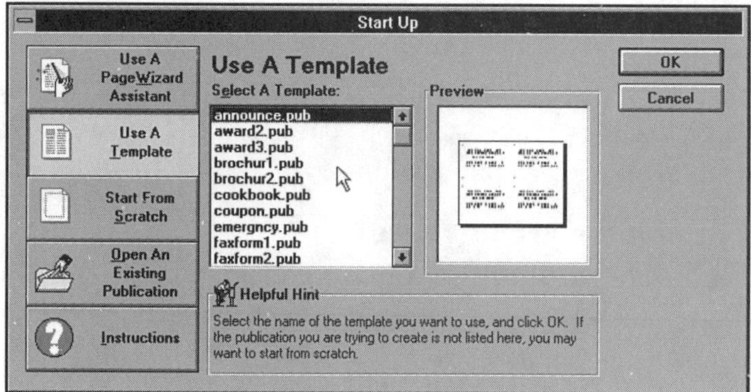

Fig. 3.13
Start the process by choosing Use A Template.

When you click on the file you want, Publisher displays the selected template in the Preview box. This allows you to get an idea of the type of file you're creating without actually opening the file. When you find the file you want, click OK.

Publisher Version 2.0 has made some dramatic changes in its templates. Version 2.0 includes new designs in a variety of styles, interesting art elements, and cool fonts. Table 3.1 lists the various template files and tells you a little about each one.

Table 3.1 Publisher Template Files

File	Description
ANNOUNCE.PUB	A horizontal page with four birth announcements. Plug in your own celebration and print.

File	Description
AWARD2.PUB	Your usual most-papers-delivered-in-the-neighbor-hood-type award
AWARD3.PUB	A more business-like award denoting excellence
BROCHUR1.PUB	A template for a three-fold brochure
BROCHUR2.PUB	A template for full-page, two-column brochure (really cool for projects with a lot of text)
COOKBOOK.PUB	A sample cookbook layout
COUPON.PUB	You guessed it—coupons
EMERGNCY.PUB	A list for emergency information
FAXFORM1.PUB	A cover sheet for faxed information
FAXFORM2.PUB	Another fax cover sheet
FLYER3.PUB	The first of two flyer designs
FLYER4.PUB	The second flyer design
INVITE2.PUB	The first of two invitation templates
INVITE3.PUB	The second invitation template
INVNTORY.PUB	A three-column inventory list
MANUAL.PUB	Another really neat design for longer documents
MEMOPAD.PUB	A full-page memo page
MENU*x*.PUB	Okay, we're getting lazy. MENU1.PUB, MENU2.PUB, MENU3.PUB, MENU4.PUB, and MENU5.PUB are all variations of your typical menu.
NAMCRD2.PUB	A template for name cards with room for four per sheet
NAMETAG.PUB	A sheet of six name tags
NEWSLTR5.PUB	A newsletter template with five—count 'em, *five*!—columns
NOTEMAIL.PUB	A template for envelope and stationery design
POSTER*x*.PUB	Three different poster designs in POSTER1.PUB, POSTER2.PUB, and POSTER3.PUB

(continues)

Table 3.1. Continued

File	Description
RESUME1.PUB	Your traditional resume. RESUME2.PUB is a little better.
SHOWPRGM.PUB	A program for a stage play (or school play, or whatever)
STATNERY.PUB	A possibility for personal stationery
THANKYOU.PUB	A folding card template with the Thank You built right in.
TODOLIST.PUB	Just what you were looking for, right? A To Do list.

Using a Template To Create Your File—Fast

Depending on what you're trying to create, the template files in Publisher can save you an enormous amount of time. You can totally customize the template so that it doesn't look anything like the file you started with. Figure 3.14 shows the template POSTER2.PUB. We're going to create an advertising flyer with this design.

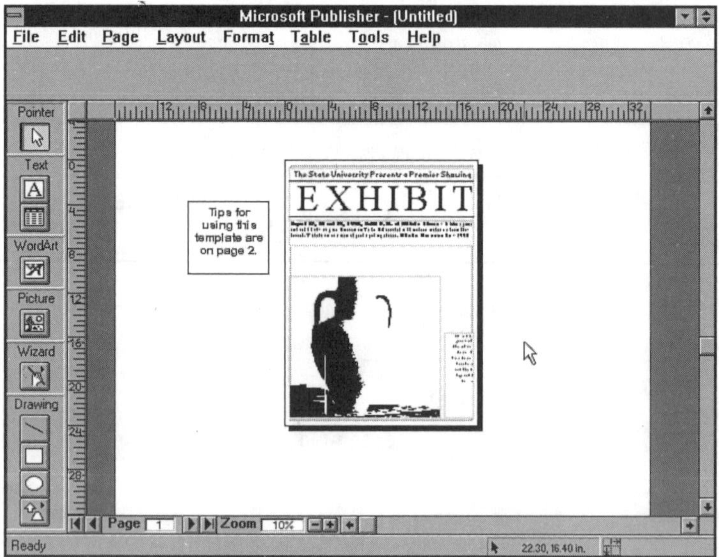

Fig. 3.14
The POSTER2.PUB template as we found it.

After opening the POSTER2.PUB template file, we added our own text, headline, sidebar, and art, while keeping the same text style and placement. The resulting flyer is shown in figure 3.15.

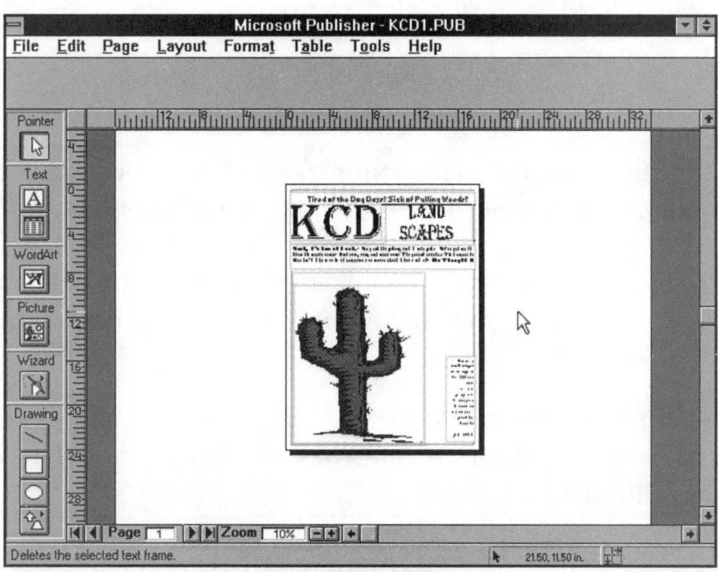

Fig. 3.15
The flyer created from POSTER2.PUB.

The entire process of changing a template into a file of your own involves two basic steps:

- Replacing the existing text with your text
- Replacing the existing art with your art

Project Tip
Don't like the way it's going? Open the **F**ile menu, choose **C**lose Publication, and when Publisher asks whether you want to save the file, click No. There. A blank screen. Now you can start again.

Replacing Existing Text

The first thing you need to do after you open a template file is replace the existing text with your own information. You can do this in two ways:

- By removing the text in each text frame as you're ready to work on that frame.
- By removing all sample text in the document and starting with an empty publication.

To replace existing text with your own, follow these steps:

1. Click on the frame you want to work with.
2. Highlight the text in the frame.
3. Press the Del key. The text disappears.
4. Zoom up to actual size.
5. Type the information for your organization. Notice that the text options selected for the template file are still in effect.

Repeat this process until you have entered all text in the publication the way you want it. If you don't want to use the existing text options, feel free to change them.

Replacing Existing Pictures

Now that you've replaced the text, you're ready to replace the pictures by following these steps:

1. Click on the picture you want to replace.
2. Open the **F**ile menu.
3. Choose **I**mport Picture. The Import Picture dialog box appears.
4. Choose the picture file you want to use.
5. Click OK.

Project Tip
Make sure that you use a recognizable file name when you save the template. Something like 81393.PUB isn't going to tell you much months from now, after you've worked with hundreds of files.

Publisher adds the picture in the frame you selected, and resizes it to fit the frame. Now that you've added your own information to the template file, you need to save the file.

Saving a Template File as Your Own

The procedure for saving the file—as a regular file—is the same one you have used before. Here's a review:

1. Open the **F**ile menu.
2. Choose the **S**ave command. The Save As dialog box appears.
3. Select the drive and directory where you want to store the file.

4. Type a name for the file.

5. Click OK or press Enter.

Publisher then saves your file. You then can print, modify, or otherwise work with the file as you would any other Publisher document.

Saving a File as a Template

In some cases, you'll want to save files you have created as templates of your own. This procedure is very similar to the routine save process. To save your file as a template, follow these steps:

1. When your publication is open on-screen, open the **F**ile menu.

2. If you have previously saved your document, choose Save **A**s. If you are saving the file for the first time, choose **S**ave.

3. When the Save or Save As dialog box appears, type a file name for the file. (Don't bother to change the drive and directory; Publisher places all template files in the TEMPLATES subdirectory.)

4. Move the pointer to the **T**emplate checkbox in the lower right corner of the screen and click the mouse button. An X appears in the box (see fig. 3.16).

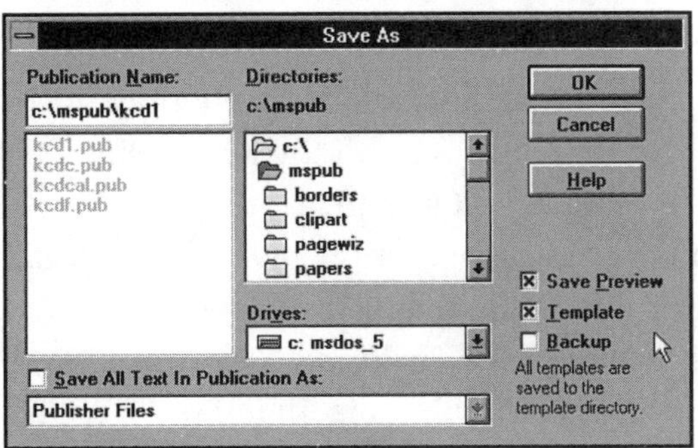

Fig. 3.16
Saving the publication as a template.

5. Click OK. Publisher then saves the file as a template.

Using a Template You Create

When you want to use the template file you have created, you can select it from the Start Up or Create New Publication dialog boxes. It's pretty neat to see the template you have created in the Preview box (see fig. 3.17).

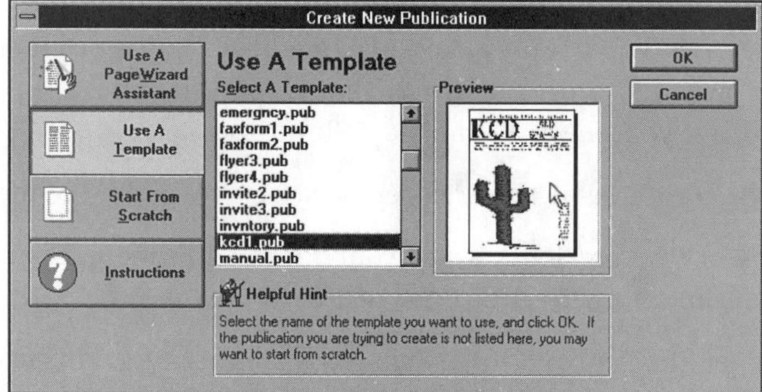

Fig. 3.17
Publisher displays the template you created in the Preview box.

When you open the template file, Publisher creates a copy and places it in the work area. The actual template remains untouched on disk. The title bar shows you that the publication you are working on is untitled and will remain so until you save the publication.

Template Tips

Use the following tips to help you tackle template issues:

- Any publication that you may use more than once makes a good template. No matter how small the task seems, creating something once is much better than creating something twice. Perhaps you are producing a simple invitation to a Christmas party. You easily could create the file and then just save it to disk as usual. But what about New Years? Valentine's Day? Your daughter's birthday? That same invitation could be reworked and used many times throughout the year. If there's a chance you'll use it again, turn it into a template.

- Invoices are particularly good for template use. Although invoices don't hold a lot of text, they require a considerable amount of work. Many text frames, columns, lines, and so on, take up small-but-accumulative bits of time. Including only the basic information and column heads in a template can give you the freedom to fill in the form by hand or on-screen later.

- Newsletters make good template candidates. Because the basic format stays the same from month to month, and other items—like the banner, major headlines, and text settings—do not change, you can save time by creating a "bare-bones" newsletter and then saving the file as a template. You may want to stop after you create the basic layout—banner, text and picture frames, table of contents, but no text or pictures—and then save the document as a template. Then, when you use the template file later, you won't need to delete last month's articles.
- You can use a template to store information you use in routine business correspondence. In your company, perhaps you send out a follow-up letter after a salesperson initially contacts a client. You can save the basic letter in a template file and, when you open the file later, fill in information specific to that client. The basic letter remains intact, but you have the flexibility to change the information as necessary.
- Anytime you are working with format-specific publications and think you'll use the publication again, save the file as a template. If you routinely work on catalogs, product listings, technical material, or any publication that involves extensive formatting, consider whether you can save time by starting with a template file.
- Save your company logo, company name, address, phone, fax number, and other important information in a template file. You then can be consistent with the various publications your company produces. Whether you're creating a promotional flyer, a brochure, or business cards, you can rest assured that your logo and important information is consistent from publication to publication.

Troubleshooting

I entered my own text in the template, but it takes up less room and looks funny.

Highlight the text and change the text size by clicking on the down-arrow button to the right of the Size box in the text settings row and choosing a new size (one or two sizes larger should do the trick).

I wasn't paying close enough attention, and I accidentally gave a new template the same name one of my old templates had.

Sorry, Charlie. That "old" template is a goner, having been overwritten by the new file with the same name.

From Here...

For information directly related to the topics covered in this chapter, you may want to review the following sections of this book:

- Chapter 4, "Working with Publisher Files." After you create your first publication—whether it's an original or a "borrowed" design—you need to save that puppy to disk. Don't risk losing it; turn to Chapter 4 to find out how to protect that file.
- Chapter 5, "Entering Text." Adding your own text to the publication is the next basic step after getting the design in place. Chapter 5 tells you how to create text boxes, enter text, and use text from other applications.
- Chapter 8, "Adding Pictures." The artwork in the PageWizard and the template file may be cool, but it isn't going to work for every one of your publication needs. When you're faced with having to add your own clip art or custom-drawn pictures, take a look at Chapter 8.

Chapter 4

Working with Publisher Files

As your experience with Publisher grows, so will the number of files you create. At first this accumulation of files may seem like no big deal. But one day, you'll try to open an existing publication and not know which one is which. You won't remember, from the names, whether REPPUB is the report you did last month or your son's science report on reptiles.

In this chapter, you learn how to work with files—from starting a new Publisher file to opening an existing one. You also learn how to organize your files and use drives and directories.

In this chapter, you learn to do the following tasks:

- Start a new publication
- Retrieve an existing publication
- Save publications

Opening Files

This section explains how to open a new file in Microsoft Publisher and how to open files you've already created and saved.

Starting a New File

Most of the time, when you sit down to work with Publisher, you are starting a new file. This section explains the various options you have when you begin a new publication in Microsoft Publisher.

When you start Publisher by double-clicking on the Microsoft Publisher icon in the Publisher group window, the Start Up window appears (see fig. 4.1). This window provides you with all the options for initially opening a publication.

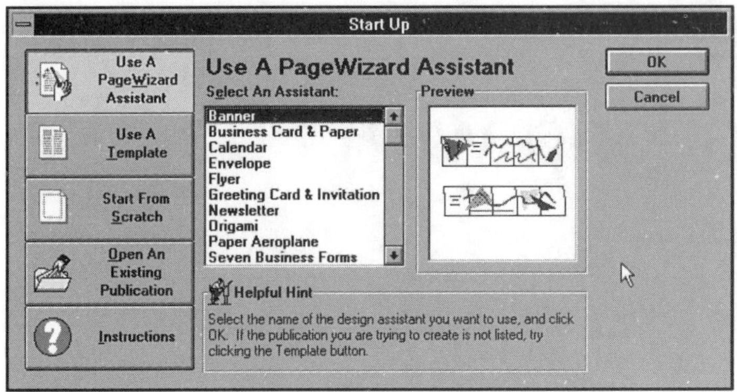

Fig. 4.1
The Publisher Start Up screen.

Your first option in the Start Up window involves using a PageWizard. A *PageWizard* is a publication-generating utility that takes the burden of creation off of you. The PageWizard asks you a series of questions and then creates the document based on your answers.

When the Start Up window first displays, Use A PageWizard Assistant is the default selection. The Select A Template list box shows that you can choose from twelve PageWizards.

To select a PageWizard Assistant, simply move the pointer to the one you want to use and click the mouse button. A miniature sample of the PageWizard you've selected appears in the Preview window. When you have the PageWizard you want, click OK. The PageWizard then leads you through a series of questions designed to help you create the publication you want.

Tip
Publisher 2.0 added 12 new templates, designed by professionals. Knock yourself out!

The second button in the Start Up window, Use A Template, gives you a choice of 36 template files. A *template* is a bare-bones publication from which you can build your own document. When you open a template, the basic format, text, picture frames, and various other publication-specific settings are already in place. You simply plug in your own text and graphics, then save the file.

To choose a template, click on the Use A **T**emplate button. The list of available files in the Select a Template list box changes to show the template files. Click on the file you want. A sample appears in the Preview box (see fig. 4.2). Select your favorite, and then click OK.

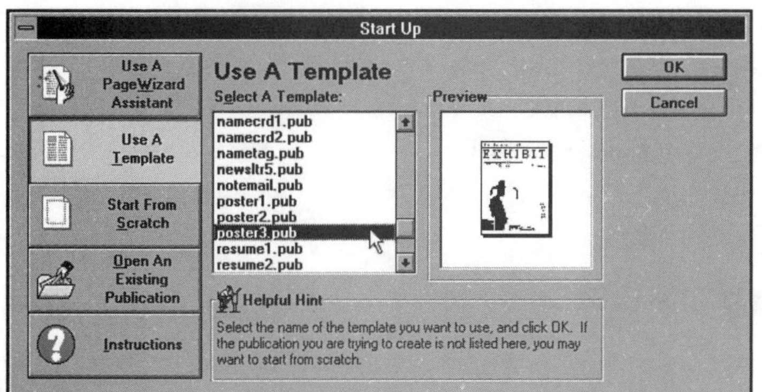

Fig. 4.2
Choosing a template.

The third option in the Start Up window is the Start From Scratch button. Use this option when you want to start with a blank page so that you can create an original document, with the settings, fonts, frames, and other options of your choice.

To start a blank publication, click Start From **S**cratch. The list box title changes to Select A Page Layout. In this list box, you see several layouts from which you can choose. You can start your publications based on any of the following layouts:

- Full Page
- Book
- Tent Card
- Side-Fold Card
- Top-Fold Card
- Index Card
- Business Card
- Banner

When you click the page layout you want, the Preview window shows you an example of your selection. If you want to choose a different layout, click the new choice. If you want to accept the layout shown in the Preview window, click OK.

After you click OK, Publisher displays the opening screen of the Cue Cards. If you want to close the Cue Cards for this session, click I Want To Work On My Own, and then click For This Session Only. (For more about working with Cue Cards, see Chapter 3.) Finally, after you've put away the Cue Cards, the blank page appears on-screen.

Retrieving an Existing File

After you save a file, you need to know how to open it again. When you saved it, you placed it on your hard disk or floppy disk. You can use three procedures to open an existing file:

- You can click the **O**pen An Existing Publication button in the Start Up window and select the file from the displayed list.

  If you don't see the file you want in the Select A File list box, click More files. Publisher displays the Open Existing Publication dialog box, in which you can change drives or directories and locate the file you want from the displayed list.

- If the file you want to retrieve is one you've worked on recently, the file name may be displayed at the bottom of the **F**ile menu. If the file you want is shown, you can open the file simply by clicking on it.

- You can use the **O**pen Existing Publication command in the **F**ile menu.

Opening a File at Startup. If you want to retrieve a file when you first start Publisher, you can open the file directly from the Start Up window. When the Start Up window appears, click on the **O**pen An Existing Publication button. The files that appear in the list box are the files in the current directory (you learn more about directories later in this chapter).

Click on the file you want. Choose OK. Publisher then loads the file you've selected.

Opening a File with the File Menu. After you create and save a Publisher file, the program makes the file easily available to you. Perhaps the easiest way to open a file during your Publisher work session is to select it from the **F**ile menu (see fig. 4.3). In the **F**ile menu, below the E**x**it Publisher command, you see a list of the files you've worked on most recently; your list will be different from the one shown in the figure.

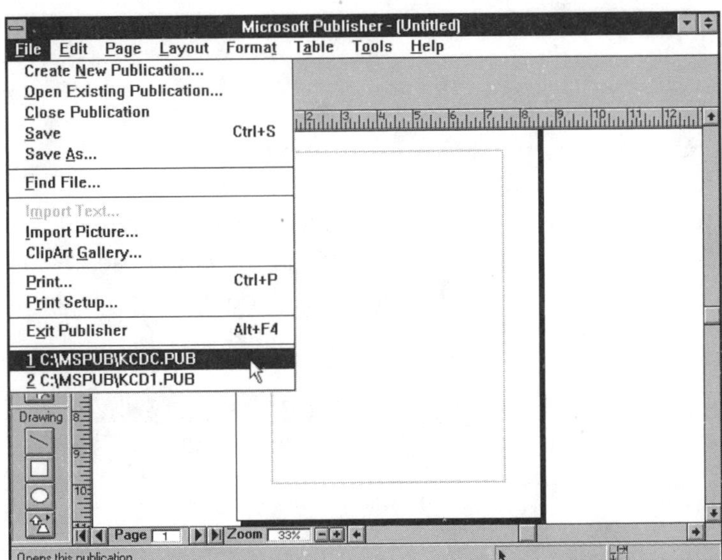

Fig. 4.3
You can select recent files from the File menu.

Publisher lists the drive, directory, subdirectory (if any), and name of the publication. Consider the following line:

C:\MSPUB\KCDC.PUB

This line tells you that the publication you want, KCDC.PUB, is found on drive C in the MSPUB directory.

To select a file, simply position the mouse pointer on the file you want and click the mouse button. If you prefer to use the keyboard, you can press the number to the left of the publication file you want. To select the file shown in the preceding example, you would press 1.

Opening Files with Open Existing Publication. It would be nice to think that you could complete a publication in one work session. Unfortunately, depending on how complex your project is, you may need to work on your document over several days or, at least, for more than one session. This means that when you're ready to stop working on the publication, you have to save it to disk (a procedure covered later in this chapter). When you're ready to start working on the publication again, you open it. To open a publication, follow these steps:

1. Open the **F**ile menu.

2. Choose the **O**pen Existing Publication command.

The Open Existing Publication dialog box appears. You can highlight the name of the file you think you want in the Publication **N**ame list and click Preview File to see the file before you open it (see fig. 4.4). When you find the file you want to open, click OK.

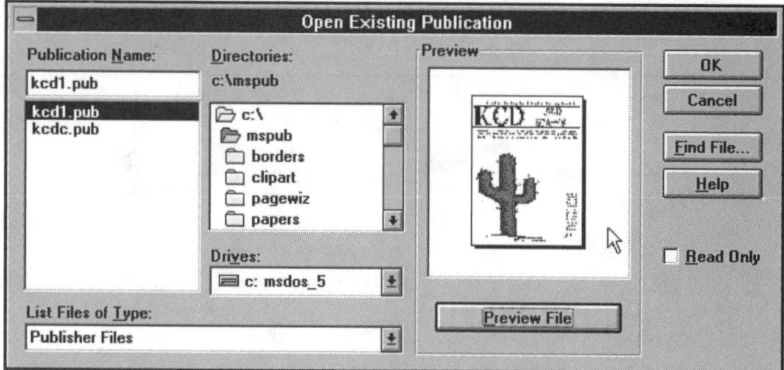

Fig. 4.4
The Open Existing Publication dialog box.

Open Options. The Publication **N**ame box, in the Open Existing Publication dialog box, enables you to specify which publication you want to open. You can type the name of the file you want to open in the text box. The entry is already highlighted, so you can simply begin typing without positioning the cursor. The characters you type will replace the highlighted text in the Publication **N**ame box. You can also select a file from the files listed in the list box beneath the Publication **N**ame box.

The type of files displayed in the Publication **N**ame list box depends on the type of files you've selected for display. The List Files of **T**ype box, at the bottom of the Open Existing Publication dialog box, gives you options for selecting the type of files you want to display. Click on the down arrow on the right side of the List Files of **T**ype box to display the types of files you can open in Publisher (see fig. 4.5).

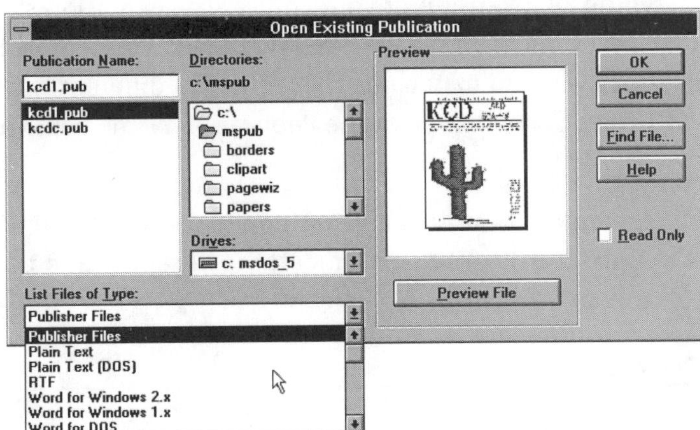

Fig. 4.5
Files you can use in Publisher.

As you can see, the types of files you can open are not limited to those you've created in Microsoft Publisher. You can open files from the following programs:

Microsoft Word 6.0
WordPerfect 5.x for Windows
Windows Write 3.0 and 3.1
Word for Windows 1.x and 2.x
Word for DOS
WordPerfect 5.x
Works for DOS
Works for Windows 2.0 and 3.0

Additionally, you can use files created and saved in the following file formats:

Plain text (ASCII)
Plain text (DOS)
RTF

After you select the file type you want to use, Publisher places the file extension (the three-character designation that follows the period in the file name) in the Publication **N**ame box. The files in the current directory having that file extension are shown in the list box.

Tip
Publisher gives you the option of making a file you retrieve a read-only file. This designation means that you can view the publication, but you cannot make any changes or write any new information to the file.

You can change the file extension by clicking in the Publication **N**ame box and typing the new extension. Most programs give you the option of typing an extension of your choice. The extension shown for WordStar files, for example, is DOC. When you create a file in WordStar, however, you may name the file with a different extension, such as RPT. To display the file in the Publication **N**ame box, you replace the DOC extension with RPT.

After you enter or click on the name of the file you want to retrieve, click OK to open the file. After a moment, the file appears in the work area.

Troubleshooting

I can't find the file I just created!

You may be looking in the wrong directory. Display the Open Existing Publication dialog box and double-click on the directory you want. You also may need to change to a different drive.

Understanding Directories

The discussion in the preceding section is fine and dandy if you see the file you want in the Publication **N**ame list box. But what if you can't remember the name of the file, and when you click the right file type, the file isn't shown in the list box? The problem could be that the file you're looking for isn't in the current directory. In this section, you learn about drives and directories and find out how to locate the files you need.

Defining a Directory

As you know, a file is something you create with a program. As you continue to work with a program, you accumulate a number of files. These files are stored in directories. You can think of a directory like a file folder that stores similar information. The directory that stores your Publisher files, for example, may be a subdirectory of another larger directory. The directories are stored on your hard drive. Table 4.1 explains the drive, directory, and subdirectories of Microsoft Publisher.

Table 4.1 Publisher Drive and Directories

Drive	Directory	Subdirectory	Definition
C:\			The hard drive that stores the Publisher program.
	MSPUB		The main directory in which all Publisher files are stored. You write this directory designation, or path, like this: C:\MSPUB.
		BORDERS	A subdirectory of MSPUB that stores BorderArt files. This path is written as C:\MSPUB\BORDERS.
		CLIPART	A subdirectory of MSPUB that stores the clip art files. This path is written as C:\MSPUB\CLIPART.
		PAGEWIZ	A subdirectory of MSPUB that stores the PageWizard files. This path is written as C:\MSPUB\PAGEWIZ.
2		PAPERS	A subdirectory of MSPUB that contains special paper designs you can use in the background of your publications (paper is available from a third-party source)
		TEMPLATE	A subdirectory of MSPUB that stores the template files. This path is written as C:\MSPUB\TEMPLATE.

Project Tip

If you work on one project at a time, you may want to create a subdirectory to store only those files specifically related to your current project. If you're working on an employee handbook, for example, you could create a directory named HANDBOOK.

When you need to specify another drive or directory in Publisher, such as when you're looking for a file in the Open Existing Publication dialog box, you first need to find out where you are in the program. The current directory is shown directly beneath the **D**irectories field in the center of the Open Existing Publication dialog box.

To change to another directory, move the pointer to the **D**irectories field, find the directory you want to see, and double-click the mouse button. The files shown in the Publication **N**ame list box change to show you the contents of that directory. You may need to change the file type chosen, in the List Files of Type box, in order to find the file you're looking for.

Tip
If you want to display all files in the current directory, you can replace the text in the Publication Name field with *.*.

You can move to any directory or subdirectory in the Directories list by double-clicking on the name or icon. After you select a directory, the icon changes, resembling an open folder.

You also can change the drive by clicking on the down arrow to the right of the Dri**v**es box. A drop-down list of drives appears. Publisher searches your hard drive during installation, so the program already knows how many drives you have set up on your computer. To choose another drive, click on the drive you want. The directories in the Directories box, and the files in the Publication Name list box, change to reflect the newly selected drive.

Saving Files

Another important step in working with files is saving files you've created. This section introduces you to the various options available to you when saving a file.

Saving a File for the First Time

When you save a file for the first time, you need to choose a drive and directory for the file and enter a file name. Follow these steps:

1. Open the **F**ile menu.
2. Choose the **S**ave command. The Save As dialog box appears (see fig. 4.6). As you can see, this dialog box looks similar to the Open Existing Publication dialog box.

Fig. 4.6
The Save As dialog box.

3. Type a name for the file in the Publication **N**ame text box. You can type up to eight characters before the period and three characters after the period. You can enter any extension you want; however, you may want to keep the extensions consistent so that you can find your Publisher files later. Publisher suggests that you use the extension PUB.
4. Change the drive, if necessary, by clicking on the down arrow to the right of the Dri**v**es box and choosing the drive you want from the displayed list.
5. If necessary, choose the directory in which you want to save the file by double-clicking on the directory in the **D**irectories box.
6. Decide whether you want to save this file as a template. If you do, move the pointer to the **T**emplate checkbox and click the mouse button. An x appears in the box.

Note

If you are saving the file as a template, remember that Publisher stores the file in the TEMPLATE subdirectory automatically. If you are going to use the current publication as a file and as a publication, save it as a regular file (in other words, don't click Template) first.

7. Decide whether you want to create a backup copy of this file in addition to the regular saved file. If you do, click on the **B**ackup checkbox.

Note

If you choose to make a backup copy, remember that the backup is one generation behind the original. Every time you save, the old version is moved to the backup and the new version is saved to the PUB file. That way, you can return to the previous version of your file if necessary. Because saving the backup file requires the use of some hard disk space, you may want to consider using this option only for very important files, if your computer is tight on storage space.

8. Click OK to save the file.

Publisher then saves the file and returns you to the publication open on-screen.

Saving Existing Files

Now you've saved the file once. But suppose that you open the file and make more changes. Now you need to save those changes—in the same file—to disk. The process is simple: press Ctrl+S or open the **F**ile menu and choose the **S**ave command. Ctrl+S is a quick-key combination that saves the publication for you without any further action.

If you want to save the publication under a different name, or change some of the settings you initially selected in the Save As dialog box, choose Save **A**s from the **F**ile menu. The Save As dialog box appears again, and you can change the settings as necessary, or enter a new name to save the file under a different name.

Saving a File to a Floppy Disk

At times you may want to copy a file to a floppy disk. Suppose that you want to give a coworker a copy of the publication you've been working on. To do this, simply insert a blank formatted disk into drive A or B. Assuming that the publication you want to copy is open on-screen, click on the **F**ile menu and choose the Save **A**s command.

When the Save As dialog box appears, move the mouse pointer to the Dri**v**es box. Click on the down arrow to the right of the Drives box. A list of available drives for your system appears. Windows determines the drives during the installation process. For this reason, the number of drives shown on your screen may differ from those shown here.

Click on the drive to which you want to copy the file. The line above the Directories box and the contents of the Directories box change to reflect the newly selected drive. You now can save the file by typing the name in the Publication **N**ame box and clicking OK.

After you save the file to the floppy disk, Publisher is logged on to the new drive. If you want to return to a file on another drive, you need to select the **O**pen Existing Publication command in the **F**ile menu, change the drive in the Dri**v**es box, and enter a new publication name or select the file you want from the displayed list.

Saving Tips

Here are a few tips to remember as you create and save Publisher files:

- Remember to save your work every 15 minutes or so.
- Save your publication each time you make significant changes to the document.
- Publisher saves all information on the pages and in the work space. If you are unsure whether you want to include a section of text or a picture in your publication, place it on the work space surrounding the page before saving the file. That way, if you want it later, the item has been saved with the file.
- When you choose to save a backup of your file by clicking on the **B**ackup box, Publisher saves both the current file and another copy as a backup.

- You can save the current file as a template so that you can later build publications based on the layout and settings saved in the current file.
- After you save a file once, you can use the quick-key Ctrl+S to save the file quickly.

Troubleshooting

I just tried to save my file to a disk and my computer said `Disk Full`.

That disk has too many files on it—choose another. You do have a formatted blank disk nearby, don't you?

I accidentally used another file's name when I saved my file! Is it gone forever?

If you checked the Backup box when you saved the file, you can recover the previous version (just look for the same file with the extension BAK). If you didn't use the Backup option, however, that file's goose is cooked.

From Here...

For information directly related to the topics covered in this chapter, you may want to review the following sections of this book:

- Chapter 5, "Entering Text." After you open a new file, the next logical step is to start entering text. Chapter 5 shows you the basics of typing and importing text.
- Chapter 11, "Printing the Publication." After the creative work is complete, you're ready to print. To pick up printing basics and learn how to step around printing problems, check out Chapter 11.

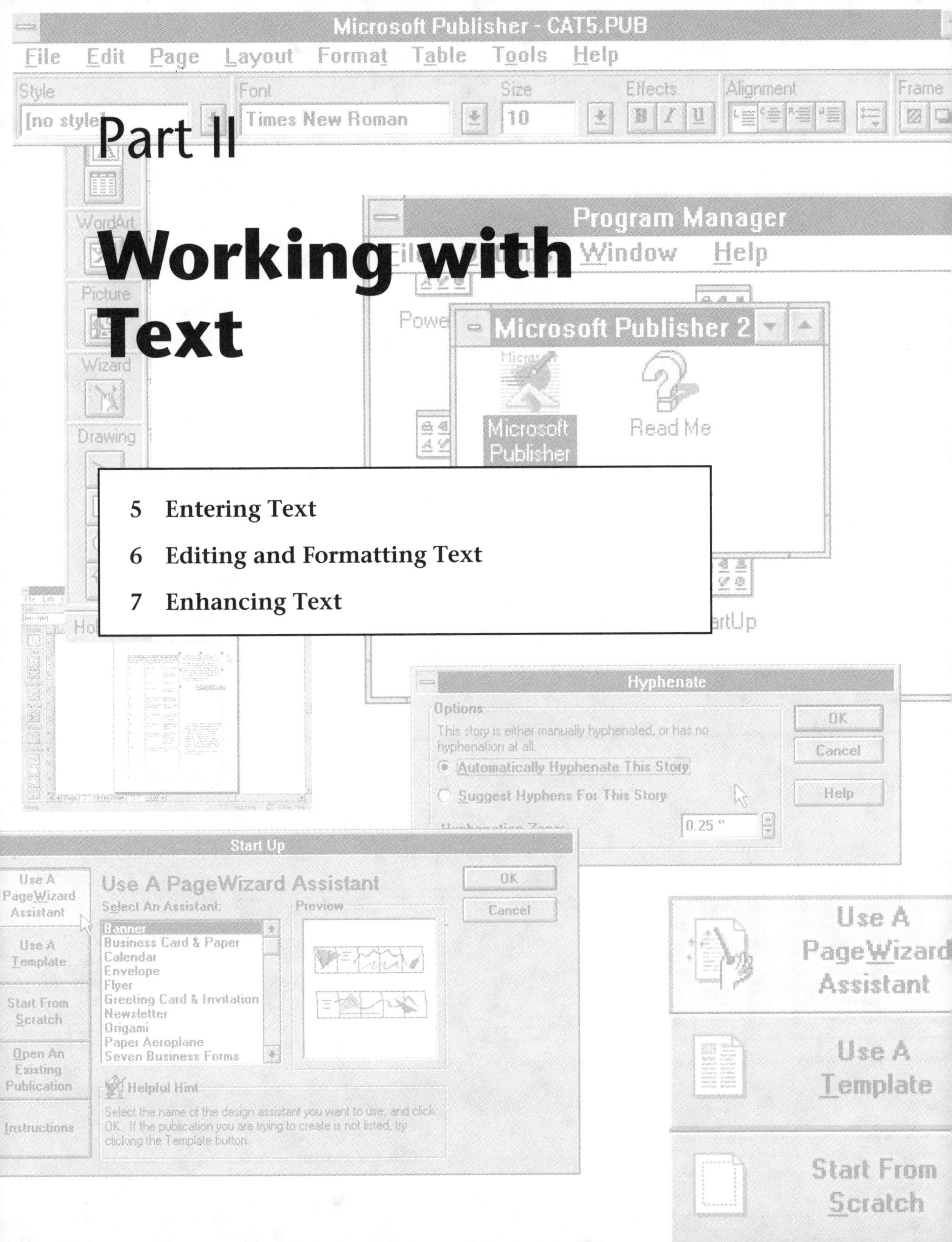

Part II

Working with Text

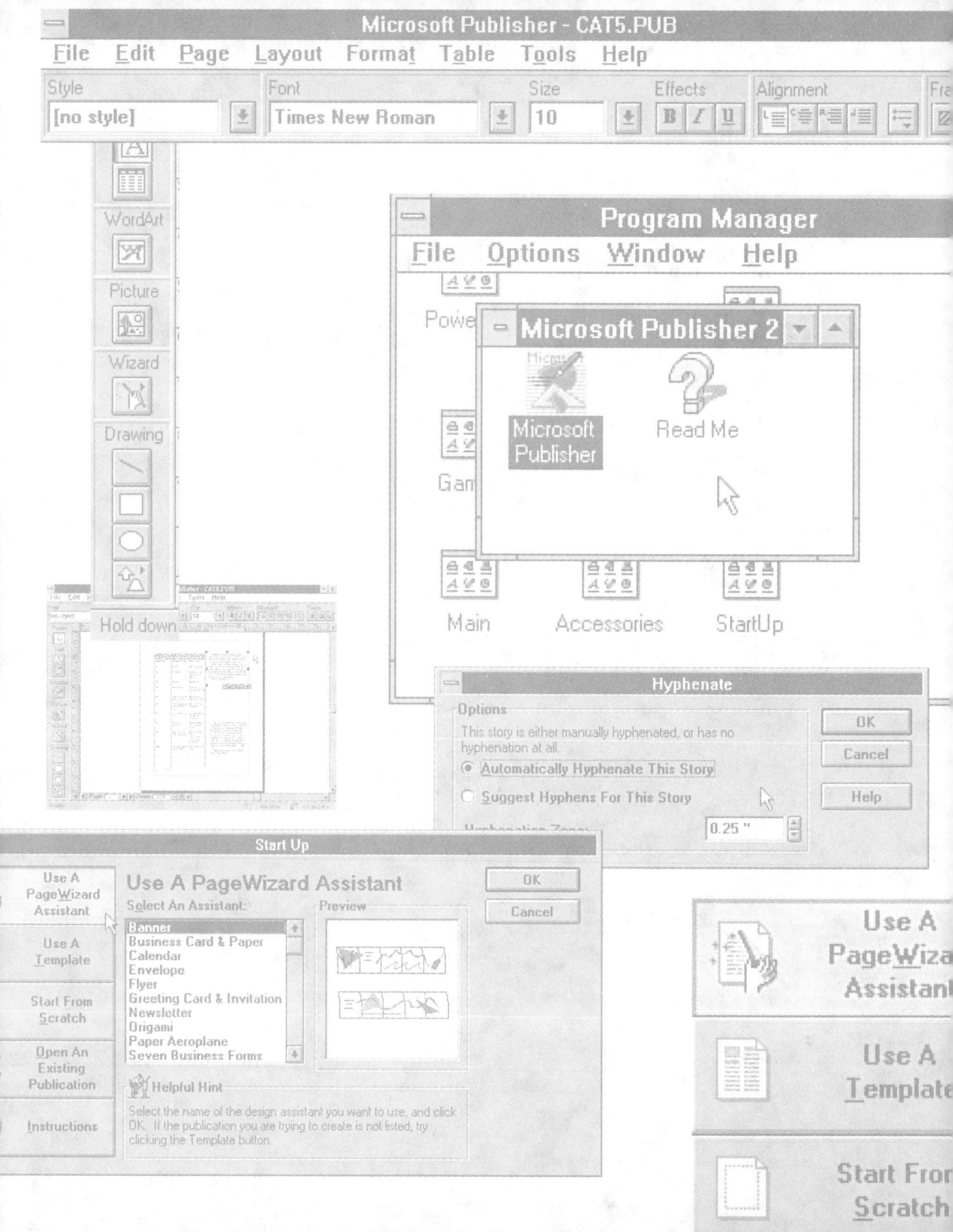
Microsoft Publisher - CAT5.PUB
File Edit Page Layout Format Table Tools Help
Style
[no style]
Font
Times New Roman
Size
10
Effects
Alignment
WordArt
Picture
Wizard
Drawing
Hold down
Program Manager
File Options Window Help
Microsoft Publisher 2
Microsoft Publisher
Read Me
Main
Accessories
StartUp
Hyphenate
Options
This story is either manually hyphenated, or has no hyphenation at all.
Automatically Hyphenate This Story
Suggest Hyphens For This Story
0.25 "
OK
Cancel
Help
Start Up
Use A PageWizard Assistant
Use A Template
Start From Scratch
Open An Existing Publication
Instructions
Use A PageWizard Assistant
Select An Assistant:
Banner
Business Card & Paper
Calendar
Envelope
Flyer
Greeting Card & Invitation
Newsletter
Origami
Paper Aeroplane
Seven Business Forms
Preview
OK
Cancel
Helpful Hint
Select the name of the design assistant you want to use, and click OK. If the publication you are trying to create is not listed, try clicking the Template button.
Use A Template

Chapter 5

Entering Text

Chapter 3 showed you how to use two Publisher features—PageWizards and templates—to make publications fast, right from the first time you use the program. You just plug in your text and graphics and go. This chapter takes care of the "plugging in" part.

There will be those times when a little extra creativity is called for. You need to come up with a design that's all yours, that relays your message just the way you envision it. That's when you will create your publications from scratch.

In this chapter, you learn how to start building your own custom Publisher publications. Although Publisher lets you start with any element—text or graphics—for the most part, it's easier to start with the text.

In this chapter, you learn to do the following tasks:

- Create a text frame
- Enter sample text
- Choose font and text size
- Select text effects
- Connect frames
- Create a table
- Enter table data

Methods of Entering Text

There's more than one way to enter text in Microsoft Publisher. You can type the text directly—the most obvious choice—or you can use text you've already entered in other programs. That's a process known as *importing* text. Publisher supports text from many different programs, including Microsoft Word. Importing text is discussed in detail later in this chapter.

With Publisher 2.0, you can create text tables in a snap. No more aligning columns with the Tab key; now you can assign a table format to your text as you create it. You then can choose from any number of preset layouts to help you enter the data correctly—the first time.

Entering Text

If you're working with a document created by a PageWizard, or you're using an already created template file, you need to remove the existing text in the document before you can add your own. If you are creating a new publication (which means that you just selected the Start From **S**cratch button in the Start Up box), your first step is to choose the type of layout you want in the S**e**lect A Page Layout list (see fig. 5.1). After you make your selection, click OK.

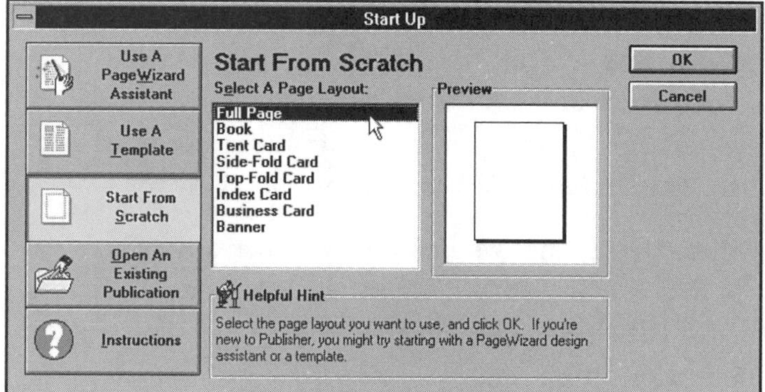

Fig. 5.1
Choosing the Page Layout.

After you make room for your own text in the publication or choose the basic page layout, you're ready to get started. If you are starting with a blank publication, you need to create new text frames to store the text you enter. If you used a PageWizard or a template, you can use the text frames already included on your publication.

Project Tip

You may feel like you have to get all the settings right—spacing, alignment, font—from the start. Relax. You can change all the text settings after you have some text to work with.

Creating a Text Frame

To create a text frame, first click on the Text tool in the Left Toolbar. The Top Toolbar appears with several options (see fig. 5.2).

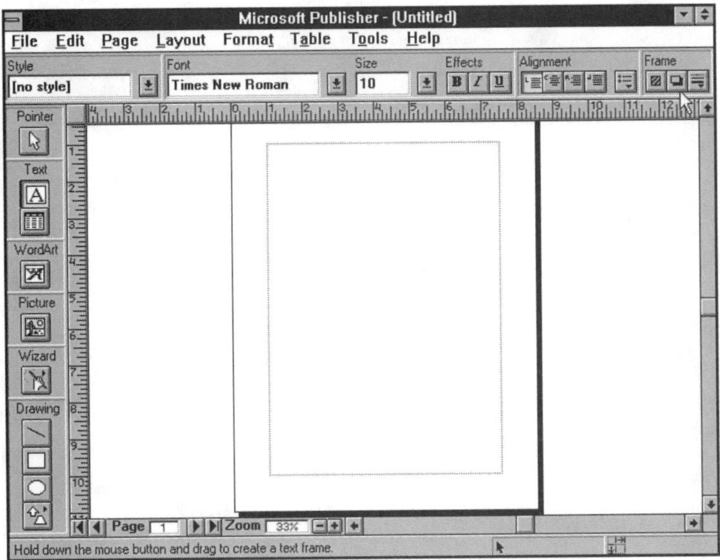

Fig. 5.2
Displaying the text options.

The Frame options—at the right end of the Top Toolbar—control the way your text frame is drawn. The first option enables you to choose a shaded background for the text, the second option creates a drop-shadowed box, and the last option controls the width of the line bordering the text frame.

Click on the options you want or don't choose anything and get the default, which is a text frame with no border. Move the pointer to a point on the document page where you want the upper left corner of the text frame to be positioned. Press and hold the mouse button. Drag the mouse down and to the right. The box is drawn on-screen.

When the box is the size you want, release the mouse button. The frame appears with black handles and a small tag at the bottom of the frame (you use this tag later to connect text frames). A small flashing text cursor is positioned in the upper left corner of the frame. This shows the point where characters will appear when you begin typing.

If the frame isn't exactly where you want it, don't worry. You can drag the frame to the right spot at any time during the creation of your publication. Just position the pointer on the edge of the frame and the small "moving van" pointer appears (see fig. 5.3). Now press and hold the mouse button and drag the frame to the desired location.

Tip
To change the size of the frame, move the mouse pointer to one of the frame handles. Use the mouse to drag the handle in the direction you want to resize the frame. If you want to resize the height and width at the same time, move one of the corner handles.

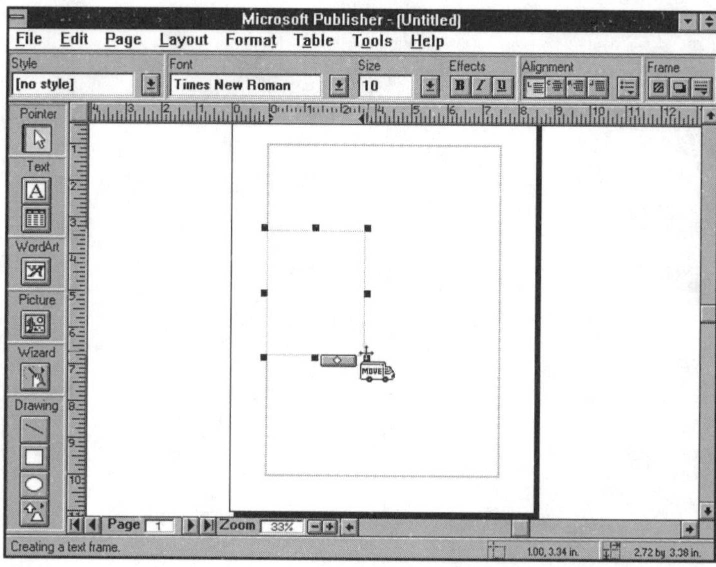

Fig. 5.3
The text frame created.

Project Tip

Remember that the text you are going to enter will completely fill the text frame, so if you're putting text frames right next to each other, leave room between the frames for column space.

Quick-and-Easy Text Entry

Now comes the fun part—entering text within the frame. Just type something. You know the keystrokes. Type a little paragraph about the vagabond wanderings of your neighbor's cat, or take a stab at politics or religion (whatever people tell you not to—might as well make it fun).

The first time you create a text frame, Publisher may pop in with a helpful message reminding you to zoom in on the text frame to see the text you enter more clearly. Use the zoom controls, in the bottom of the work area, to zoom the display.

Here are a few things to remember when you start typing in your text:

- Don't press Tab at the beginning of the paragraph. If you want a paragraph indent, you use the Indents and Lists command to take care of that for you.

- No need to press Enter at the end of the line. Publisher moves the cursor (any necessary characters) to the next line for you. That's a cool feature called *word wrap* that virtually every word processing program worth its salt now has.
- You can press Enter to leave a blank line between paragraphs (if you enter more than one, you industrious person), but you don't need to; instead, you may prefer to adjust spacing with the Line Spacing command.

Project Tip

Can't see what you're typing? Click the plus button in the Zoom controls at the bottom of the screen once or twice.

Figure 5.4 shows some text plugged into the text frame. (An available text frame is a terrible thing to waste.)

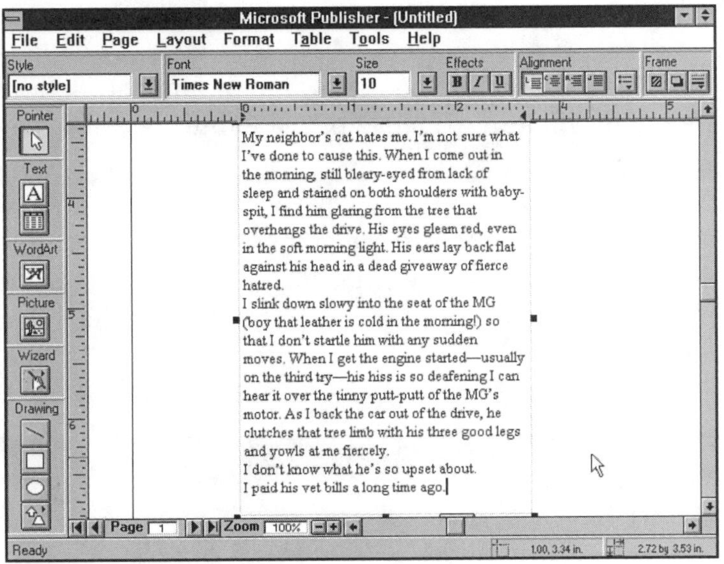

Fig. 5.4
Okay, so we're filling space.

Note

If you're the type of person who likes to have all your ducks in a row before you take the plunge yourself, you may feel more comfortable getting all your text options set just the way you want them before you enter text. These options include choosing the text font, size, and effect you want for the characters you type. If you make these choices before you type, the characters you enter will appear in the font, size, and style you want. If you just blaze away and start typing before you make your choices, you get Publisher's default text settings, which you may want to change at a later point. Either way works. The next section explains how you can set the text options you want before you enter text. If you've already entered text and want to change what you've done, check out Chapter 7, "Enhancing Text."

Choosing Text Font and Size

In addition to the Frame options in the Top Toolbar, a whole slew of other text options awaits your attention:

- *Style.* You can use a text style to apply certain settings you use over and over again.

- *Font.* The text font is the typeface you use for the text you enter. Depending on the capabilities of your printer, you may have many different fonts available (as is the case if you are using a PostScript laser printer) or you may have just a few fonts available. The default font used earlier in figure 5.4 is Times New Roman. Your font may be different. To display a list of available fonts, click on the down arrow to the right of the Font box (see fig. 5.5).

Project Tip

Make sure that the font you use reflects the tone of your publication. As a general rule, use what you think looks good. Show it to a couple of objective people and get their opinions.

To change the font selected, simply open the Font box by clicking on the down arrow at the right end of the box and click on the font you want to use. Your choice is shown in the Font box. When you begin typing, the font you selected is used.

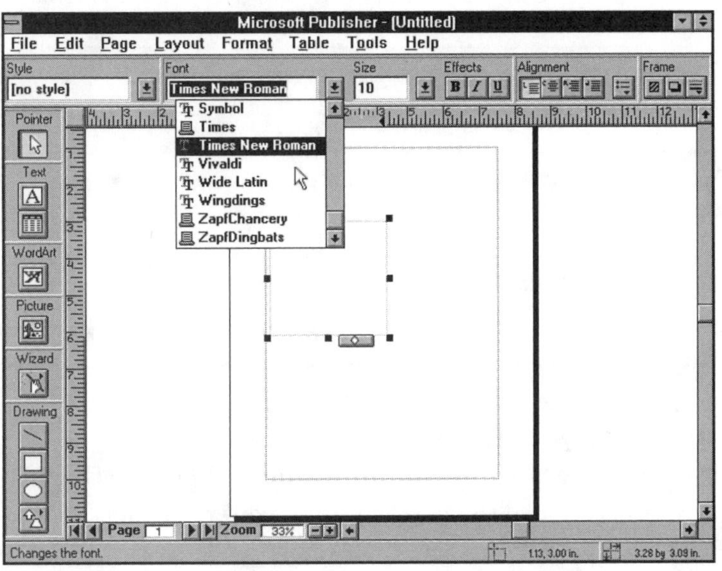

Fig. 5.5
Displaying other font choices.

■ *Size*. The font Size box is found to the right of the Font box. Again, to see a list of available sizes, click on the down arrow to the right of the font Size box. The number of sizes you have available depends on the type of printer you are using and the fonts available to your printer. Select the size you want; the new size appears in the Size box. You can use the size guidelines in table 5.1 to help you choose the text size for your publications.

Tip
You can change any text option (font, size, style, alignment, and spacing) at any time during your work session. To change existing text, highlight the text and then choose the option you want to change.

Table 5.1 Choosing Text Sizes

Point size	Use for
6	Copyright information, trademark information, or disclaimers
8	Catalog information or required statistical information too small for readable body text

(continues)

Table 5.1 Continued

Point size	Use for
10	Standard size for body text
12	Standard size for body text—easier on the eye in some formats than 10-point type
14	Small headlines, kicker lines, and pull-quotes
16	Medium headlines, pull-quotes
18	Headlines or large text for promotional flyers
20	Headlines or small titles (banners)
24	Banners
30	Banners (use only if the banner has few characters)

Being Bold about Text Effects

To the right of the Size box, you see a series of buttons. The first three Effects buttons control the personality of your characters. In the past, Bold, Italic, and Underline were called *text styles*. Now that Publisher has a different feature using that name, these buttons are called *effects*. (Hmmmm. The jury's still out.)

You can use bold, italic, or underline to change the look of your words. Here's an example of each:

Boldface

Italic

Underline

Generally, boldface is used to make a text item stand out. Headlines are usually boldfaced, as are product names (in press releases) and information in headers and footers.

Italic is used in different professions for different reasons. Typically, people use italic to stress an important word, to indicate a term that is going to be defined, or to call attention to a new concept.

Underlining is used much like italic, again depending on your application. Underlining often is used when names of publications or book titles are included in a published work.

Project Tip

Remember that if you emphasize too much text too often, everything in the publication can be de-emphasized. If you use too much bold, italic, or underlining, your text will have a cluttered look.

To select bold, italic, or underline, simply click on the button of the style you want. You can select more than one style; for example, you can use boldface italic to make a defined term stand out; you can italicize an underlined word in a publication quote. If you want to deselect a style you've chosen, simply click on the button again.

Let's Get Things Straight

The alignment of your text controls the way the text is placed in the frame. You can choose from four Alignment buttons:

Option	Alignment
Left	Along the left edge of the frame with a ragged right edge
Center	Centered in the frame (both edges are ragged)
Right	Along the right edge of the frame with a ragged left edge
Justified	Along both the left and right edge of the frame

To select the alignment of the text, click on the appropriate Alignment button. Like the other settings in the text options row, you can change the alignment of your text before or after you enter the text.

Project Tip

Justified text is often used for multiple columns of text; left alignment is by far the most common alignment used. Centered text is chosen most often for headings, and Right is used in special situations like figure captions, subheads, or specially designed text used as graphics.

Bulleted Lists, Numbered Lists, and More Lists

That little button sitting all alone at the right edge of the Alignment buttons is the List button. Behind that button lurks a number of options. When you click the List button, the screen shown in figure 5.6 appears.

You can make numbered lists or bulleted lists. Choose a variety of bullet characters. Control line spacing. Change the size and alignment of text. And when you click More, you see another palette of choices—lots of things you only dreamed about (see fig. 5.7).

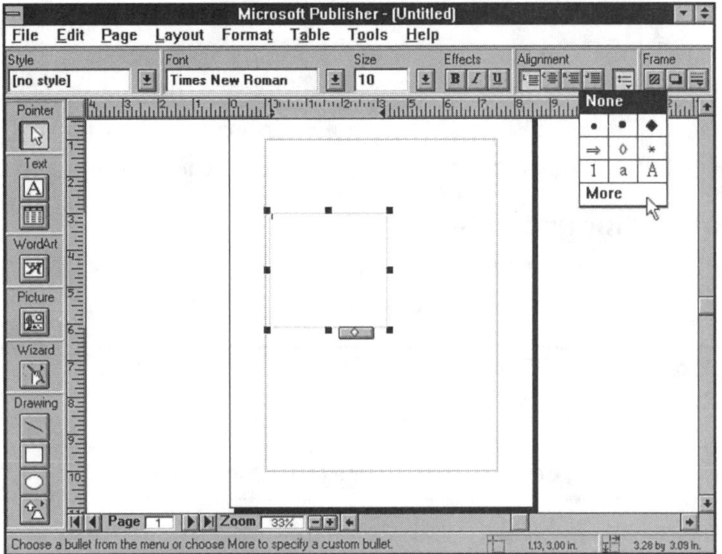

Fig. 5.6
A little button with a lot of punch.

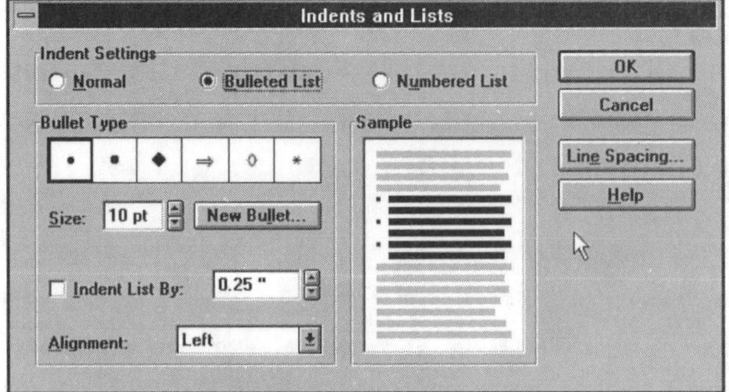

Fig. 5.7
Look at all those choices in the Indents and Lists dialog box.

Project Tip

Bulleted lists and numbered lists are very effective in helping readers find important information quickly. Put the things you want your readers to remember in a bulleted list.

Changing the View

Entering text is an up-close-and-personal issue. If you can't read the characters you're typing, how are you sure what you're really saying? Don't take a chance. Zoom in.

The process is simple, and Version 2.0 makes it easier than ever. You can use commands in the Page menu to enlarge the view, or you can use the Zoom controls in the status bar at the bottom of the screen (see fig. 5.8).

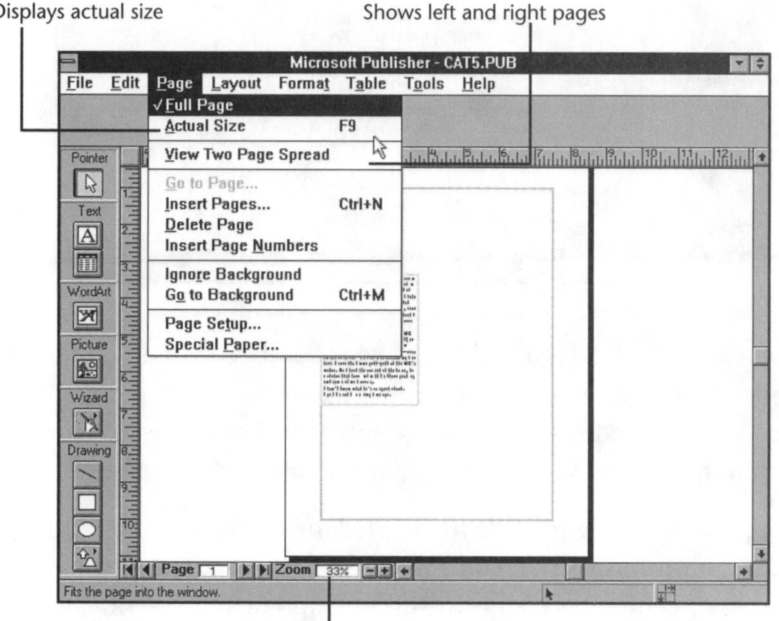

Fig. 5.8
Zoom choices.

In the Page menu, you have three different view choices:

- ***Full Page***. Shows the entire current page in the Publisher work area (the default).

- *Actual Size*. Displays the selected frame in the size it will appear in print (the easiest way to display Actual Size is to press F9). Figure 5.9 shows the entered text in Actual Size.

- *View Two Page Spread*. Shows you the left and right pages of your document, so, needless to say, the text is displayed smaller than it is in Full Page view. Figure 5.10 gives you a taste of View Two Page Spread.

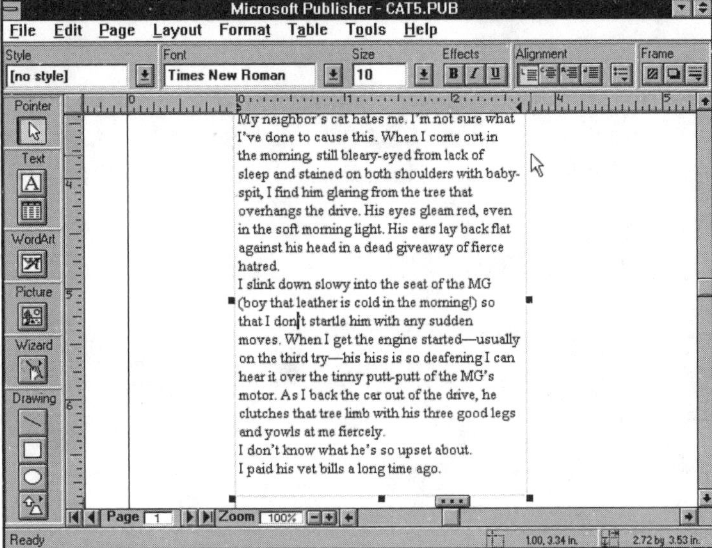

Fig. 5.9
A little bit of reality: Actual Size.

For up-close text work, Actual Size is your best bet. When you want to see how the text and graphics elements balance on your page, whether you included enough white space, and to resolve other overall layout questions, View Two Page Spread comes in handy.

If you prefer working in increments, clicking either the plus (+) or minus (-) buttons in Zoom controls at the bottom of the screen does the trick. Clicking plus zooms the display up one increment; clicking minus reduces the display one increment.

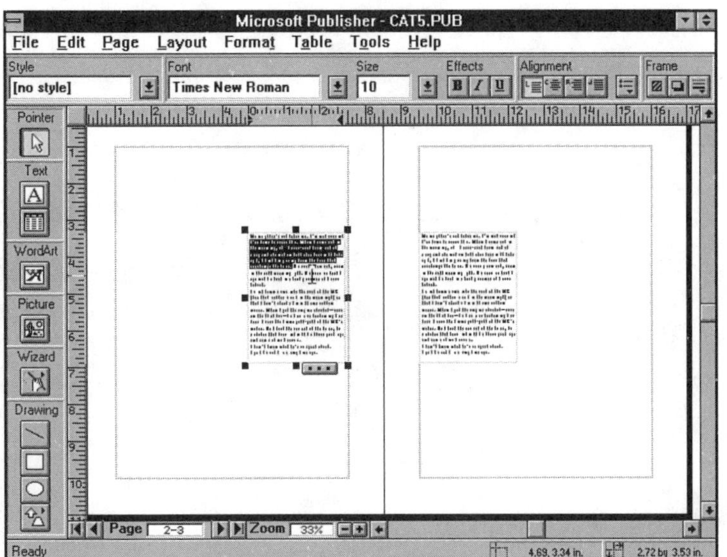

Fig. 5.10
The big picture: Two Page Spread.

Connecting Text Frames

When you have entered all you can type in the first text frame, you need to know how to move to the next frame. You could keep each story in an individual text frame, but if you later make additions or deletions to one frame, the text in subsequent frames will not be connected to the first frame. This could result in gaping holes at the end of the first frame (if you delete information), or it could cause some information from the first frame to be bumped off the display into oblivion (actually, the text is stored in an unseen overflow area). Connecting your frames, therefore, is best: it is simple to do, is sugar-free, and makes sure that none of your text gets lost.

To link frames, follow these steps:

1. First create the second frame, if you haven't already done so. (You may need to change the view first.) In this example, another text frame has been added to the right of the first frame (which was shortened so we'd need another frame).

2. If you changed the view, return to Actual Size.

3. Select the frame that currently is storing the text. If you have entered more text than the frame can display, the button at the bottom of the frame displays three dots in a button (see fig. 5.11).

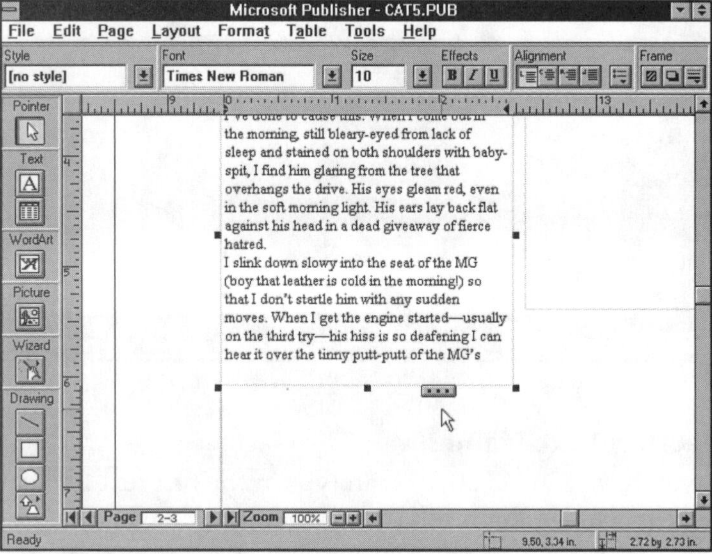

Fig. 5.11
The dots mean that the frame has more text to pour.

4. Click the button. The cursor changes to a pitcher.

> **Note**
>
> After you click the button, Publisher helpfully pops up a box on-screen, telling you what you're about to do and asking if you'd like a quick demo of the procedure. Go ahead, if you want. We can wait.

Tip
The drag-and-drop text feature is used for moving a section of text quickly from one place to another. Highlight the text you want to move, and drag the text to the other frame.

5. Move the cursor to the new frame. Now the pitcher changes to show it pouring characters into the frame.

6. Click the mouse button. The additional text is entered in the frame (see fig. 5.12).

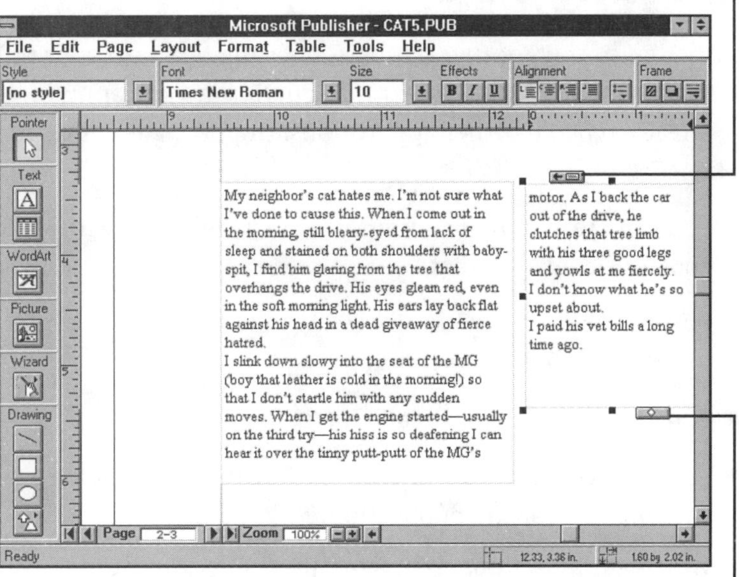

Fig. 5.12 Entering text in the linked frame.

Now, whenever you change any information in the first frame, the text in the second frame moves to reflect the change.

Troubleshooting

Oh, jeez—I really messed up that last sentence.

No biggie—just use the Backspace key to delete back to the problem and retype things correctly. And if the last sentence is many words back, check out Chapter 6 to find an easy way to make bigger editing changes.

I clicked on the down-arrow beside the Style box, but my screen just says [no style].

You have to create a style before you can apply it to your text. (The first time you click the style down-arrow, Publisher intervenes and asks if you'd like a quick demonstration. Click OK if you do.) A style records text settings, like font, size, and alignment, that you want to apply to other text. For more about creating styles, see Chapter 7, "Enhancing Text."

Importing Text

Publisher gives you another option for getting text into your publication. Rather than typing the text into Publisher, you can use text you have already typed in other applications. Importing text files has several benefits:

- You can create long documents in a fast program with which you are already familiar.
- You can use other word-processing benefits, such as a built-in thesaurus or grammar checker.
- You can use files you already have on disk.
- You can accept files from other people who are helping you prepare the text for the publication.
- You can import tables you have already created in other programs like Excel or Word.

What Types of Text Files Can I Import?

As you know, Publisher supports many types of popular word processing programs. Because of the number and popularity of Windows programs, this is a major benefit for users of the following programs:

Microsoft Word 6.0
WordPerfect 5.x for Windows
Windows Write 3.0 and 3.1
Word for Windows 1.x and 2.x
Word for DOS
WordPerfect 5.x
Works for DOS
Works for Windows 2.0 and 3.0

You also can import files saved in ASCII (American Standard Code for Information Interchange) format. Most popular word processing programs have techniques you can use to save your file in ASCII form. Consult your word processor's instruction manual for details.

Project Tip

The possibility of using text later is a great incentive for keeping backups of all your documents. Sure, maybe you were sick of that booklet when you finished it last year, but who knows—maybe next you will want to import it into Publisher.

Importing a Text File

To import a text file into your Publisher document, follow these steps:

1. Create a text frame (or, to use an existing frame, click in the frame you want to use).
2. Open the **F**ile menu.
3. Choose I**m**port Text. The Import Text dialog box appears (see fig. 5.13).

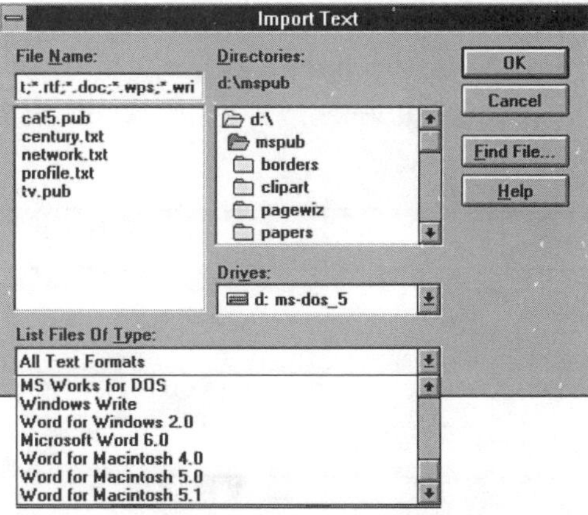

Fig. 5.13
The Import Text dialog box.

Note

If the text frame you selected is part of a connected chain of frames, the Import Text command is available only if you select the first frame in the chain.

4. To specify the file you want to import, first move the pointer to the Drives box.
5. Change the drive, if necessary, by clicking on the down arrow to the right of the Drives box and choosing the drive you want.
6. Change the directory, if necessary, by double-clicking on the name of the directory in the **D**irectories list.
7. Select the type of file you want to import by clicking on the down arrow to the right of the List Files Of **T**ype box. Click on your selection.
8. Locate the file you want in the File **N**ame list and highlight it.
9. Click OK to import the file.

Publisher tells you that the file is being converted. After a moment, you return to the publication and the text is flowed into the frame. If the imported text takes up more room than one text frame allows, Publisher asks you if you want the text to be flowed in all text frames or if you want to place text in only this frame and connect other frames yourself. To have Publisher flow all text, click Yes. To flow the text yourself, click No.

Troubleshooting

I don't see my file anywhere.

Try clicking the **F**ind File button and letting Publisher help you locate the timid file.

Adding and Importing Tables

Creating tables was one of the last great headaches word processing users had to deal with. Aligning text in a columnar fashion was a task just begging for trouble. You press Tab a few times, get the text to line up on-screen, and, when you print, you have columns that look nothing like columns.

Luckily, you have Publisher. The addition of the Table tool—new with Publisher 2.0—makes it easy for you to set up the table any way you want it. How many columns and rows do you want? Just enter the numbers in the Create Table dialog box (see fig. 5.14). When you click OK, Publisher puts the table—with the number of columns and rows you selected—at the point you drew the frame (see fig. 5.15).

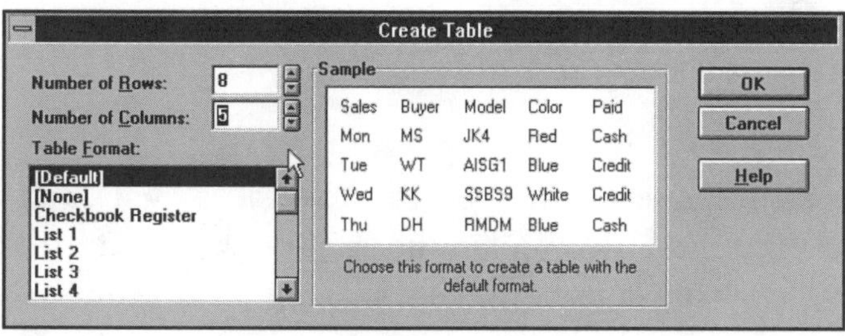

Fig. 5.14
Choosing the number of columns and rows.

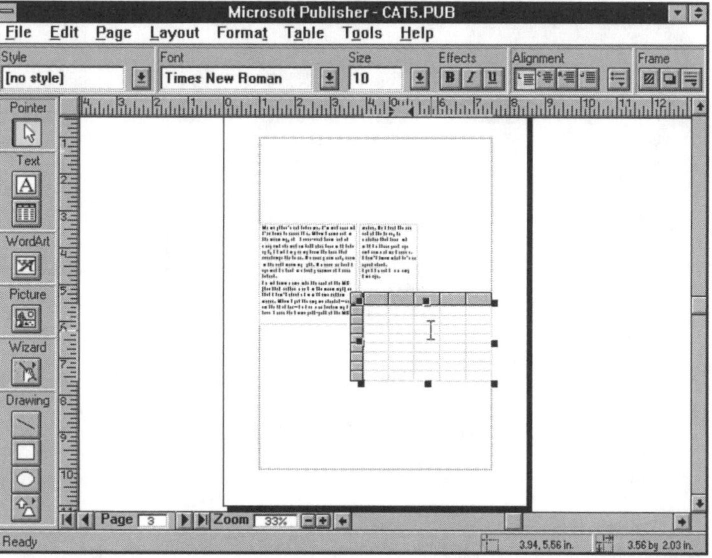

Fig. 5.15
The added table.

Bet you're just dying to try this out. The following sections explain how to add a table and enter and import data.

Creating a Table

The first step in creating a table is, of course, to think about the type of data you want to display. A table is different from a text frame because there must be some order to the way you're presenting the information; otherwise, you wouldn't be interested in putting it in a table. Think about how you want the table to appear before you start creating it.

Project Tip

Sketching out a rough draft of possible columns and rows can help you create the table right the first time. You might also look at reports or tables you've done in the past to see what worked and what didn't.

The next step is to select the Table tool to create a frame. The Table tool is just under the Text tool in the Left Toolbar (see fig. 5.16). When you click the button, the cursor changes to the traditional crosshair.

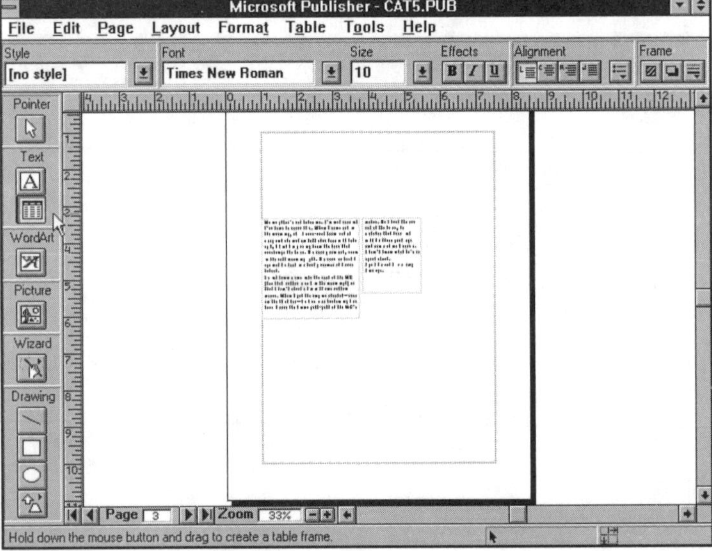

Fig. 5.16
Selecting the table tool.

Now draw the frame as you would any text frame. The difference? When you release the mouse button, the Create Table dialog box appears (see fig. 5.17). Publisher makes a best guess at the number of rows and columns you might want, based on the way you created the frame. You can click the up or down arrows beside the Number of **R**ows or Number of **C**olumns boxes if you want to change the settings.

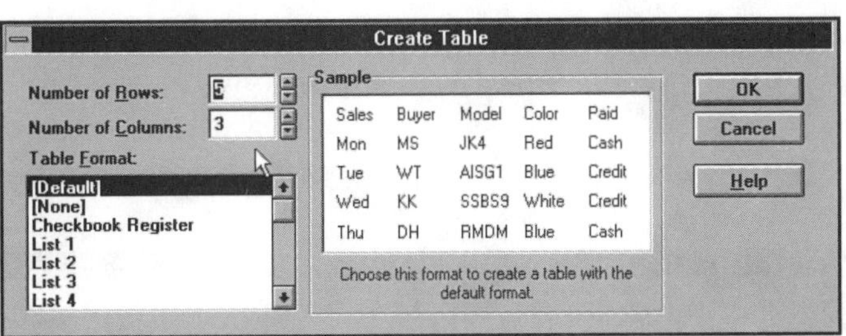

Fig. 5.17
The Create Table dialog box.

The Table Format list box controls—you guessed it—the basic table format. You can choose from a number of different table styles—some with titles and colors, some without—in a variety of different configurations. You can choose from the following table types:

- Checkbook register style with room for monthly column headings
- Lists with column headings only and various shading selections for rows and columns
- Lists with titles and column or row labels
- Spreadsheet-style lists with column and row labels, as well as a totals line
- Table of Contents table that includes a heading and space for TOC entries
- A checkerboard table that could drive your boss crazy

When you finish making selections, click OK. Publisher then draws the table on-screen (see fig. 5.18).

Entering Table Data

This is the easy part. The cursor is already positioned in the new table for you; just zoom in (press F9) and start typing. Here are a few rules for entering table data:

- Type the information without pressing Enter at the end of a line. Publisher lengthens the cell to accommodate any spill-over data.
- Press Tab to move to the next cell.
- Press Shift+Tab to move back to the previous cell.

- Don't press Enter to get to the next line of the table. Publisher moves the cursor one line down in the same cell.

Figure 5.19 shows the table after data has been entered.

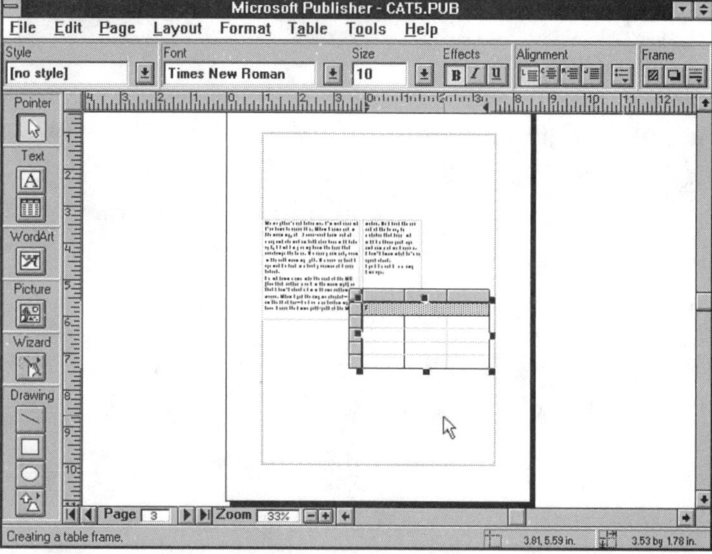

Fig. 5.18
The new table.

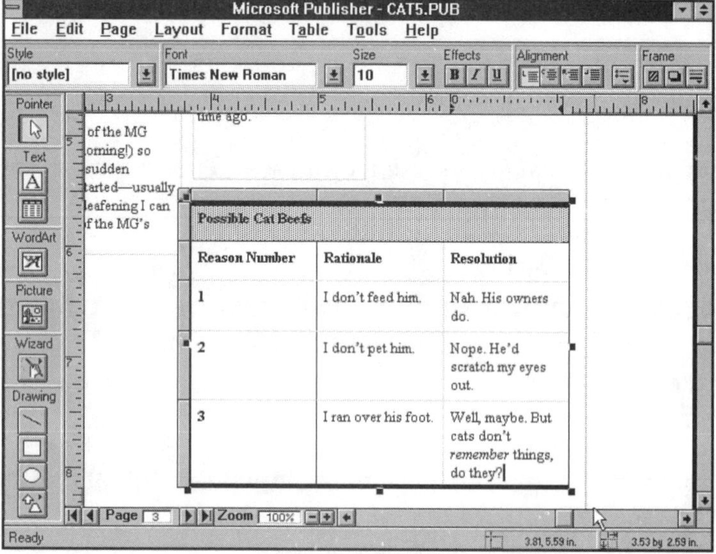

Fig. 5.19
Table with entered data.

Importing Table Data

Importing table data into Publisher really is a glorified way of saying that you're copying table data from one application into another. You might, for example, want to use a table you've already created in Microsoft Word, Works, or Excel. Why retype the data when you don't have to?

First, create the basic table (see fig. 5.20). Next, open the other application (minimize Publisher first) and highlight the data you want to copy. Use the trusty old **C**opy command in the **E**dit menu; then return to Publisher.

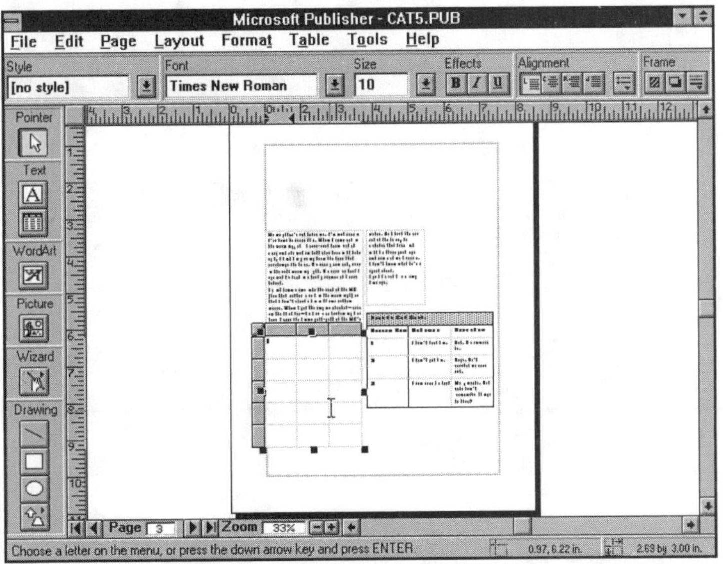

Fig. 5.20
The table, waiting for data.

Make sure that the table is selected, and then open the **E**dit menu and choose Paste **S**pecial (see fig. 5.21). This special kind of Paste command preserves any special format the incoming data might have. The Paste Special dialog box appears so that you can choose how you want the data imported (see fig. 5.22). You can have the data placed in the document in the table you created, in a new table, or in a text frame. For this example, the first option, Table Cells With Cell Formatting, was selected. When you click OK, the table is created (see fig. 5.23).

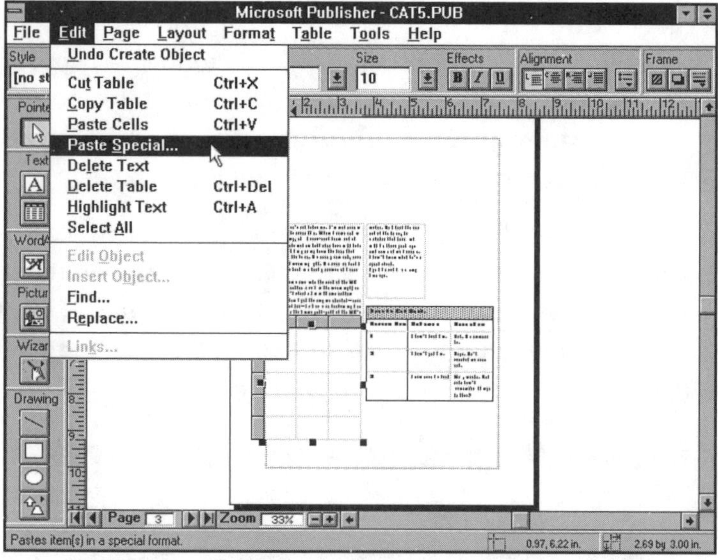

Fig. 5.21 Using Paste Special to preserve the table's format.

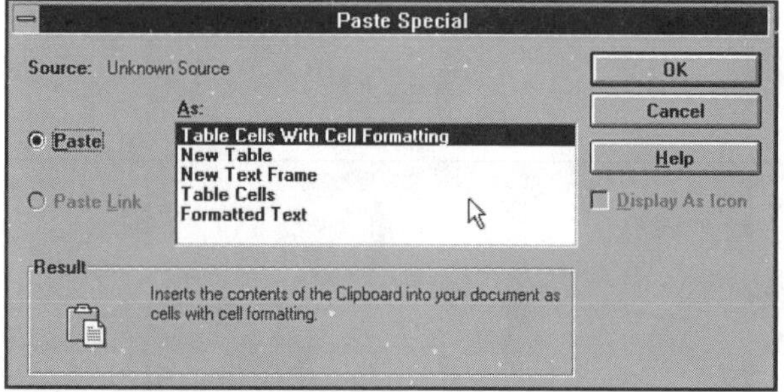

Fig. 5.22 The Paste Special dialog box.

Project Tip

You can also add graphics to your Publisher tables. See Chapter 8, "Adding Pictures," for more details.

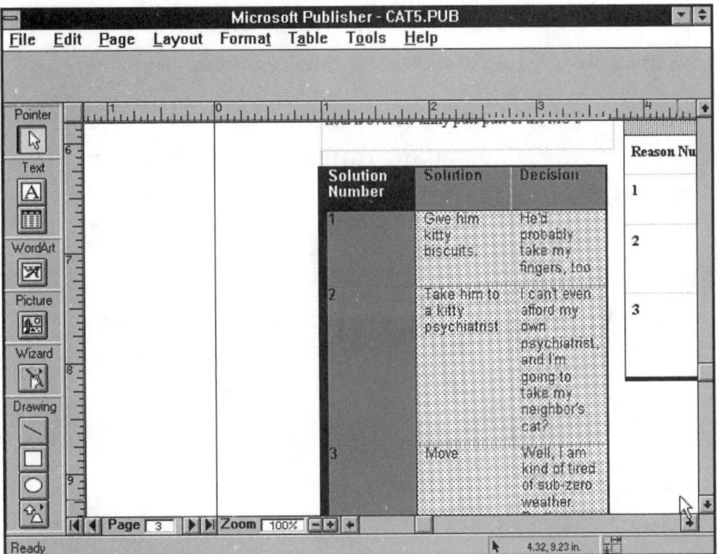

Fig. 5.23 The completed table.

> **Troubleshooting**
>
> *I created the table, but now that I see it in the document, I don't like it.*
>
> If you want to blow a table away and start again, press Ctrl+Del. If you simply want to change the format of the table and choose a different type, open the Table menu and choose AutoFormat.
>
> *I forgot to enter column heads.*
>
> You can easily cut and paste information, move data, or add columns and rows to your table. Use the Table menu to find the necessary commands (or turn to Chapter 6, "Editing and Formatting Text," to find out more about editing tables).

From Here...

For information related directly to working with text, you may want to review the following sections of this book:

- Chapter 6, "Editing and Formatting Text." Now you know the basics of getting the text in there. But do you know how to make it presentable? Clean up those typos. Align the text. Get the spacing right. Chapter 6 covers all those editing tasks, and more.

- Chapter 7, "Enhancing Text," shows you how to change the look of your text by making different font choices, working with WordArt, and using those cool TrueType fonts.

Chapter 6

Editing and Formatting Text

Nobody does anything perfectly (present company especially). Sometimes you need to see things on-screen—just get the idea up there—before you can start identifying what's wrong with it. Anyone standing around the water cooler will be glad to tell you where you've missed the mark:

> "Oh, you misspelled orangutan."
>
> "Maybe you should talk about *this* before you talk about *that*."
>
> "I think this report would be a lot better if you used fewer adjectives."

Before you get discouraged, remember: you've already done the hardest part. You have entered the basic text of your publication. The rest of the process is just about arranging and editing the text and making it look its best. This chapter helps you identify areas that might need editing and then helps you edit them.

In this chapter, you learn to do the following tasks:

- Perform simple text editing techniques
- Select text blocks
- Cut, copy, paste, and delete text blocks
- Use find and replace
- Use the spelling checker
- Edit tables

What's Editing?

Anyone who's ever received a paper or report that is bloody with red-pen markings knows how it feels to be edited. But what does it mean to edit? And how does that apply to Publisher?

For our purposes, editing is fixing what's wrong or what could be better. Editing might include the following things:

- Fixing typos
- Rearranging sections
- Moving paragraphs
- Revising text
- Running a spelling checker
- Substituting stronger words for weaker ones

In short, editing makes the overall publication a cleaner, stronger, more focused version of its former self.

The way you edit depends on the type of editing you're doing. If you are simply changing this character to that one, you're doing a kind of "keystroke editing"; that is, you can edit by using a simple keystroke or two. If you are moving a section of text, the edit is more complicated. That process requires that you first mark the section of text—called a *story* in Publisher—before you do anything else. This kind of editing is called "block editing."

Keystroke Editing

The phrase *keystroke editing* refers to the editing of individual words or characters. The following editing problems, for example, require keystroke editing:

- Letters transposed in a word
- An omitted word
- Extra space in a paragraph
- The use of a wrong word in a sentence
- Punctuation errors
- Grammatical errors

When you correct this type of editing problem, you use a certain set of keys to navigate through the document and fix the error. Table 6.1

lists the various keys you use for moving the text cursor and correcting problems.

Table 6.1 Using Keystroke Editing Keys

Key	Description
For moving the cursor:	
↑	Moves text cursor up one line
↓	Moves text cursor down one line
→	Moves text cursor right one character
←	Moves text cursor left one character
Ctrl+↑	Moves cursor to beginning of text block
Ctrl+↓	Moves cursor to end of text block
Ctrl+→	Moves cursor to beginning of word to the right
Ctrl+←	Moves cursor to beginning of word to the left
Home	Moves cursor to beginning of line
End	Moves cursor to end of line
PgUp	Scrolls page up
PgDn	Scrolls page down
For performing keystroke edits:	
Tab	Adds tab space at cursor position
Enter	Adds line space; takes cursor to next line
Backspace	Deletes character left of cursor
Del	Deletes character right of cursor

These basic cursor-movement and editing keys are common to all Windows applications, so after you get comfortable with them in Publisher, you can use them in all your other Windows programs as well.

Controlling Hyphenation

Publisher also gives you options for controlling the way your words are hyphenated. You can specify how you want Publisher to hyphenate words before you add text, or you can choose a specific word you want Publisher to hyphenate in a certain way. Either way, whether you're controlling hyphenation globally or only in one instance, you use the **H**yphenate command in the Tools menu to tell Publisher how, and where, you want words to be hyphenated.

With Publisher, you can specify a *hyphenation zone*, which is an area measured from the edge of the frame, in which a word will be hyphenated. If the word *Publisher*, for example, falls within the hyphenation zone, the program will hyphenate the word for you.

To set the hyphenation for a particular frame (or connected frames), follow these steps:

Tip
If you want to bypass the menu selections, you can press the quick-key combination Ctrl+H.

1. Click on the frame that contains the text you want to hyphenate.

2. Open the T**o**ols menu.

3. Choose the **H**yphenate command. The Hyphenate dialog box appears, as shown in figure 6.1.

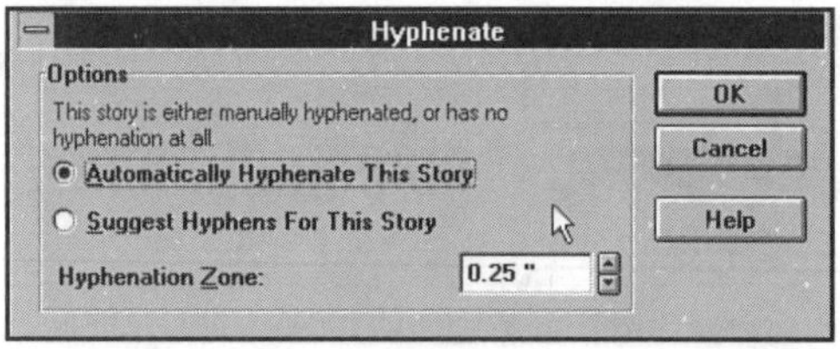

Fig. 6.1
Selecting hyphenation of entered text.

The hyphenation zone is the area you specify from the end of the text to the edge of the frame. The default, 0.25, tells you that if a long word falls within 1/4 inch of the frame edge, Publisher will ask you if you want to hyphenate the word.

Version 2.0 changes the Hyphenate dialog box a little. Now you see the Confirm option only if you choose **A**utomatically Hyphenate This Story. If you choose the Confirm Every Automatic Hyphen option, Publisher displays the Hyphenate box whenever it encounters

a word that falls within the hyphenation zone. The word is displayed in the Hyphenate **A**t box.

When you click OK to turn on hyphenation, for example, Publisher begins looking through your document for words that need to be hyphenated. When a word is found, Publisher displays the word in the Hyphenate **A**t box and shows you where the hyphen would be placed (see fig. 6.2). You can click **Y**es to have Publisher add the hyphen in the text or click **N**o to continue to the next word.

Tip
If you have a problem with the hyphenation procedure, you can get more information at any time by clicking the **H**elp button in the Hyphenate dialog box.

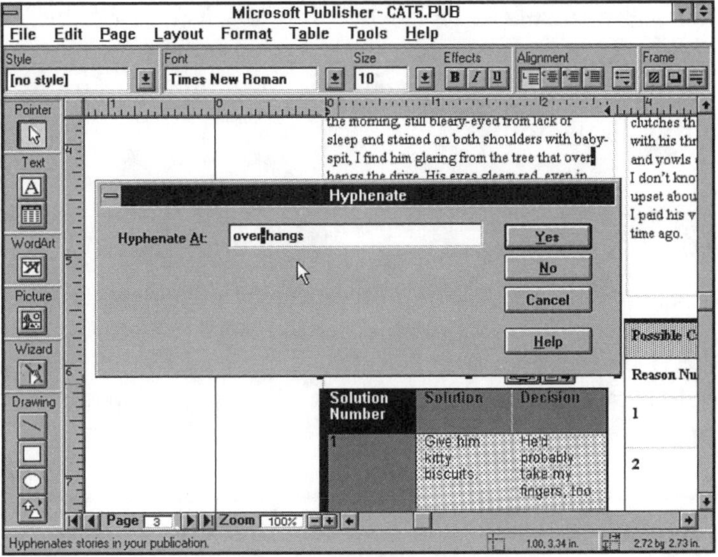

Fig. 6.2
Choosing hyphenation of the found word.

If you do not select the Confirm Every Automatic Hyphen option (after selecting Automatic Hyphenation), Publisher goes through your document and hyphenates words automatically, without any further action from you, after you initially click the OK button.

Selecting Text

Before you can work with a section of text (which can be anything from two characters to the entire publication), you first must select the text with which you want to work. You can select (or highlight) text in one of four ways:

- Click the Pointer tool and drag the mouse to highlight the section of text you want.

- Click the frame you want, open the **E**dit menu, and choose **H**ighlight Entire Story (or use the quick-key combination (Ctrl+A). This highlights not only the text in the selected frame, but also the text in all frames connected to the one you selected.

- Position the cursor at the point you want to begin highlighting; then press and hold the Shift key while using the arrow keys to expand the highlight.

- You can also use the Shift+click method. Position the cursor at the beginning of the block you want to select, move the mouse pointer to the position (within the same frame) where you want the block to end, and while holding down the Shift key, click the mouse button.

Note

It may seem silly, but sometimes the most obvious procedures are the easiest to stumble over. How do you select a frame? Click it. What if you want to select more than one frame? Press Shift and hold it down while you click subsequent frames. All frames you click are selected, shown with gray—rather than black—handles.

Try using the mouse and the Pointer tool to select some text. Open a publication with which you have been experimenting. Now highlight a section of text by following these steps:

1. Click the Pointer tool.

2. Select the frame that contains the text you want to use. Handles appear on the frame. ***Note:*** If you are looking at Full Page view, you need to zoom up on the publication to Actual Size view so that you can see the section of text you're selecting (see fig. 6.3). You should see the flashing text cursor as well as the I-beam pointer .

3. Move the I-beam pointer to the place in the text where you want to begin highlighting.

4. Press and hold the mouse button.

5. Drag the mouse until the text you want is highlighted.

6. Release the mouse button. The text remains highlighted (see fig. 6.4).

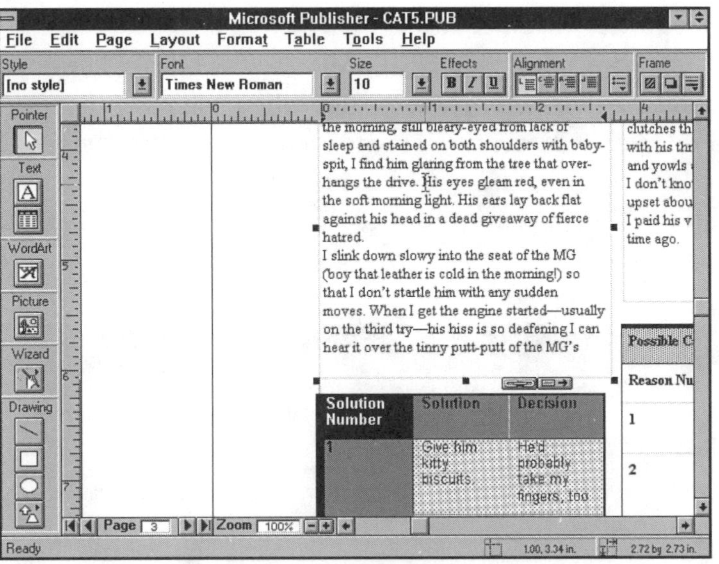

Fig. 6.3
Positioning the cursor.

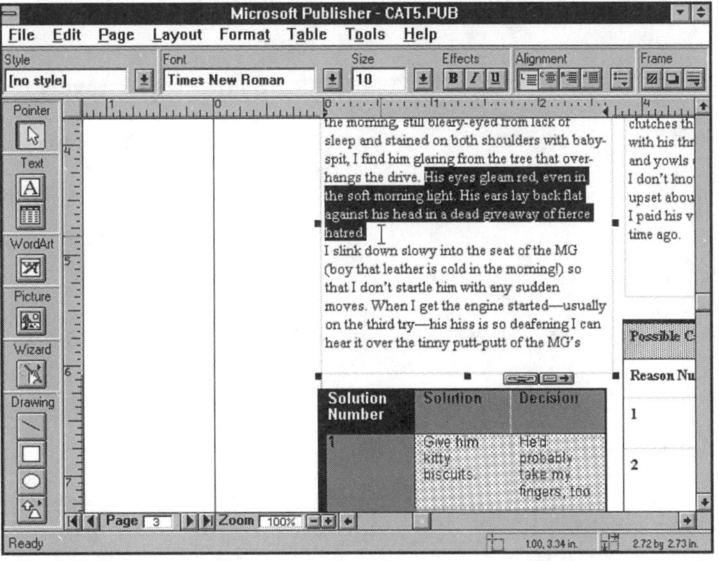

Fig. 6.4
The selected text block.

Now that the text block is selected, you're ready for some text juggling fun. Want to move some paragraphs around? Cut and paste text? Exchange words? Now that you know how to mark the text as a block, your editing horizons have expanded.

Copying and Pasting Selected Text

When you copy selected text with Microsoft Publisher, the text is placed on an invisible clipboard. Then when you paste the text, Publisher retrieves it from the clipboard. Remember, however, that Publisher stores only one item on the clipboard at a time. If you copy a sentence to the clipboard and then copy a headline, for example, the headline replaces the sentence you copied earlier.

Note

Here are just a few examples of when you may need to use a copy-and-paste operation:

- When you want to copy information from one frame to another
- When you are placing Publisher information into other Windows programs
- When you are bringing into Publisher text from other Windows applications
- When you want to change the order of sentences in a paragraph
- When you need to move a word or a string of words to another paragraph within a text frame

Tip

To copy text quickly, simply highlight the text you want to copy and press Ctrl+C. Publisher places the copy on the clipboard without any further action from you.

To copy text, follow these steps:

1. Highlight the text you want to copy.
2. Open the **E**dit menu.
3. Choose the **C**opy Text command.

You don't see any obvious change to your publication, but Publisher has placed the copy on the unseen clipboard. Obviously, you need to do something else in order to place the copied text elsewhere in your publication—that's where the **P**aste Text command comes in.

Project Tip

If you create a section of text that you really like but you're just not sure it fits in your current publication, don't throw it away; save it for another possible creation. Highlight the block and then copy it to a new publication for safe-keeping. It might come in handy someday.

To paste text, follow these steps:

1. Move the text cursor to the position in the text where you want the copy to be placed.
2. Open the **E**dit menu.
3. Choose the **P**aste Text command.

Tip
As an alternative to using the menu selections to paste text, you can position the cursor and press the quick-key combination Ctrl+V.

Publisher places the text in your document at the cursor's position. Text that was in that spot before you pasted text is moved to the right to accommodate the inserted text.

If you paste the copied text at the wrong place in your document, you can easily fix the problem. Open the **E**dit menu and choose **U**ndo Paste Text. The text is removed from the publication. You then can position the text cursor in the right place and press Ctrl+V to repaste the text.

Remember, however, that Undo can change only your *last* operation. If you copy another section of text, for example, and *then* realize that you pasted the last section of text in the wrong place, you're too late. The copy operation already has replaced the paste operation as the last operation performed.

Project Tip

If you are working with several blocks of text that you swap in and out of documents, keep a separate file for odds and ends. You can use that file like a clipboard and, because you can minimize and maximize Publisher documents easily, you don't lose a lot of time opening and closing files.

Copying and Pasting Text Frames

You also can copy and paste text frames. When you copy a text frame, the *text* in the frame isn't copied—only the frame itself. You may want to copy a frame, for example, if you have created one text frame of specific dimensions and want another frame of equal size. This procedure is similar to copying and pasting selected text, but one less step is required. Follow this procedure:

1. Zoom up to Full Page view.
2. Click the frame you want to copy.
3. Open the **E**dit menu (see fig. 6.5).
4. Choose the **C**opy Text Frame command. The frame is copied to the clipboard.
5. Again, open the **E**dit menu and choose **P**aste Object(s). The frame is placed in the center of the page. You then can move and resize the frame as necessary.

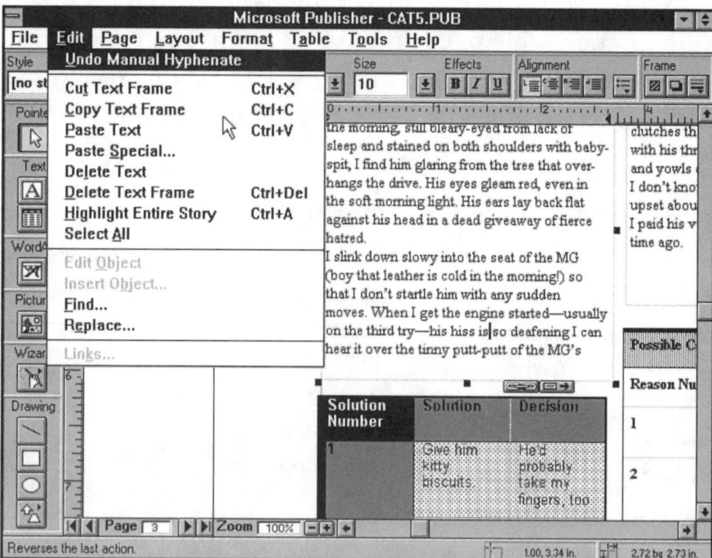

Fig. 6.5
Copying a text frame.

You may be surprised to find the **C**opy Text Frame command in your **E**dit menu; it wasn't there a minute ago. Some commands come and go depending on what you've selected. There's no point in displaying the **C**opy Text Frame command in the **E**dit menu if you've already highlighted a text block, for example. Publisher knows you're going to copy (or cut or delete) that block or you wouldn't have highlighted it. Scary, isn't it?

Cutting Selected Text

Another operation that involves selecting text enables you to cut text out of one place in your publication. You then can use Paste Text to put the text in another place. To cut text, follow these steps:

Tip
You can use Ctrl+X, the quick-key combination, for cutting text.

1. Click the frame containing the text you want to use.
2. Display the page in Actual Size view.
3. Highlight the section of text you want to cut.
4. Open the **E**dit menu.
5. Choose the Cu**t** Text command.

The highlighted text is removed from your publication and placed on the clipboard. To insert the cut text into the document, position the text cursor and use the **P**aste Text command. (See "Copying and Pasting Selected Text," earlier in this chapter, for more information.)

Cutting Frames

To cut a frame from your document, follow these steps:

1. Display the page in Full Page view.
2. Select the frame you want to cut.
3. Open the **E**dit menu.
4. Choose Cu**t** Text Frame.

The frame is removed, and the text from the frame moves to the next connected frame. The text in subsequent frames is reflowed.

Remember that you can reverse your last operation by using the **U**ndo command from the **E**dit menu.

Deleting Selected Text

At first glance, you may think that the process of deleting text is the same as cutting text. In essence, they are the same process: both operations remove the selected text from the publication. With a cut operation, however, you have the intention of placing the cut material elsewhere; in this case, *cut* is more akin to *move*. When you delete text, you still can undo the procedure if you choose (as you can with Cut), but you cannot paste the text back into the document (as you can with Cut). When you delete text, in other words, the text is not placed on the clipboard.

You can delete text in two ways:

- Highlight the text you want to delete and press the Del key.
- Highlight the text and select the De**l**ete Text command from the **E**dit menu.

Deleting Text Frames

The process for deleting text frames is similar to deleting selected text. The frame is not placed on the clipboard for easy placement later, although you can recover a deleted frame by using Undo immediately after the deletion. When you delete a text frame, the text inside the frame is moved to the next connected frame.

Tip
You can remove a text frame quickly by selecting the frame and pressing Ctrl+Del.

To delete a text frame, follow these steps:

1. Display the page in Full Page view.
2. Click the frame you want to delete.
3. Open the **E**dit menu.
4. Choose **D**elete Text Frame.

The frame is removed from the publication, and the text is placed in the next connected frame.

Resizing and Moving Frames

You probably know the procedure for resizing windows: just point at the corner or the edge of the window, press and hold the mouse button, and drag the window to the size you want.

You use the same procedure for Publisher text frames. Just click the frame you want to resize and move the pointer to a handle on an edge or a corner. You then can

- Click and drag the handle on the edge if you want to shorten the frame (vertically or horizontally).
- Click and drag the handle on the corner if you want to shrink the frame proportionally.

If you want to move a text frame from one place to another, move the pointer to the outer edge of the frame until the pointer changes to the moving van symbol. Then press and hold the mouse button and drag the frame to its new location. When you release the mouse button, the frame is set down in its new place.

Using Find and Replace

Another editing procedure that Publisher offers you is the capability to search for certain characters, words, or phrases and replace the found items with different words. You can use this feature, for example, if you discover that you have misspelled a manager's name throughout a publication. You can have Publisher find every occurrence of the name and replace it with the correct spelling.

Because Publisher breaks the find-and-replace operation into two commands—Find and Replace—you can use these commands in different ways:

- You can use the Find command to locate a certain word in your publication.
- You can use Find to move to a place in your document that you need to review.
- You can place a marker (such as your initials) in the publication when you stop working one day, and use Find in your next Publisher session to find the section where you stopped.
- You can use Replace to locate characters, words, or phrases that you want to replace with another item.

Project Tip

Before you make any big changes to your publication, it's a good idea to save the file, just in case you want to return to an earlier version later.

Finding Text. To display the Find dialog box so that you can have Publisher find a word or phrase for you, follow these steps:

1. Select the text frame (or frames) you want to search.
2. Display the page in Actual Size view.
3. Open the **E**dit menu.
4. Choose the **F**ind command. The Find dialog box shown in figure 6.6 appears.

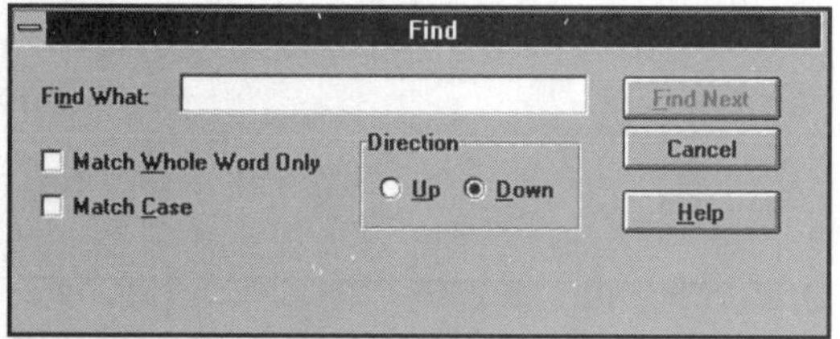

Fig. 6.6 The Find dialog box.

As you can see, the Find dialog box offers several options. Use the first option, Fi**n**d What, to enter the word (or words) you want to find. When you select the Match **W**hole Word Only box (it is unselected by default), Publisher finds the specified text only where it is used as a stand-alone word. If you are searching for the word *bus*, for example, and you do not click the Match **W**hole Word Only box, Publisher may find the following words:

business
Columbus
busted

If you click the Match **W**hole Word Only box so that an X appears in the box, Publisher finds only the word *bus*.

The Match **C**ase option enables you to tell Publisher that you want to find a word only if it matches the exact upper- and lowercase letters you have entered in the Find What box. With the Direction box, you can specify in which direction you want Publisher to search; **D**own is the default. If you click **U**p, the document is searched backward—toward the front of the document—from the current cursor position. If you choose **D**own, the document is searched from the cursor position to the end of the publication. After the search is completed in one particular direction, Publisher asks whether you want to search the remainder of the publication.

After you enter the text and select the necessary options, click Find Next to begin the search. Publisher asks you to wait a moment while the search is being performed. Then if the program finds the word you entered, Publisher highlights it in the publication.

If you enter a word that Publisher cannot find, the program first displays the following message:

```
Reached end of story. Continue searching at the beginning?
```

(or `...end?`, depending on the direction of your search). Click Yes to continue the search. If the text still is not found, Publisher alerts you of this fact, and you can click OK to return to the Find dialog box.

When you finish finding things, you need to close the Find dialog box to return to the publication. To do so, click Cancel or double-click the control menu box in the upper left corner of the Find dialog box.

Replacing Text. The R**e**place command, also on the **E**dit menu, performs a similar operation to Find but goes one step further. In addition to finding the text you specify, Publisher replaces the found text with something else you specify.

Note

You can move the dialog boxes (Replace, Find, Spelling Check) to see your text more clearly by positioning the mouse pointer in the title bar of the box and pressing and holding the mouse button while you drag the box in the direction you want.

To replace text, follow these steps:

1. Click the text frame you want to search.
2. Display the page in Actual Size view.
3. Open the **E**dit menu.
4. Choose the R**e**place, command. The Replace dialog box appears (see fig. 6.7).

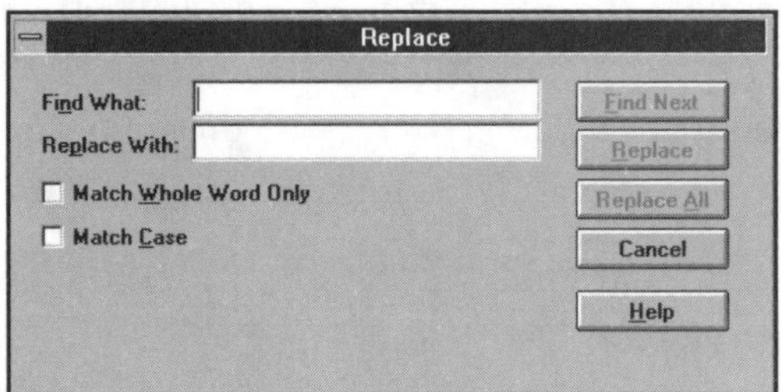

Fig. 6.7
The Replace dialog box.

5. In the Find What box, type the text you want to find.
6. In the Replace With box, type the text you want to replace the found text.
7. Choose Match **W**hole Word Only if you want Publisher to find the text you entered only when it appears as an entire word.
8. Choose Match **C**ase if you want Publisher to find text with the same upper- and lowercase letters you entered.

   Publisher then searches the document for the text you specified. When the text is found, Publisher highlights it and waits for your next command.

9. To continue the find-and-replace operation, choose one of the buttons along the right edge of the Replace dialog box. The Find Next button enables you to find—but not replace—the next occurrence of the specified text. The Replace button enables you to replace the found occurrence of the text. The Replace All button tells Publisher to find and replace all occurrences of the text in the publication. Or, with the Cancel button, you can halt the operation.

10. When you finish, click Cancel or double-click the control menu box to return to the publication.

Project Tip

Everybody has certain grammatical or spelling mistakes that they make repeatedly. As you discover those somethings in your own writing, make a list of them so that you can find and replace them in your finished documents. Common usage mistakes include using the word *since* when you mean *because*, *if* instead of *whether*, and *while* instead of *and* or *although*.

Using the Spelling Checker

Publisher has another great feature—a 120,000-word spelling checker. Publisher can check the spelling accuracy of your document without you ever having to turn to your dictionary.

What types of errors can the Spelling Checker find? First and foremost: typos. Entering *freidnship* when you meant *friendship*, or typing *Mr. Meany* when you meant *Mr. Mead*. (Yeah, *sure* it was a mistake. Of course we believe you.)

Publisher will count as "misspelled" any word it does not recognize after looking in its own internal dictionary for the correct spelling. You can teach Publisher new words by adding them to the dictionary, however, so words that you use often in your own publications—such as the name *Mead*, for example—can be added to the speller so Publisher won't count them wrong.

Luckily for you, the spelling checker finds the following offenses:

- Misspellings
- Weird capitalization (Sr. Editor HiNeY)
- Numbers in strange places (skid23oo!)

To start the spelling checker, follow these steps:

1. Select the frame (or frames) you want to check.
2. Zoom up to Actual Size view.

3. Place the text cursor at the beginning of the story.

4. Open the T**o**ols menu.

5. Choose the Check **S**pelling command. Publisher immediately begins searching your document for misspelled words. When such a word is found, Publisher displays the dialog box shown in figure 6.8.

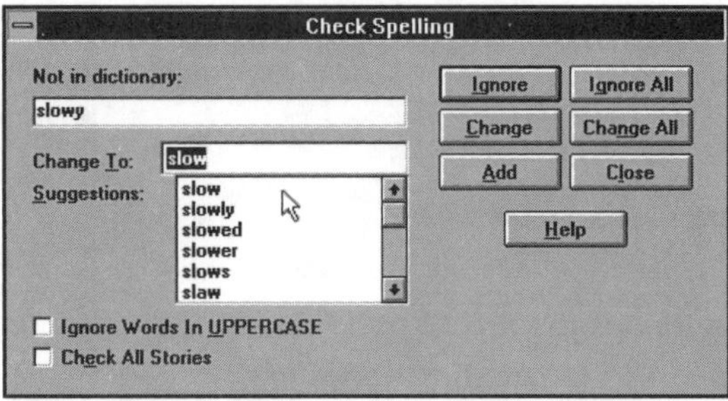

Fig. 6.8
Egad! A misspelled word.

In the top left corner of the box, you see the culprit: in this case, *slowy*. In the Change **T**o box, you can type the corrected spelling if you know it. Or you can click one of the entries in the **S**uggestions box to choose a substitute spelling.

The Ignore Words in **U**PPERCASE option enables you to have Publisher bypass all words that consist of capital letters. Spelling checkers usually find acronyms confusing—words like ASCII, CGA, VGA, CPU, and so on. If your text contains many of these types of words, your spell-checking process may be littered with numerous unnecessary pauses. To have Publisher bypass these ALL-CAPITAL words, click this box.

The Ch**e**ck All Stories option provides you with a quick and easy way to have Publisher check all the text in your publication. If you don't select this option, Publisher checks only the text in the selected frame.

On the right side of the Check Spelling box, you see a series of seven buttons. Table 6.2 explains the functions of these buttons.

Table 6.2 Using the Check Spelling Dialog Box Buttons

Button	Description
Ignore	Ignores the spelling of the found word. You may need to use this button, for example, if Publisher finds a word that is used specifically in your line of business but is not in Publisher's dictionary.
I**g**nore All	Ignores the spelling of the found word for the rest of the publication.
Change	Accepts the changes you have made in the Change **T**o box and returns you to the document.
Cha**n**ge All	Accepts the changes you have made and applies the same changes to any other occurrences of the found word.
Add	Adds the found word to Publisher's dictionary and leaves the word as is in the publication.
C**l**ose	Closes the spelling checker without making changes.
Help	Displays help topics related to the spelling checker.

After you make the corrections, Publisher asks you whether you want to continue checking other items in the publication. If you do, click Yes. If you don't, click Cancel. Publisher then returns you to the beginning of the publication.

Project Tip

Remember that the spelling checker doesn't replace that oh-so-important final read-through. Although the speller can catch words it doesn't recognize and words you've accidentally misspelled, it won't find situations where you've used a real word in the wrong context.

Troubleshooting

I turned hyphenation on, and Publisher stops at the end of almost every line.

You may have set your hyphenation zone to too narrow a width. Try widening the box, if possible. Otherwise, turn hyphenation off. Too many hyphens spoil the soup.

I highlighted a block, but I highlighted the wrong block.

Just move the mouse off the area and click. The highlight will disappear.

I copied a block to the clipboard and then forgot and copied another block to the clipboard. Now I want the first block back.

Sorry—that first block is history. Windows only stores one block on the clipboard at a time.

I moved a frame from one place to another, but it looks funky.

You can move the frame right back to its previous position by opening the **E**dit menu and choosing Undo.

Arg! I replaced all occurrences of "if" with "whether" and wound up with words like "rwhetherle," "wwhetherfle ball," and "whetherfe"!

Undo won't handle the correction for you this time. With sweeping changes such as this, it's better to have Publisher ask for confirmation before Replacing. In other words, stay away from the Replace All button unless you're really, really sure you won't be sorry later.

Editing Tables

Publisher Version 2.0 added the easy tables feature so that you can plop data down in just about any format that makes sense. Business publications often use tables heavily because they can communicate information quickly that might otherwise take pages to explain. For example, if I were trying to compare three different products, you might understand what I was getting at if I wrote a long dissertation about each product and then tied them all together at the end with a comparison of one kind or another. But wouldn't it be a lot easier to look at a table that compared the three choices?

This section explains how to select and edit the tables you've created. You can make simple text changes by doing keystroke editing, or you can mark blocks and copy, cut, and paste them. Additionally, you can insert and delete rows and columns from your table.

Selecting the Table

The first step in editing a table involves selecting the table. In this case, you'll edit the table created in Chapter 5, as shown in figure 6.9. First, move to the page the table occupies, and then click the table. The handles appear, as shown in the figure.

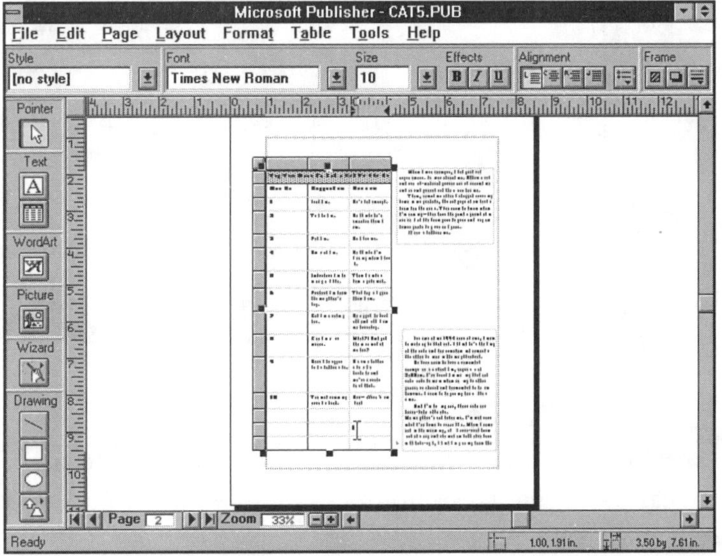

Fig. 6.9
Selecting the table to be edited.

Project Tip

Remember that you can also cut, copy, and paste tables. Save a table you like to a file of reusable items so that you don't have to create the table again when you want to add a similar table to another publication.

Modifying Table Data

If you're working in Full Page view, you need to zoom in on the table by using the Zoom controls at the bottom of the screen or by pressing F9 to move to Actual Page view. For information about using the Zoom controls, see Chapter 2, "Starting Out with Publisher."

You then can position the cursor at the point you want to change and use the Backspace key or the Del key to remove unnecessary characters. Figure 6.10 shows table text in Actual Page view, ready for editing.

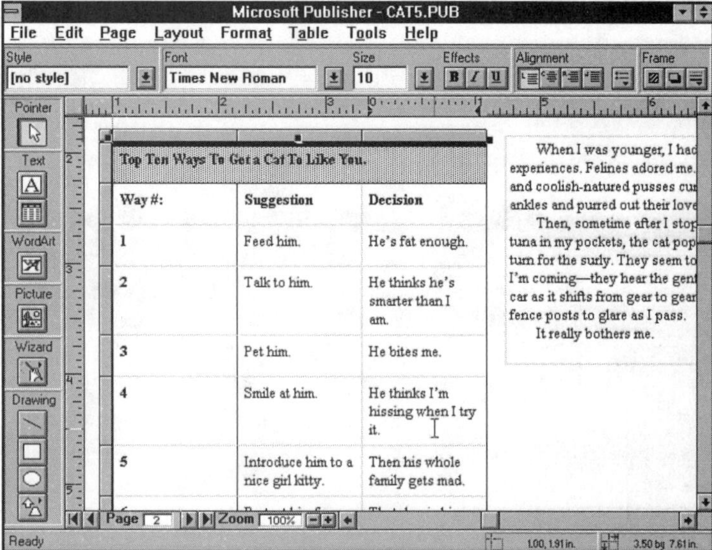

Fig. 6.10
Table text in Actual Page view.

Cutting and Pasting Table Data

Suppose that you want to change the order of the items in the table. You can easily highlight a section as a block and move it to the place you want it. Here's how:

1. First, highlight the block you want to move (see fig. 6.11).
2. Open the **E**dit menu and choose Cut Cells.
3. Move the cursor to the point you want to insert the data.
4. Open the **E**dit menu and choose Paste Cells.

The data is then placed in the new position. But wait—there's an easier way. (Now you tell me.) Right after step 1, when you've highlighted the block, position the mouse pointer inside the block and press and hold the mouse button. What happens? The pointer changes to show a small box. Now drag the pointer to the place you want the text and release the mouse button (see fig. 6.12).

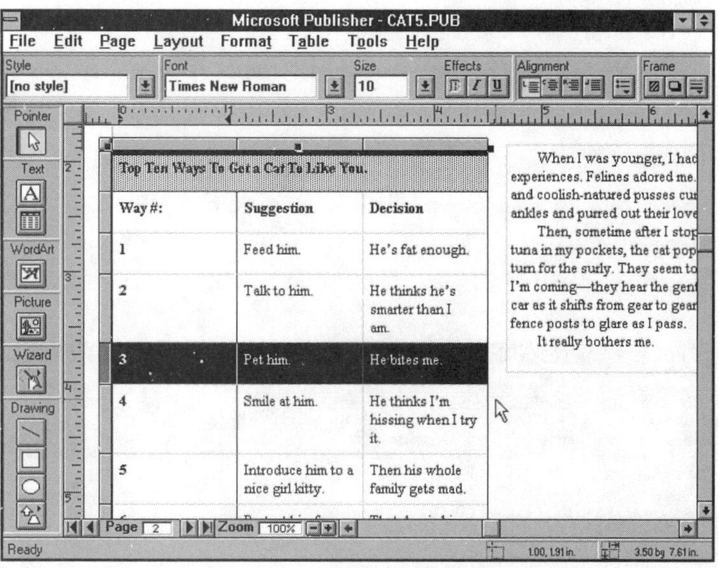

Fig. 6.11
Highlighting the table text to be moved.

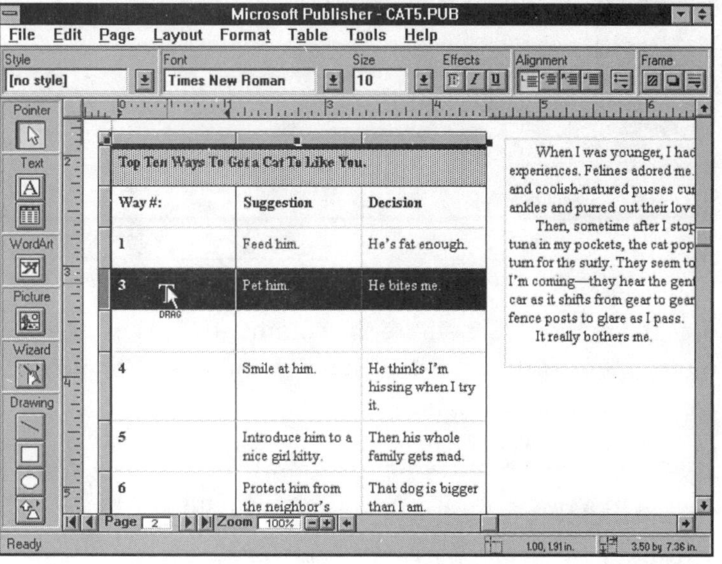

Fig. 6.12
The moved text.

You just dragged-and-dropped table text. Congratulations!

Adding and Deleting Columns and Rows

Publisher does a good job of anticipating the number of columns and rows you need. You get your own chance to decide how many you want in the Create Table dialog box. Sometimes, however, you just don't know what you need until you've created the table, and then you still might need to make some adjustment. You might need to add a column and delete a few rows. This section shows you how to do just that.

Deleting Rows and Columns. In the sample in figure 6.11, the table has too many rows. A look at the bottom of the table reveals that there's just too much extra space (see fig. 6.13).

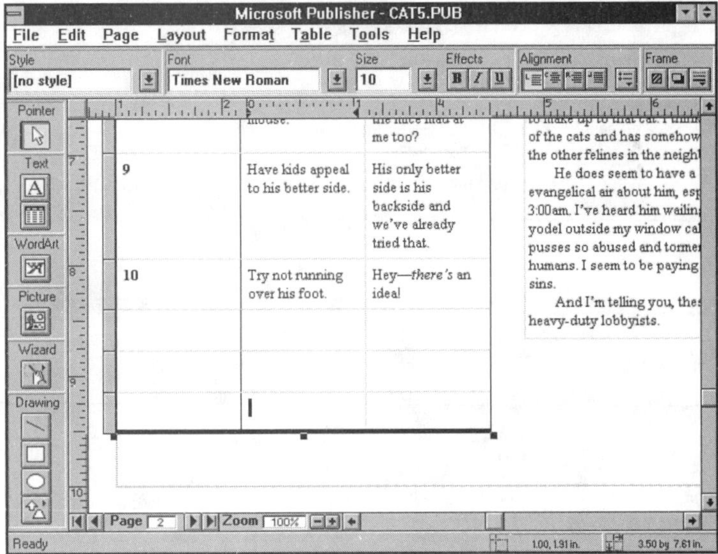

Fig. 6.13
The extra rows in the table.

To delete the extra rows, you use the commands in the T**a**ble menu. First make sure that the table is selected (handles appear along the edges and in the corners). Then follow these steps:

1. Highlight the row or column you want to delete. (If you want to highlight a block or rows or columns, highlight the block.)

2. Open the T**a**ble menu (see fig. 6.14).

3. Choose **D**elete Rows or Columns.

4. When the Delete dialog box appears (see fig. 6.15), choose the item you want.

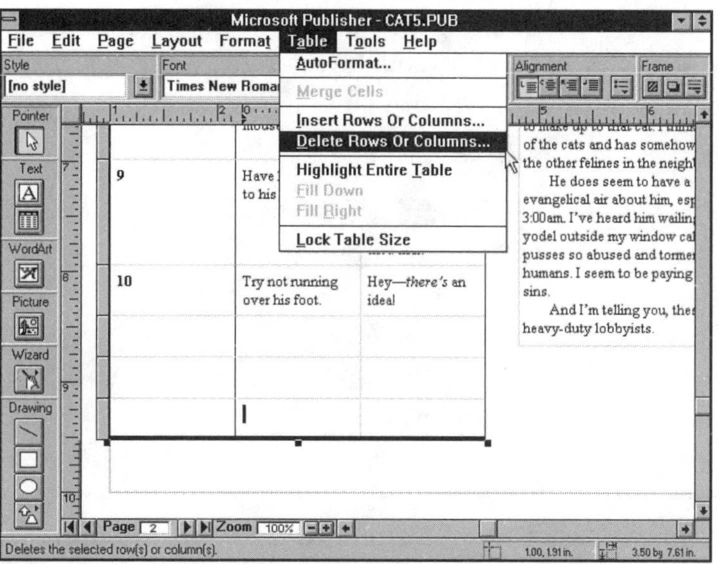

Fig. 6.14
You can use the Table menu to modify table formatting.

> **Note**
>
> If you have highlighted rows or columns before you open the Table menu, the command in the Table menu is Delete Rows (or Delete Columns). No dialog box appears. The rows or columns are simply deleted. The Delete dialog box appears only if nothing has previously been highlighted.

5. Click OK.

Publisher removes the extra rows or columns from your table.

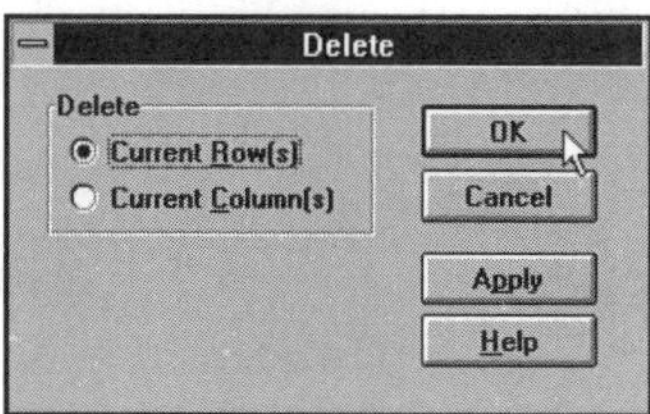

Fig. 6.15
The Delete Rows or Columns dialog box.

Adding Rows and Columns. If someone asked you "How similar do you think adding rows and columns is to deleting rows and columns," what would you say? Pretty similar, huh? The only real difference is the command you select.

You can start by positioning the cursor at the point either after which or before which you want to add the columns or rows. Open the **T**able menu, choose **I**nsert Rows Or Columns, and make your choices in the Insert dialog box (see fig. 6.16).

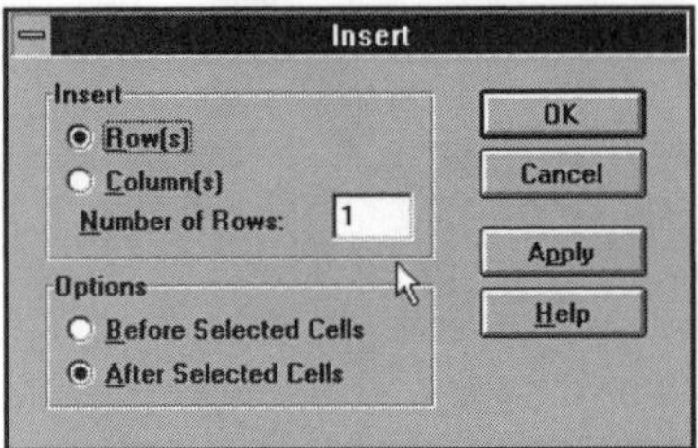

Fig. 6.16
Inserting rows and/or columns.

Troubleshooting

The rows I inserted popped up at the wrong spot.

Before you do anything else, open the **E**dit menu and choose **U**ndo Insert Row. Those rows will be picked back up and you can insert them in the right place. Be sure to position the cursor accurately first.

From Here...

For information directly related to finishing hands-on text work, you may want to review the following sections of this book:

- Chapter 7, "Enhancing Text," tells you how to concentrate on the aesthetics of your text. Did you use the best font possible? What about WordArt? Do you have a cool banner? Add these things and more in Chapter 7.

- Chapter 10, "Finishing the Layout," explains more about fine-tuning the layout of your publication. Now that you have text boxes and tables, things are starting to fill up. Find out about aligning columns, working with guides, and using the layout checker in Chapter 10.

Chapter 7

Enhancing Text

In this chapter, you learn to do the following tasks:

- Create and use styles
- Change fonts
- Choose font size and effect
- Control text alignment
- Work with tabs and spacing
- Enhance documents with WordArt

Even the best documents will fall flat if they don't look right. You may have done hours and hours of research. You might have a really great concept. But unless you put the document together so that it all looks inviting to your readers, your publication may not have a chance. There are just too many other things competing for your readers' attention.

One of the most obvious changes you may want to make to your publication involves changing the look of text. In this chapter, you learn to enhance the appearance of your text by changing text attributes and character spacing; by working with tabs, indents, and paragraph spacing; and by using WordArt.

Changing Text Attributes

In Chapter 5, "Entering Text," you learn to choose the attributes of your text before you enter it. But what happens if you enter the text and then decide that you want to change the way it appears? You can change the font, size, style, alignment, and spacing of text in text frames at any time you're working with a publication.

The first step in changing text attributes is to select the area of text you want to change. Whether you want to change a character, a word, or an entire document, you need to highlight the text first. Follow these steps to get started:

1. Open the publication with which you want to work.
2. Click the frame containing the text you want to change.

3. Change to Actual Size view.

4. Highlight the text you want to change.

After you highlight the text, you can change the attribute you want by using the text attributes in the Top Toolbar (see fig. 7.1).

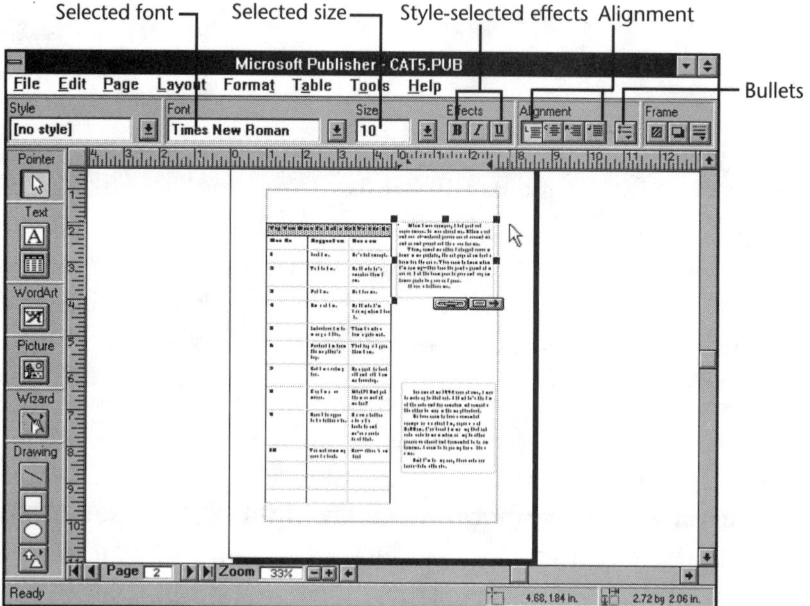

Fig. 7.1
Choosing text attributes.

Table 7.1 describes the text attributes you can choose from the Top Toolbar.

Table 7.1 Text Attributes

Attribute	Description
Style	A style is a certain preset definition you can apply to a character, paragraph, or section. You create styles for formats and text selections you use often. For example, in this table, a style was used to automate the format of the left and right columns.
Font	The text font is the typeface you choose. Depending on the capabilities of your printer, you may have many different fonts available, as is the case if you are using a PostScript laser printer, or you may have just a few. To display a list of available fonts, click the down arrow beside the Font box.

Attribute	Description
Size	The font Size box (to the right of the Font box) controls the size of the characters. Again, to see a list of available sizes, click the down arrow. The number of sizes you have available depends on the type of printer you are using and the fonts available to your printer.
Effects	Several Effects buttons enable you to choose bold, italic, or underline text style. You also can mix styles and use such combinations as bold italic and bold underline.
Alignment	The alignment of your text controls the way the text is placed in the frame. Four alignment types represented by four alignment buttons are available: left, center, right, and justified.
Bullets	The Bullets button lets you choose a bullet type from a displayed palette.

Project Tip

It's always a good idea to use some variety in your publications; however, too much variety can confuse readers. Before you begin changing fonts, sizes, and effects, think about what you're trying to accomplish; then choose two or three changes to try. A clear, easy-to-follow design will help keep your readers' attention.

Creating and Using Styles. Think of a style as a cookie-cutter you use on text. When you apply the style, it makes that text look like other text of a similar style. When you record a style, Publisher takes note of the spacing, indents, text font, styles, and effects applied to the style. Then, when you apply the style to selected text, Publisher assigns those same settings to the selected text.

Suppose that you are working on a document that includes quotations from famous people (or cats). Each time you use one of these quotations, you want to indent the text on the left and on the right (see fig. 7.2).

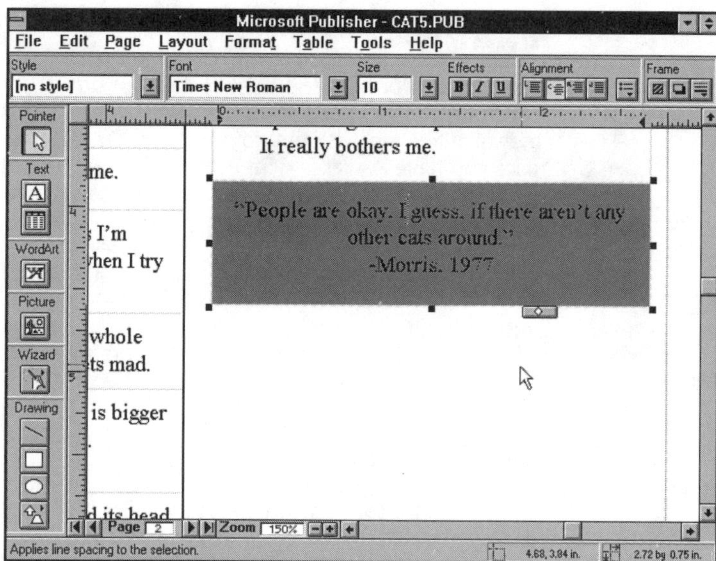

Fig. 7.2
Setting up style.

The example shown here uses several different attribute settings:

- Centered text
- Bold text
- Spacing of 4 points before the paragraph

Creating Styles. If you know that you're going to have 20 or so quotations in a single document, it's to your advantage to create a style that automates the format for you. To create a style that can apply the necessary settings to your quotations, you follow these steps:

1. Open the Forma**t** menu.
2. Choose Text **S**tyles. The Text Styles dialog box appears (see fig. 7.3).
3. Click the Create a **N**ew Style button.

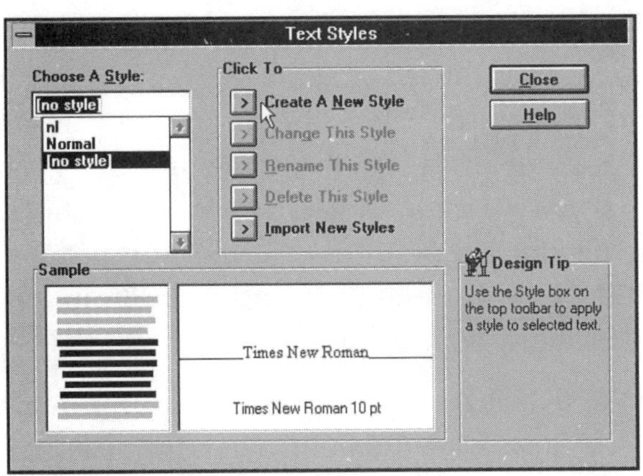

Fig. 7.3
Starting a new style.

Another pop-up window appears, the Create New Style dialog box, that gives you a choice of elements you can set for the style (see fig. 7.4).

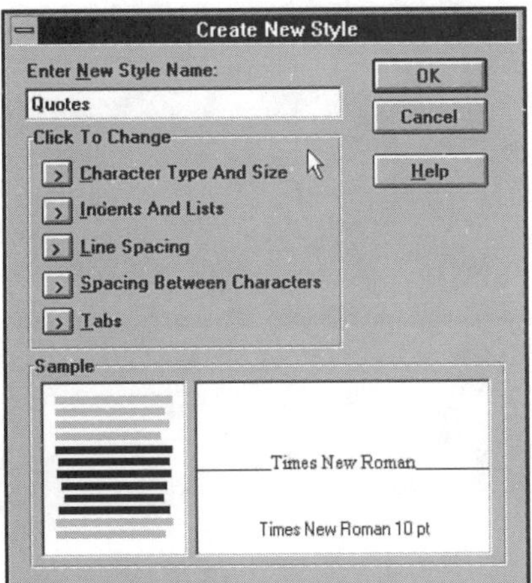

Fig. 7.4
Creating a new style.

Note

If you highlighted text before you chose Text Styles, Publisher has taken note of the settings and automatically applies these settings to the style you are creating.

The first thing you do in creating a new style is name it. In this example, you're creating a style to handle the way the quotations will look in your document. Therefore, the sample style is named *Quotes*. When entering a style name, think of something that applies to what you're doing. If you're creating a style to handle headlines, for example, use something like *head1* or *headline1*. For special notes, use *Note*. You get the idea. To enter the name, just click in the Enter **N**ew Style Name box and type the name.

The Create New Style dialog box presents you with a number of additional buttons you can click to specify the individual settings for the style. You can change the character type and size, the indents, the line spacing, the character spacing, and the tabs by clicking the appropriate button in the Create New Style box. When you click one of these buttons—such as the **C**haracter Type And Size button—another dialog box appears. Figure 7.5 shows the Character dialog box that appears when you click the Character Type And Size button.

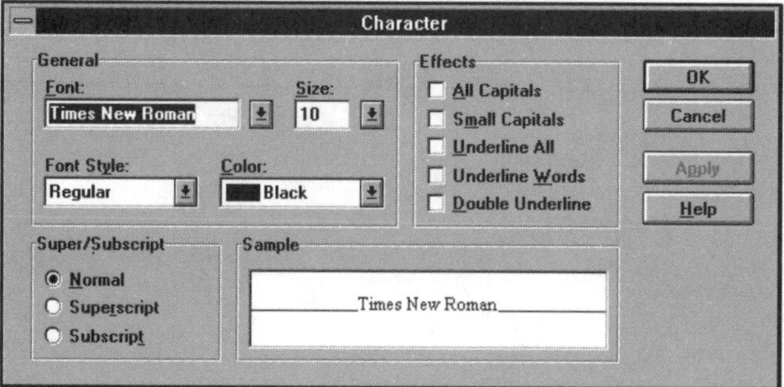

Fig. 7.5
The Character dialog box.

Now you can enter the settings you want for the style—font, size, style, effect, and so on. Click OK when you're done. You return to the Create New Style dialog box, where you can set additional settings by choosing another button. The Sample window in the bottom left corner of the box shows the alignment and indents of your text; the preview window on the right shows a sample of the text the way it will appear in your document.

Figure 7.6 shows the effect of the Quote settings in the Sample and preview windows.

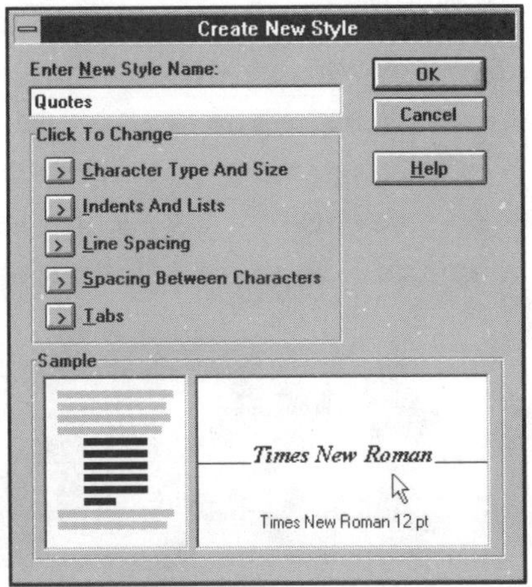

Fig. 7.6
The effects of the new style settings.

When you've entered all the style settings the way you want them, click the OK button.

Applying Styles. When you want to apply a certain style to text in your document, just highlight the text and click the down arrow in the Style box. A list of styles appears. Click your choice, and the highlighted text is changed accordingly (see fig. 7.7).

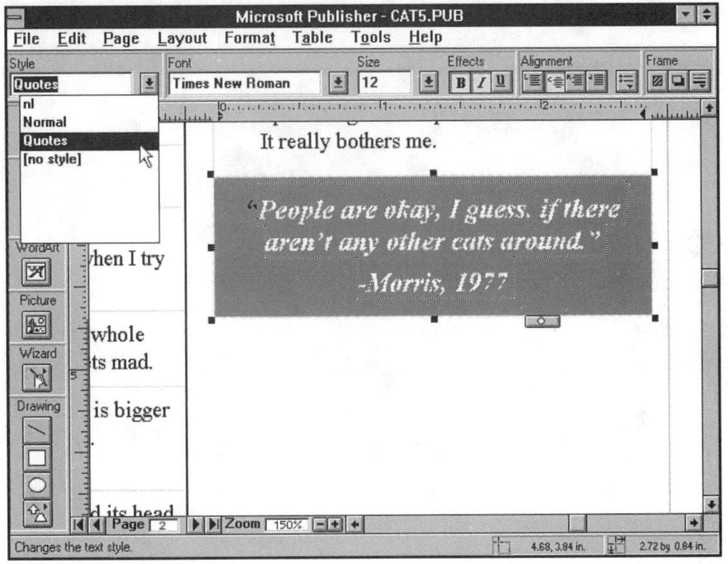

Fig. 7.7
Applying a style.

Changing Font and Size. To change the font or size of selected text, begin by highlighting the text you want to change. Next, simply open the Font or Size box by clicking the down arrow to the right of the box. Then click the font or size you want to use. Depending on the type of printer you're using, you may see quite a number of font choices (see fig. 7.8). You may also see little icons beside the font names, showing you that some fonts are printer fonts and some fonts are TrueType fonts.

Note

TrueType is a revolutionary new font technology included with Windows 3.1. TrueType fonts (indicated by the TT symbol beside the font name) allow you to print Windows files (which of course includes Publisher publications) on virtually any printer, at the highest quality available on your printer type. TrueType fonts also look the same on-screen as they do in print. Printer fonts, on the other hand, may look slightly different printed than they do displayed on-screen.

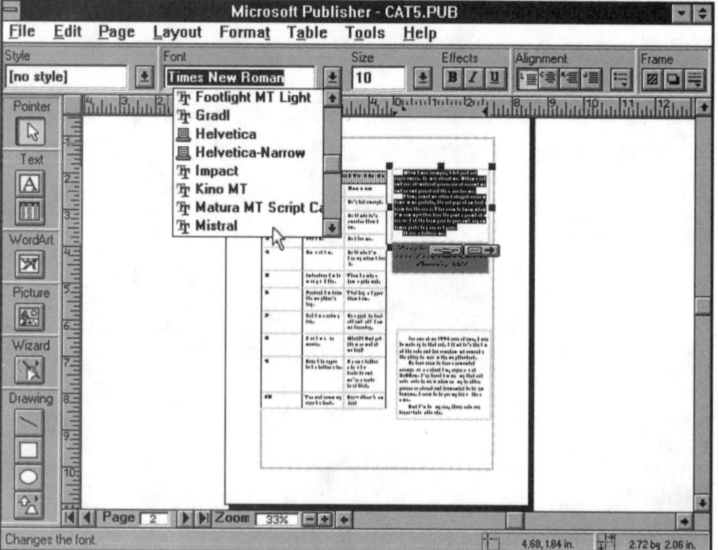

Fig. 7.8
Displaying font choices.

You may need to scroll through the list to find the font you want. Click it to select it. Your choice is shown in the Font box, and the highlighted text in your document changes to reflect this choice.

Project Tip

Use a certain font to help establish an identity for your company. For example, if you use the script font Mistral for your logo, use Mistral at key points in your publication to help reinforce the identification.

Changing Text Effects. To select bold, italic, or underline, simply click the Effects button you want. You can even click all three buttons to have a bold, italicized, and underlined phrase (but that's overdoing it just a bit). To deselect an effect, click the appropriate Effects button again.

You can use the text effects either before or after you enter text. If you want to change already entered text, highlight the text and click the button you want. If you want to set the effect for text you are about to type, click the button, and then type your text; the characters appear in the chosen effect. When you want to turn off the effect, click the button again.

Changing Text Alignment. To select the alignment of the text, highlight the text and click the Alignment button you want. You can tell which alignment is which by noticing the letter designations (L for left, R for right, C for center, and J for justified) and by looking closely at the pictures in the buttons. After you choose the button you want, the text you've selected aligns itself according to your selection.

Choosing Bullets. The last set of text options is the type of bullets you use in bulleted lists. When you click on the Bullet button, a small palette of choices appears (see fig. 7.9). You can choose one of the displayed bullet types or click More to see the Indents and Lists dialog box.

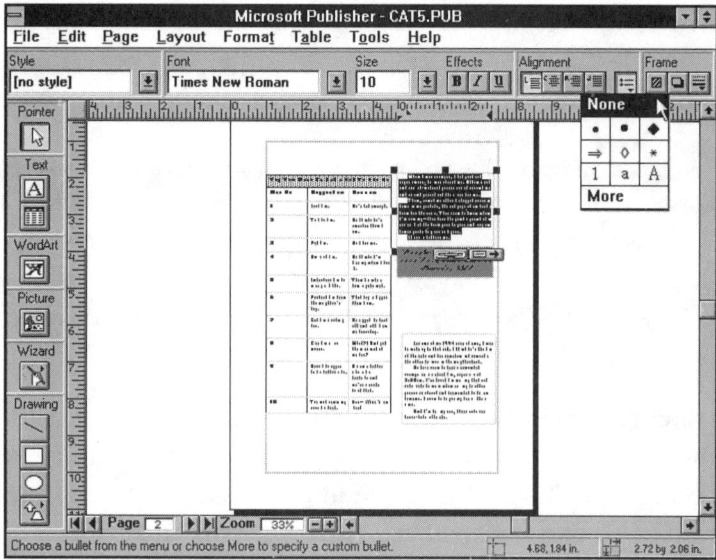

Fig. 7.9
The bullet palette.

Project Tip

The temptation is very great to go hog-wild with bullets and use a different art piece for every bullet in a publication. If you can, resist the temptation. Bullets are meant to be functional—that is, to point readers to information they can understand at a glance.

Character Formatting

You can take things a step further by changing the position and color of individual characters or sections of text. Suppose that you want to add a superscript character to indicate a footnote. A superscript character appears slightly above the rest of the text, as in the following example:

```
¹This is an example of a superscript character.
```

To change the placement or color of a character or group of characters, follow these steps:

1. Select the text you want to change.
2. Open the Forma**t** menu.

3. Choose the **C**haracter command. The Character dialog box appears, as shown in figure 7.10.

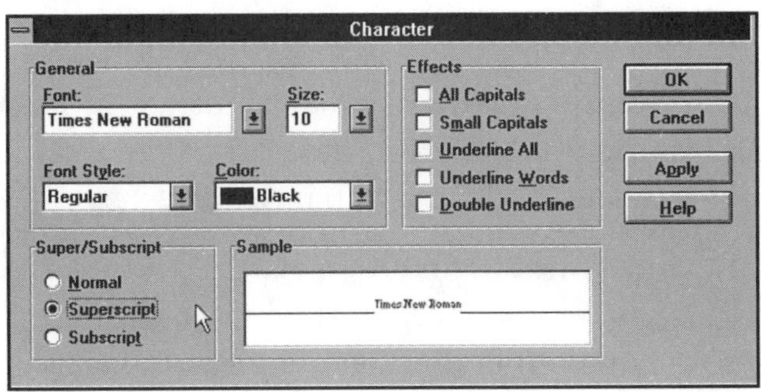

Fig. 7.10
The Character dialog box.

4. Select the **F**ont, Font St**y**le, **S**ize, **C**olor, Effects, and Super/Subscript options you want to change.

5. Click OK to accept your changes and return to the publication.

Changing Indents and Lists

A second option in the Forma**t** menu, **I**ndents and Lists, controls the type of lists you use in your publication and the way you indent them. If you want to indent the first line of a paragraph, for example, you don't need to press Tab at the beginning of every paragraph. The Indents and Lists option lets you format your publication so that the first sentence of every paragraph will automatically indent. Figure 7.11 shows the Indents and Lists dialog box.

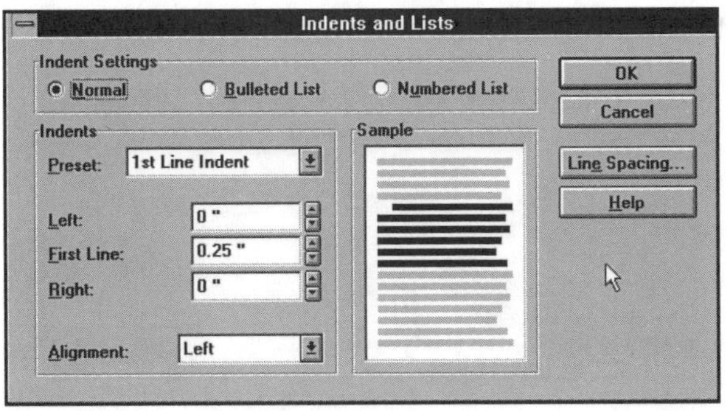

Fig. 7.11
The Indents and Lists dialog box.

At the top of the dialog box, you choose the Indent Settings you want. **N**ormal is for regular body text, **B**ulleted list is for a bulleted list, and N**u**mbered list is for—you got it—a numbered list. Simple enough?

Under Indents, you see whether any preset indent is in effect. In the figure, an across-the-board, first-line indent has been specified. You can cancel that indent by clicking in the **F**irst Line box and typing **0**.

If you want to indent text from the left margin, you enter a value in the **L**eft box. If you want to indent text from the right margin, enter a value in the **R**ight box. The **A**lignment setting tells Publisher how you want the text to line up after you decide on the indents.

The sample box in the middle of the dialog box shows what you're doing. If your indents look strange, chances are, they are. Watch that sample box closely to see how your publication may wind up looking.

Changing Line and Paragraph Spacing

The amount of space between lines of text is another matter. Text that is scrunched and hard to read is a real turn-off for readers. A paragraph that is crammed together gives readers the impression that, whatever it is they're looking at, it's just too difficult to comprehend. When you're creating something that you want people to see, give your characters some room to breathe. Your readers' eyes will thank you for it.

To control the spacing in your publication, choose **L**ine Spacing from the Forma**t** menu. The Line Spacing dialog box appears (see fig. 7.12).

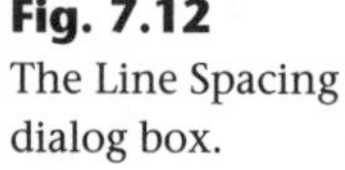

Fig. 7.12
The Line Spacing dialog box.

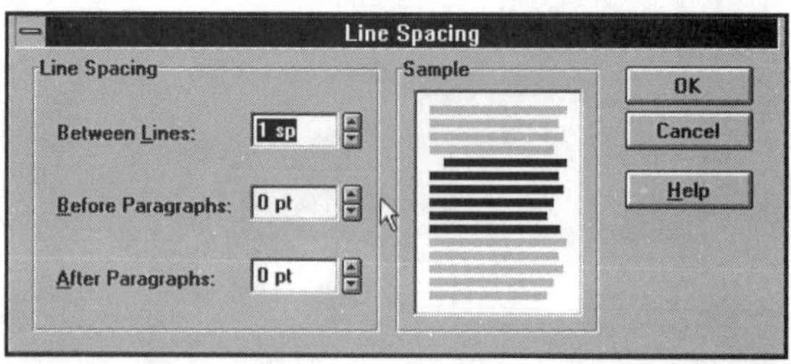

You have three simple choices here:

- Spacing Between **L**ines
- Spacing **B**efore Paragraphs
- Spacing **A**fter Paragraphs

Of course, the setting you enter for the line spacing controls the amount of space between the lines in the publication. Unless you're doing something academic, meaning that you need to leave spaces between the lines so that your instructor can mark it up, you may rarely use double-spaced text.

The Before and After Paragraph settings, however, control how much space is inserted before the paragraph begins and after the paragraph ends. In most text-intensive documents, including corporate reports, newsletters, and even this book, spacing is used before and after paragraphs to give your eyes a rest. It helps make the page look less intimidating, less boring, and more inviting.

Note

In the Line Spacing dialog box, you enter the amount of space between lines and before and after paragraphs. In the Between **L**ines option box, you type the number of line spaces you want to insert between text lines. You can enter a setting from 0.25 to 124 lines. Points, shown as `pt`, is the measurement used for the **B**efore Paragraph and **A**fter Paragraph options. 72 points equal one inch.

If you are uncomfortable entering the spacing in points, you can delete the *pt* characters and type the number of spaces you want, followed by the characters *sp*. If the setting shows `0 pt`, for example, click in the box and type the number of spaces you want to use, press the space bar, and type **sp**. When you click OK or press Enter, Publisher converts your setting into points.

Changing Character Spacing (Kerning)

Publisher gives you another sophisticated desktop publishing capability you might not expect: kerning. *Kerning* refers to the process of fitting letters together so that an unnecessary amount of white space isn't left between characters in a line. As you may know, some characters take up more space than others. A capital *W*, for example, is much wider than a capital *I*. You can have Publisher push characters together or move them apart in order to create the best look for your words.

To change the amount of space between characters, follow these steps:

1. Highlight the text you want to change.
2. Open the Forma**t** menu.
3. Choose the Spacing **B**etween Characters command. The dialog box shown in figure 7.13 appears.

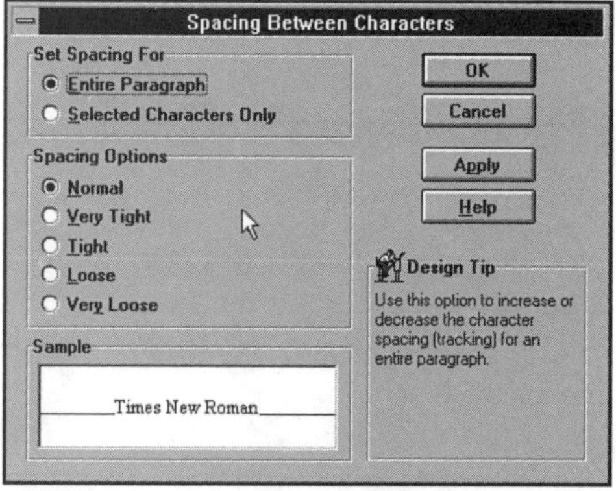

Fig. 7.13
Changing spacing between characters.

4. Choose whether you want to change spacing for the **E**ntire Paragraph or **S**elected Characters Only.
5. Select the Spacing Option you want. Choose from **N**ormal, **V**ery Tight, **T**ight, **L**oose, or Ver**y** Loose.
6. Click A**p**ply.

Project Tip

The bigger the characters are, the more you need kerning.

Working with Tabs

Another feature offered by all word processors, including the word processor in Publisher, is a tab feature. You use tabs to align columns and other items in your publications. Tabs come in handy, for example, in the following cases:

- Lining up text items in a list
- Including a bulleted list in your publication

Publisher includes preset tabs at every one-half inch across the width of your publication. Each time you press the Tab key, the cursor moves to the next tab stop.

Adding Tabs

With Publisher Version 2.0, you can change the default setting so that tabs are distributed in increments you specify. To change the default, choose **T**abs from the Forma**t** menu and change the value in the De**f**ault Tabs box.

With Publisher, you can add four types of tab stops:

Tab	Effect
Left	Aligns text along left edge
Center	Centers text
Right	Aligns text along right edge
Decimal	Aligns text at the decimal point—for example, in numbers such as 3.25

Additionally, you can include leader characters with the tabs you create. *Leader characters* are characters that lead the reader's eye to the material at the tab stop. A typical example of a tab with leader characters is found in the table of contents of a book; the dots that stretch from the chapter name to the page number are the leader characters.

To add tabs to your publication, follow these steps:

1. Position the cursor in the paragraph at the point where you want to add the tab.

2. Open the Forma**t** menu.

3. Choose **T**abs. The Tabs dialog box appears (see fig. 7.14).

4. In the box under the Tab **P**ositions line, type the position, which corresponds with the cursor placement in the ruler line, where you want the tab to appear. If you want to place the first tab 1/4 inch from the left margin, position the text cursor in the box and type **.25**.

Fig. 7.14
The Tabs dialog box.

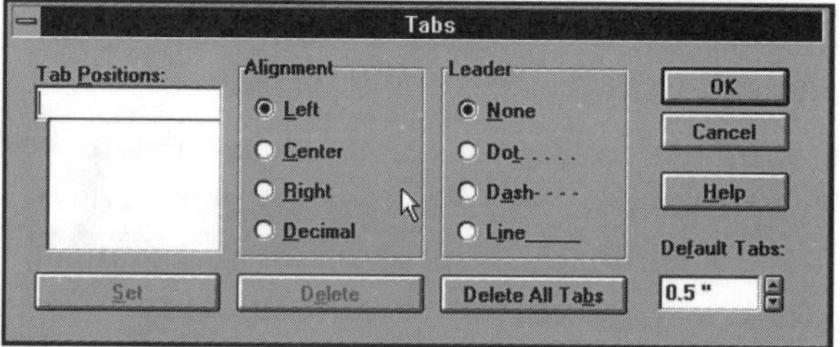

5. In the Alignment box, choose **L**eft, **C**enter, **R**ight, or **D**ecimal as the alignment for the tab.

6. In the Leader box, select **N**one if you choose not to have a leader. Otherwise, choose Do**t**, D**a**sh, or L**i**ne as the leader character for your publication.

7. Click **S**et. The tab is then added to the text frame.

8. Set additional tabs if necessary.

9. Click OK to return to the publication.

Deleting Tabs. As your experience with Publisher grows, you may want to make some modifications to the text settings in your publication. One of these changes might involve deleting tabs that you've set.

To remove a tab from your text, follow these steps:

1. Highlight the paragraph containing the tab you want to change.

2. Open the Forma**t** menu and choose **T**abs.

3. When the Tabs dialog box appears, select the tab in the Tab **P**ositions box that you want to delete.

4. Click the D**e**lete button.

5. Click OK to return to the publication.

Tip
If you want to get rid of all the tabs you've set for that highlighted block, click the Delete All Ta**b**s button.

Project Tip

Use dot leaders or lines with tabs to help lead the reader's eye from one side of the page to another. Leaders can be helpful in tables of contents, menus, and text-intensive catalogs.

Troubleshooting

I don't have any text attributes.

Click on a text frame. The text attributes appear just below the tools in the Top Toolbar.

I tried a new text alignment, but it adds too much space between letters.

You must be using the justified alignment. If you can't use left alignment, which allows only one space between words and doesn't space out letters, try resizing the text frame to shorten the distance the text is expanded.

These bullets are all boring. I want something cool.

You can add your own bullets from clip art or choose any one of the available symbols in Zapf Dingbats. Click the More button in the bullet palette to see additional choices.

I guess I messed up the indents. I only have about a one-inch strip of text in the middle of my text frame.

Remember that if you specify a 0.5 indent for **L**eft and a 0.5 indent for **R**ight, both edges will be indented one-half inch. Only enter the amount that you want Publisher to indent the text.

I tried kerning my characters and they look mutated.

First, undo the spacing change by opening the **E**dit menu and choosing **U**ndo Format. Next, when you try to change the spacing, change only selected characters instead of the entire paragraph. If you are set on doing a block of text at once, try a "lighter" option, such as **L**oose or **N**ormal.

Using WordArt

One problem with many other desktop publishing programs is that you can only do so much with the text. Oh, sure, you can put it in different fonts, styles, and formats. But what about when you want to curve it, color it, or sweep it in an arc? That's where WordArt comes in.

WordArt gives you the flexibility you need to put more creativity and flexibility in your text layout. You can use WordArt to

- Add a fancy first letter to an article.
- Make a special headline.
- Create special text for an invitation.
- Design a company logo.
- Make a company letterhead.
- Create business cards.

In the following paragraphs, you learn how to access the WordArt feature and how to use the WordArt dialog box to create, format, and edit WordArt objects.

Starting WordArt

You add a WordArt frame to your publication by using the WordArt tool in the Left Toolbar. The procedure is simple; just follow these steps:

1. Open the publication with which you want to work.
2. Click the WordArt tool (the fourth tool in the Left Toolbar).
3. Choose any Frame options that you want from the Top Toolbar.
4. Move the pointer to the page where you want to draw the WordArt frame.
5. Press and hold the mouse button while dragging the mouse down and to the right.
6. When the frame is the size you want, release the mouse button. The WordArt screen shown in figure 7.15 appears.

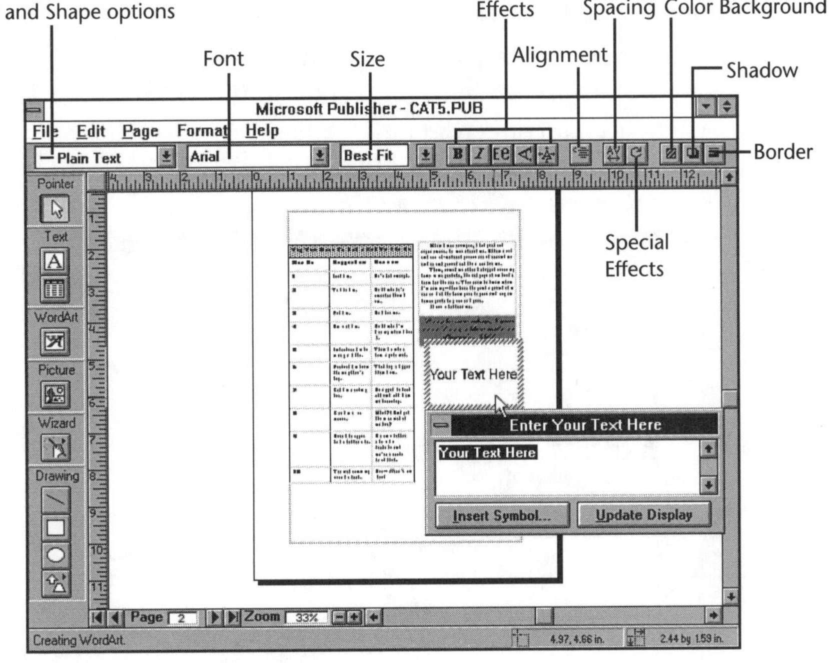

Fig. 7.15 The WordArt screen.

Understanding the WordArt Screen

The WordArt screen contains all the options you need to create and edit your WordArt text. Beside the frame you created, you see an area where you enter the text you want WordArt to display. Initially, the highlighted words `Your Text Here` appear. When you begin typing, the highlighted text is replaced with what you type.

The WordArt tools row is made up of seven different settings: the Line and Shape tools; the Font, Size, and Effects options; the Alignment, Spacing, and Special Effects buttons. The following paragraphs explain each of these tools.

Project Tip

Unless you have coordinating WordArt elements, using one WordArt item per page is plenty.

Selecting Line and Shape. Perhaps the coolest thing you can do in WordArt is pull, push, stretch, and squish text into just about any shape you can imagine. The text you enter in the WordArt box becomes clay that your command molds when you select one of the options from the Line and Shape gallery (see fig. 7.16).

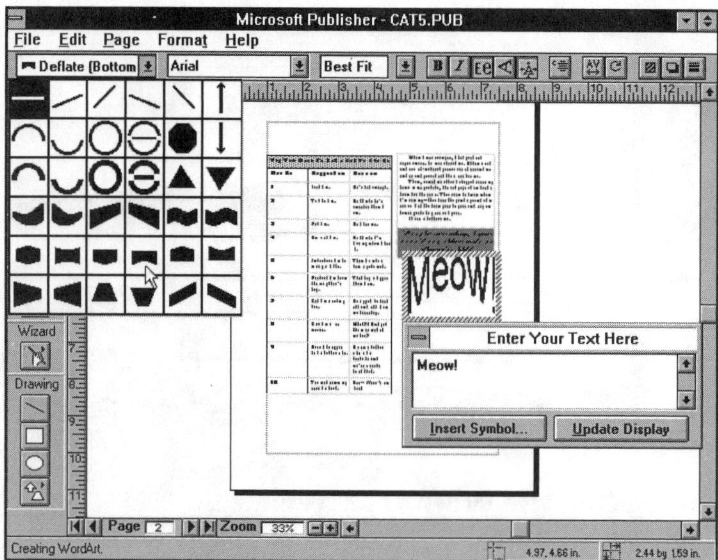

Fig. 7.16
The Line and Shape choices.

Choosing the Font. With the Font option, you choose the font in which you want to display the WordArt text. Publisher 1.0 offered you a wide variety of graphics fonts, but Version 2.0 improves on that by adding a full family of matching TrueType fonts (see fig. 7.17).

To choose a new font, simply click the down-arrow symbol at the end of the Font box; then select the font you want to use. The text in the box changes to show your selection.

Choosing the Size. You can control the size of the text in your WordArt object, or you can let Publisher make the decision for you. When you first enter text, the setting `Best Fit` appears in the Size box. With this setting selected, WordArt uses whatever space you created in the WordArt frame to determine the best size for the text in your publication. You also can choose from several specific sizes. Table 7.1 explains your choices and suggests when you may want to use those sizes.

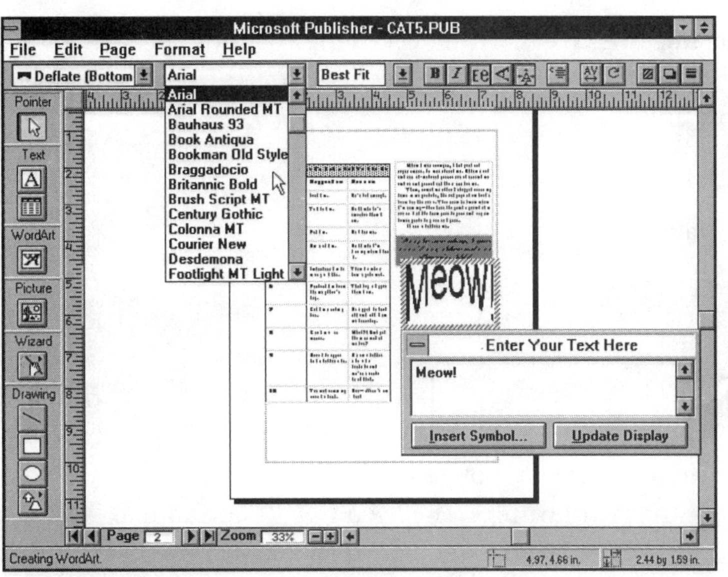

Fig. 7.17 WordArt font choices.

Table 7.2 Using Point Sizes

Point size	Used for
6	Trademarks, copyrights, or "small print" notices
12	Basic text, small headlines, or kickers
18	Headlines or promotional flyer copy
24	Large headlines or banners (masthead)
36	Titles or banners
48	Large-type items such as titles or banners
60	Specialty items
72 and up	Special large-type logos or banners

You probably won't use the largest sizes very often. Most publications use text a bit smaller than 120 or 128 points. But Publisher gives you the option, just in case.

To choose the size you want, click the down-arrow symbol at the end of the Size box in the WordArt dialog box. Then click the size you want to apply to the WordArt text.

Tip

Some font letters have small cross-lines at the top and bottom. In some typefaces, for example, the lowercase letter *n* has cross-lines that look like feet. These lines are *serifs*. So, the typefaces that have these cross-lines are called Serif typefaces; those that do not are called Sans Serif typefaces.

Choosing the Effect. The effect of the WordArt text determines the way the text is placed on the page. The effects from which you can choose are

- Bold
- Italic
- Even Height
- Flip
- Stretch

You can imagine what bold and italic do—of course, they boldface or italicize the WordArt text. The Even Height button makes all the characters in the WordArt box of equal height, whether those characters are uppercase, lowercase, or a combination of both.

The Flip button flips the text to the left, turning the characters horizontally, and the Stretch button spreads out the letters so that they fill the WordArt box.

Choosing the Alignment. The Alignment options enable you to choose the way the text is aligned within the WordArt frame. Similar to any other text-alignment options, Alignment gives you the following choices:

- Center
- Left
- Right
- Stretch Justify
- Letter Justify
- Word Justify

The alignment you choose affects your WordArt text even if you have chosen different styles. The first three alignment options—Left, Center, and Right—should look familiar from your work with text frames. The next few options—Stretch Justify, Letter Justify, and Word Justify—are options new with Version 2.0. If you choose Stretch Justify, Publisher spreads the text out to fit the frame. Letter Justify adds space between letters so that the text fills the width of the frame. Word Justify adds space between each word to make the text fill the width of the frame. In other words, the text stretches from one end of the frame to the other.

To select a different alignment, simply click on the down arrow to the right of the Alignment box. When the drop-down list of alignment options appears, click on the alignment you want. Figure 7.18 shows you the different alignment options.

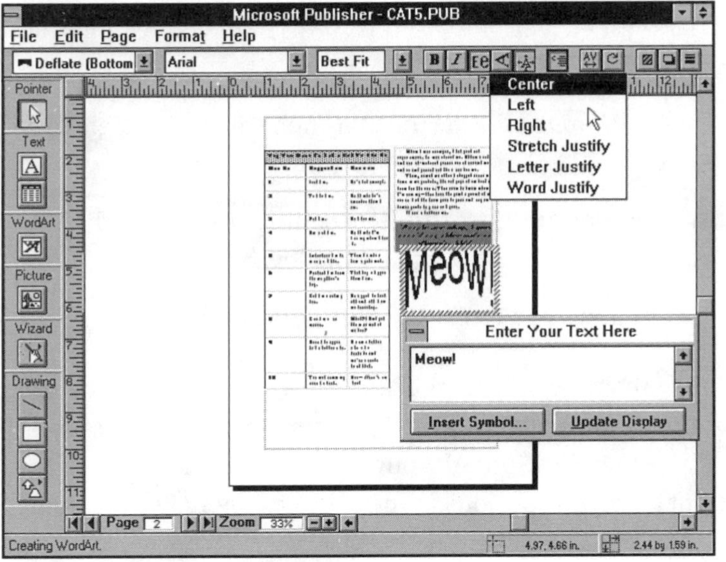

Fig. 7.18 Choosing WordArt alignment.

Controlling Character Spacing. The next button in the WordArt row controls the spacing between characters, the same as the kerning discussed earlier in this chapter. You can specify whether the characters are positioned from Very Tight to Very Loose by clicking the tool and selecting your choice.

Project Tip

Kerning is even more important when you're working with oversized letters. This is because oversized letters need to fit together well in order to look right. Experiment with the character spacing settings until you get it just the way you want it.

Adding Special Effects. The Special Effects button rotates text or adjusts text along a curve. First select the text you want to work with, and then click the Special Effects button. Enter the degree of rotation and angle (or adjustment, if you're working with a shape) and click OK. The first few times you try using Special Effects, don't get discouraged; a good amount of trial and error is usually needed to get things positioned properly.

Adding WordArt Options

At the far right edge of the WordArt tools row, you see three additional buttons (refer to fig. 7.15):

- *Color Background* fills in the text frame area with a gray shaded pattern.
- *Shadow* adds outline characters behind the text in the WordArt frame, giving the illusion of a shadow.
- *Border* allows you to choose a specific border style.

You know the process: Just click the button and choose the style you want. The Shadow effects can be really dramatic when used in the right type of publication. Although you can mix and match these additional WordArt options, remember that *overdoing* it is sometimes worse than not doing it at all.

Troubleshooting

I don't see the same fonts in my Font list.

It may be that you have a different type of printer installed or that you or someone else has added additional third-party fonts. One of the great things about TrueType fonts is that you can print any font on any printer. Something you create on another machine should print fine on your own.

From Here...

For information directly related to enhancing your publication, you may want to review the following sections of this book:

- Chapter 8, "Adding Pictures." Now that you've taken the text part of your publication as far as you can go, try adding some artwork to spruce things up. Chapter 8 explains how to import clip art, create your own graphic, and design a custom logo.

- Chapter 11, "Printing the Publication." Even though you're not finished with the entire document, you may want to take a test run at the printer. How's that text look? Do you need to make any major modifications before you start adding graphics? Find out how to print in Chapter 11.

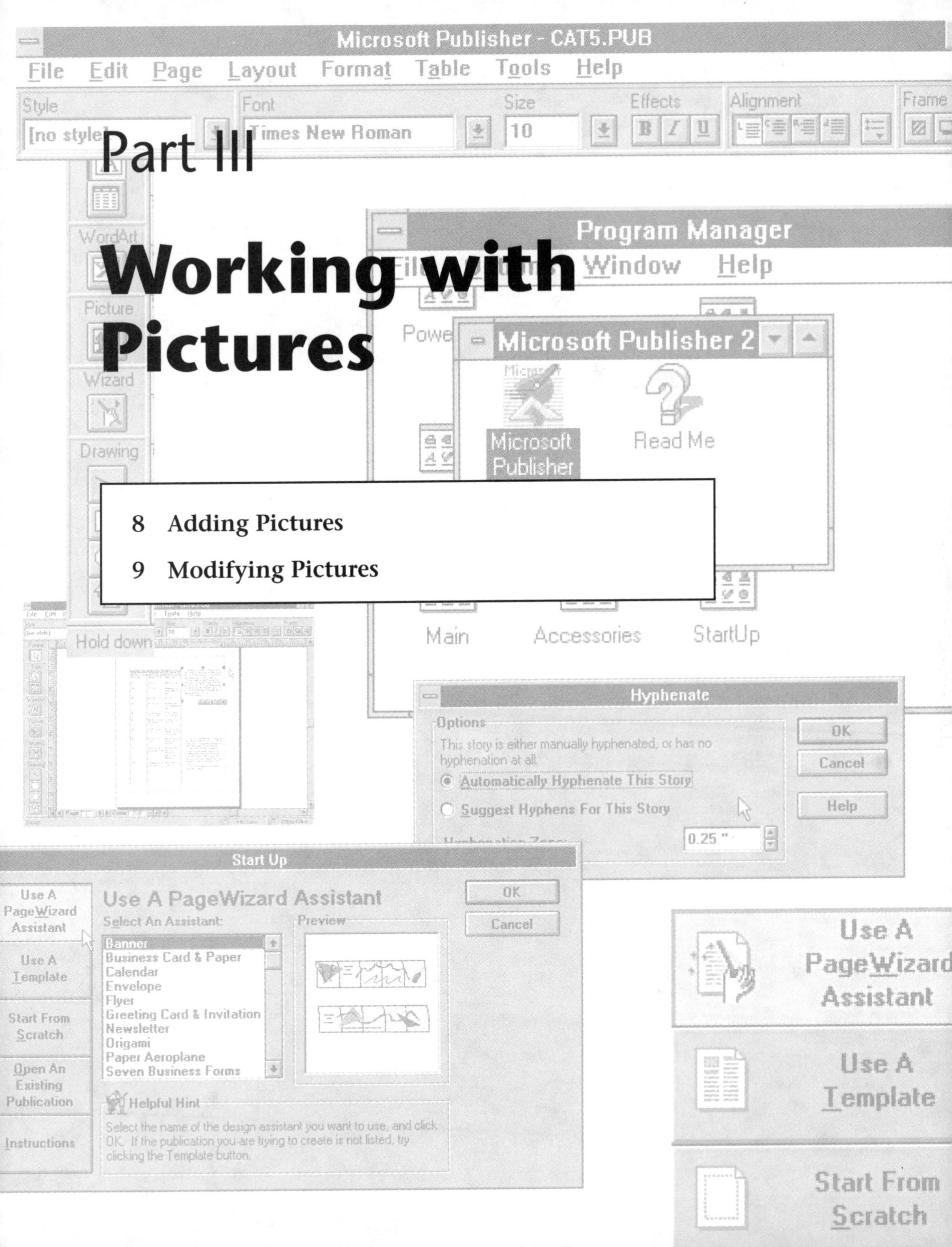

Part III

Working with Pictures

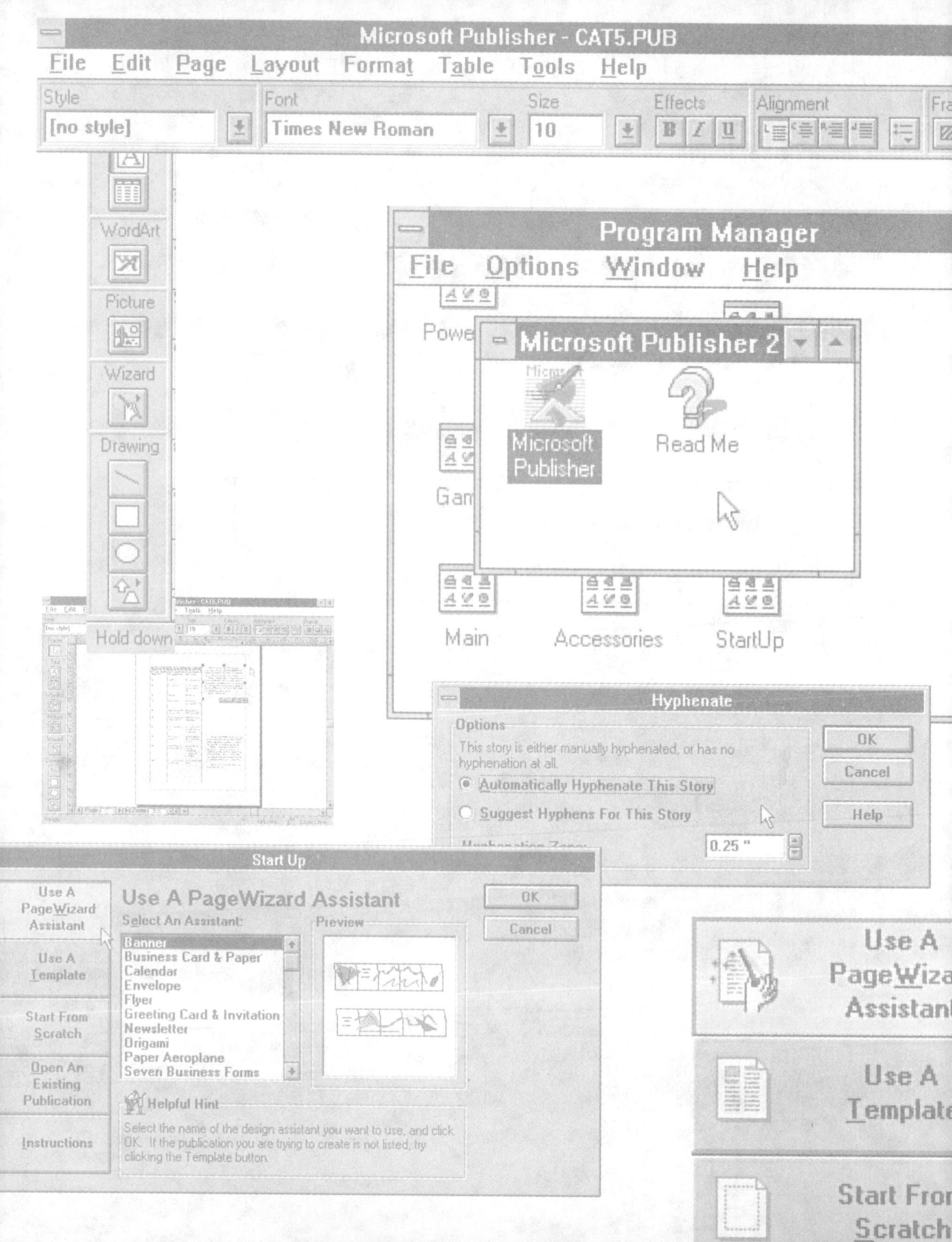

Microsoft Publisher - CAT5.PUB
File Edit Page Layout Format Table Tools Help
Style
[no style]
Font
Times New Roman
Size
10
Effects
Alignment
WordArt
Picture
Wizard
Drawing
Hold down
Program Manager
File Options Window Help
Microsoft Publisher 2
Microsoft Publisher
Read Me
Main
Accessories
StartUp
Hyphenate
Options
This story is either manually hyphenated, or has no hyphenation at all.
Automatically Hyphenate This Story
Suggest Hyphens For This Story
0.25 "
OK
Cancel
Help
Start Up
Use A PageWizard Assistant
Use A Template
Start From Scratch
Open An Existing Publication
Instructions
Use A PageWizard Assistant
Select An Assistant:
Preview
Banner
Business Card & Paper
Calendar
Envelope
Flyer
Greeting Card & Invitation
Newsletter
Origami
Paper Aeroplane
Seven Business Forms
OK
Cancel
Helpful Hint
Select the name of the design assistant you want to use, and click OK. If the publication you are trying to create is not listed, try clicking the Template button.

Chapter 8

Adding Pictures

Art adds life to your publication. Nobody wants to look at page after page of nothing but letters. Pictures help to break up the page and take the monotony out of reading a long publication. Text used as graphics, or WordArt, can also serve this purpose. You can use quotations that stand out in text and fancy first letters in your stories, for example, to make your publications more interesting.

Some graphics are just plain fun. When it's appropriate, cartoons or light-hearted pictures can make your publication more appealing and enjoyable. Remember to consider your audience; placing a funny picture in a serious publication may not cause the results you want.

Graphics also can draw attention to a specific article or element within an article. Because so many things in your readers' lives compete for their attention—the boss, the kids, the bills, TV, school, grandparents, the dog—sometimes readers need to be "courted" into spending time reading an article they may otherwise toss aside. If you receive a newsletter that has an article about a recent high school football game, for example, you might throw it out without a second look. If there is a graphic image of a grandstand full of fans waving pennants madly on a crisp October afternoon, however, you might pause a moment to look at that picture. As soon as the thought "I wonder what they're so excited about?" crosses your mind, you're hooked. You may not read the entire article, but the picture did spark your interest.

In this chapter, you learn to do the following tasks:

- Understand art basics
- Create a picture frame
- Add clip art
- Import a picture from another program
- Create your own art
- Create a logo with Logo Creator Plus

In this chapter, you learn the basics of understanding graphics, which Publisher refers to as *pictures*. After an overview of different graphic types, you learn about several options for including pictures in your Publisher documents.

Introducing Graphics

You'll use two different kinds of pictures in your publications: *bit-mapped* or *draw-type* pictures. The type of picture you choose to use depends on the quality of the picture you want and what you plan to do with it.

Bit-Mapped Pictures

Bit-mapped pictures consist of a series of square dots that are arranged to form a picture (see fig. 8.1). Because the picture is actually made up of a set of dots called *pixels*, when you enlarge the picture, the dots become more noticeable, resulting in a choppy-looking piece of art. Even if the art isn't enlarged, the quality of bit-mapped pictures is poorer than the quality of draw-type pictures. Undoubtedly, if you look closely enough, youll be able to see the individual dots that comprise a bit-mapped picture.

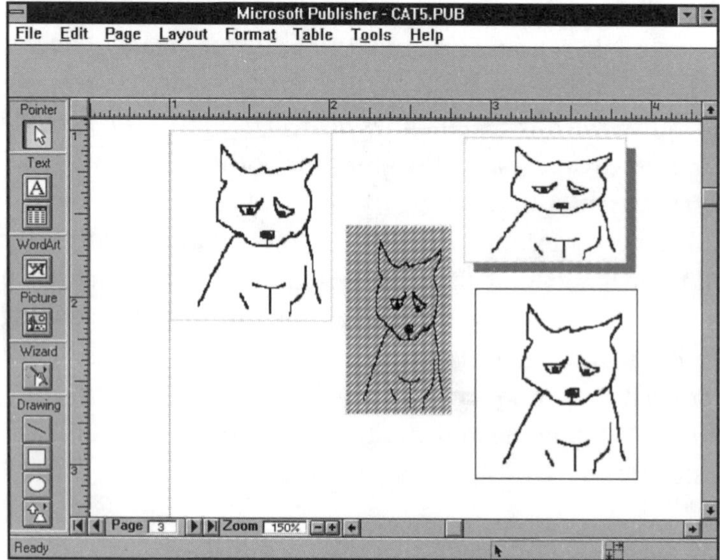

Fig. 8.1
A sample of a bit-mapped picture.

You can import bit-mapped picture files into Publisher. Many popular programs—and Windows Paintbrush is one of them—create bit-mapped files. Some extensions for bit-mapped pictures are BMP, TIF, and PCX.

You can use a scanner to bring a photograph into your publication. *Scanners* are devices that make an electronic copy of the dot patterns in a photo or piece of art and save these patterns in a file. These types of bit-mapped pictures are saved with the extension TIF.

Draw-Type Pictures

Draw-type or *object-oriented* pictures are the highest quality of art currently available. Rather than storing your picture as a series of dots, draw-type pictures store the picture as a complex set of instructions that describe how the picture is put together. Because these equations and descriptions are retained in the instructions, you can resize, move, or change the draw-type pictures without any loss of quality. Each time you resize the picture, the computer refigures the equations so that the picture is drawn clearly and in proportion (see fig. 8.2). As you can see in the figure, the resized version loses no visual quality.

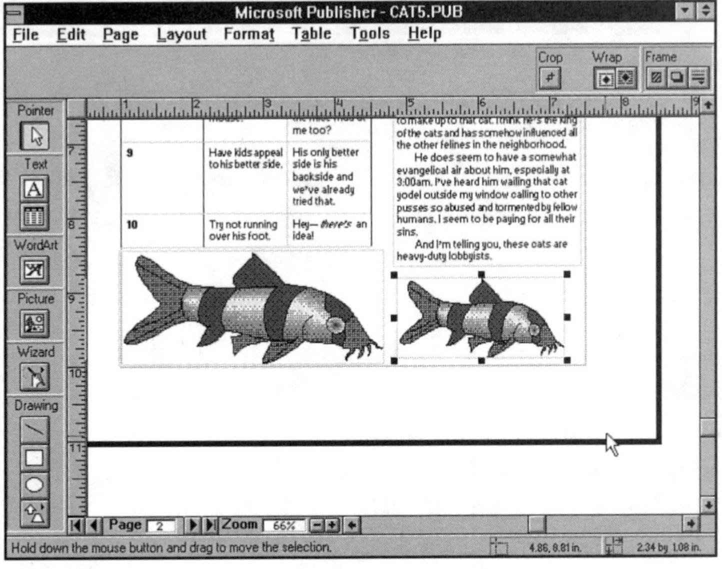

Fig. 8.2
A sample of a draw-type picture resized with no loss of quality.

Draw-type pictures are available with many high-level graphics programs. You may have heard of EPS graphics. Other draw-type picture formats include those with the extensions CGM, DRW, and WMF. These formats—and many more—are supported by Microsoft Publisher.

Table 8.1 lists the picture types and some programs that produce those types of images.

Table 8.1 Picture Types Produced by Different Programs

Picture type	Description	Program used
Bit-mapped	Picture is formed with a series of dots	Logitech Paintshow PC Paintbrush Windows Paintbrush
Draw-type	Picture is formed by a complete set of instructions and equations	CorelDraw Excel charts Harvard Graphics Microsoft Designer Windows Draw PowerPoint Freelance Graphics

Project Tip

If you use a lot of clip art for various programs, you may want to create a CLIPART directory to store often-used files that different software programs can share. If you do that, however, be sure to specify in the directory where the clip art files can be found; otherwise, your program may not be able to find the clip art when it needs it.

Clip Art

Microsoft Publisher comes equipped with over 100 files of *clip art*—pictures you can use as is or modify to fit your publications. These clip art files include pictures for all sorts of subjects, such as people, animals, computer equipment, sports, and much more. You'll find an incredible range of clip art that is bound to fit some of your publications at one time or another. All clip art in Microsoft Publisher has the extension CGM, which means that the pictures are high-quality, draw-type art.

Using Pictures Effectively

Before you begin adding pictures to Microsoft Publisher, take a few minutes to review the following guidelines for using pictures effectively:

- *Don't overwhelm the reader.* One well-placed well-planned picture makes a more favorable impression than six what-the-heck-let's-put-these-here graphics. Think about the type of pictures you want to use, and then limit yourself to only one or two pictures per page.
- *Make sure that the picture relates to the text.* Make sure that the picture fulfills a purpose. Obviously, in the example of the newsletter that showed a picture of an enraptured crowd at a football game, a picture of an ice cream cone would be inappropriate. Occasionally though, you see this type of gimmick used in advertising. This is because they want you to wonder "Why is this here?" so that you'll spend more time looking at the ad.
- *Use enough white space to showcase the image.* Although most people don't think about it, the white space they see on the page is as important as the text and the pictures. White space helps to display pictures, set off columns, and improve the look of headings. Size your pictures so that they allow an appropriate amount of white space as a border; don't make them so large that they look scrunched against the text.

Adding Pictures

Now that you know the basics, you're ready to try your hand at adding art. In Microsoft Publisher, you can add pictures in three ways:

- You can use Publisher's clip art.
- You can import picture files you create or scan from other programs.
- You can use Publisher's drawing tools to create your own art.

Creating a Picture Frame

The first step in adding a picture is to create a picture frame. When you're working with Publisher pictures, you have the option of adding a picture without first creating a frame. If you import a picture file without first creating a frame, however, the picture will be placed in your publication in the size it was originally created. In some publications, this size may take up the entire page. You then must resize the picture to fit the publication, which may result in a distortion of the picture. So, for the best fit, create a frame in the size and place you want the picture to appear, select the frame, and then place the picture. The picture is inserted into the frame in the size and place you specified. Creating a picture frame is basically the same as creating any other type of Publisher frame, except that you use the Picture Frame tool. To create a picture frame, follow these steps:

Tip
If you are importing a picture, you may want to resize the frame to the size you want before you add the picture. This saves you from having to resize everything later.

1. Open the Publisher file you want to add the picture to. Use the **O**pen Existing Publication or Create **N**ew Publication command in the **F**ile menu to open the file.
2. Open the **P**age menu and choose **F**ull Page.
3. Click on the Picture tool in the Left Toolbar. The framing options appear on the right end of the Top Toolbar. You can choose the wrap settings, shading, and line thickness for the picture frame.
4. Choose the option(s) you want, if any, by clicking on the appropriate button(s).
5. Move the pointer to the place on the publication where you want to begin drawing the picture frame.
6. Press and hold the mouse button and drag the mouse down and to the right.
7. When the frame is the size you want, release the mouse button. The frame is created; handles appear on the corners and the sides, indicating that the frame is selected (see fig. 8.3).

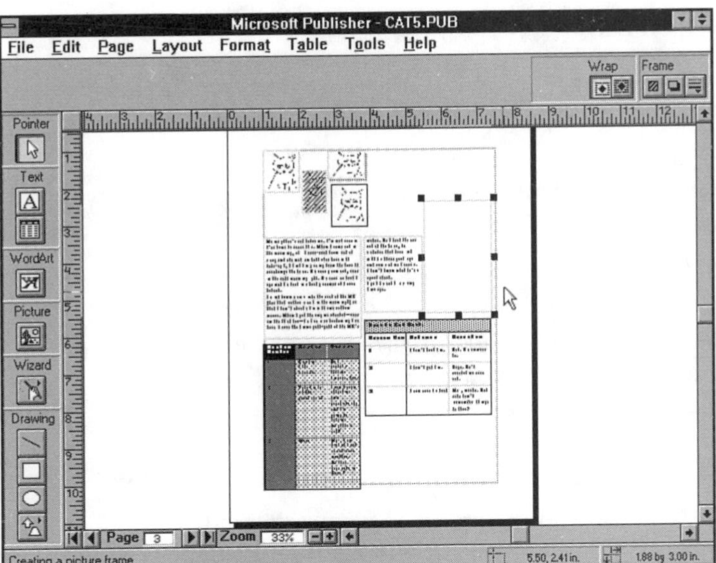

Fig. 8.3
The new picture frame

Inserting a Clip Art Picture

There's no cutting corners when it comes to illustrating your document. Publisher gives you the option of using clip art—not just from Publisher—but from a wide variety of sources. You can use Publisher's ClipArt Gallery, which includes over 100 different pieces of art, or you can use clip art from other programs like Microsoft Works, PowerPoint, or Freelance Graphics. You can also purchase additional clip art from a variety of manufacturers, including Microsoft.

Using the Publisher ClipArt Gallery

Publisher has an incredible library of clip art images. You can access these items either by using the **I**mport Picture command, if you know the file name of the art you want, or by browsing through the images in the ClipArt Gallery. The clip art items are organized into specific categories so that you can easily find the images you want. To insert a clip art picture, follow these steps:

1. Make sure that the publication is displayed in Full Page view. This view helps you see the proportion and placement of the picture in relation to the other items on the page.

2. Make sure that the picture frame you want to use is selected.

3. Open the **F**ile menu.
4. Choose the ClipArt **G**allery command (see fig. 8.4). The ClipArt Gallery dialog box appears.

> **Note**
>
> If this is the first time you're using Publisher's ClipArt Gallery, a message appears asking whether you'd like to add Publisher's clip art to the Gallery. Click Yes, and go get a Coke. The addition of the art files may take several minutes, depending on the speed of your machine.

5. Choose the category of art you'd like to see. If you're not sure what you want, click All to see all available art.
6. Choose the art you want from the displayed gallery of choices.
7. Click OK to return to the publication.

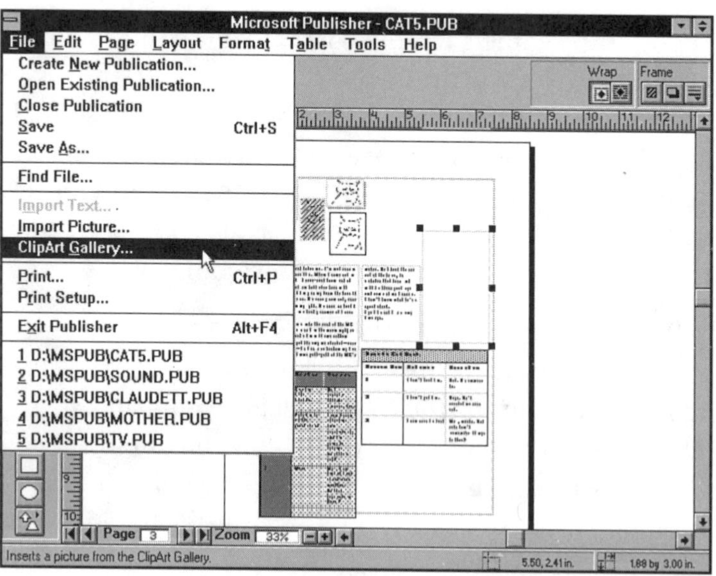

Fig. 8.4
Starting the ClipArt Gallery.

To use the ClipArt Gallery, simply click on the category you want and then scroll through the images until you see the one you want. Publisher includes a variety of different styles, so you should be able to find one that fits the bill. When you find it, click OK to add it to the picture frame in your publication.

Troubleshooting

I clicked the wrong piece of art and Publisher imported it.

That's okay. Make sure that the picture frame is selected, and then just press Delete. Publisher deletes the art but leaves the frame. Make sure that the frame is still selected and start the ClipArt Gallery again.

Importing Pictures

Another method of putting pictures into your publication is to import pictures from other applications. As you read earlier, Publisher accepts a wide range of picture files created in almost any graphics program. This section explains the various types of pictures you can use in your Publisher publication and shows you how to bring the pictures into your document.

Learning Which Picture Files Publisher Accepts

Publisher is a friendly program; you can use all kinds of files with Microsoft Publisher without much hassle. As you know, Publisher accepts both bit-mapped and draw-type pictures.

Although bit-mapped pictures produce graphics of lesser quality, they give you a certain benefit, as well. When you create a bit-mapped graphic, you are actually painting individual pixels on the screen. This means that you have a great amount of control over the picture you create. If you want to change a pattern, add a highlight, or fill in a shape, you can do so by enlarging the view and working with the individual pixels. On the flip side, however, this flexibility has its cost. The loss of quality that can result when you enlarge bit-mapped graphics makes them a less attractive option when you need high-quality smooth-line art.

Because bit-mapped pictures are used in most paint programs, however, they give you the choice of using a wide range of paint programs currently available. In fact, one paint program, Windows Paintbrush, is included with Windows (in the Accessories window in the Program Manager). With Paintbrush, you can create bit-mapped graphics for use in your publications.

Virtually any file format you can create in another program—even on Macintosh computers—you can use in Publisher 2.0. Version 2.0 now supports the following formats (considerably more than Version 1.0):

BMP
CGM
DRW
EPS
PCX
TIF
WPF
WMF

Even with the incredible range of graphics programs available in the market today, these formats pretty much cover all available popular programs. Chances are, your particular graphics program has the capability to output your picture files in one of these formats. Check your program's documentation for instructions. If you're using a program that does not output files in one of these formats, the makers of Publisher urge you to try the file anyway. In the best-case scenario, Publisher will recognize the format and import the file; in the worst case, Publisher will display a message saying it doesn't understand the file format.

Importing the Picture

The way in which you import a picture into Publisher from another application depends, in part, on how you created the file. If you created the picture in another program, such as Windows Paintbrush, and you now want to import the file into Publisher, you have two options:

- You can save the file in Paintbrush and then import the file into Publisher.
- You can copy the picture to the Windows clipboard and then paste the picture into Publisher.

Importing a Saved File. When you're ready to import a file you already saved, follow these steps:

1. Create the picture frame, if you haven't already done so.
2. Make sure that the frame is selected.
3. Open the **F**ile menu.
4. Choose the **I**mport Picture command. The Import Picture dialog box appears (see fig. 8.5).
5. Click on the List Files of **T**ype box to select the file type you're looking for. A drop-down list showing all the supported types appears (see fig. 8.6). If you're unsure what the extension of the file is, select All Picture Types. This displays all files with the extensions supported by Publisher.

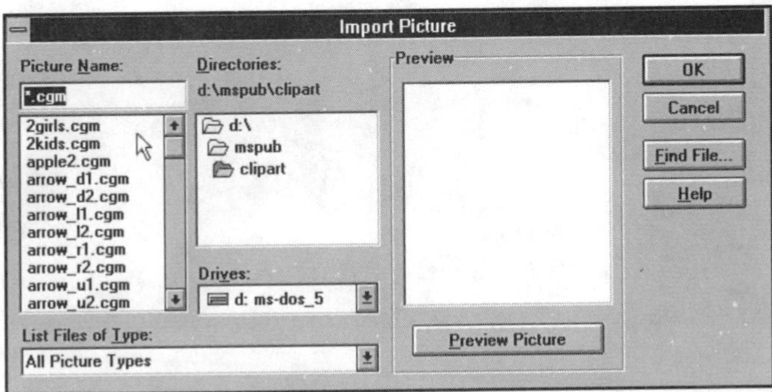

Fig. 8.5
The Import Picture dialog box.

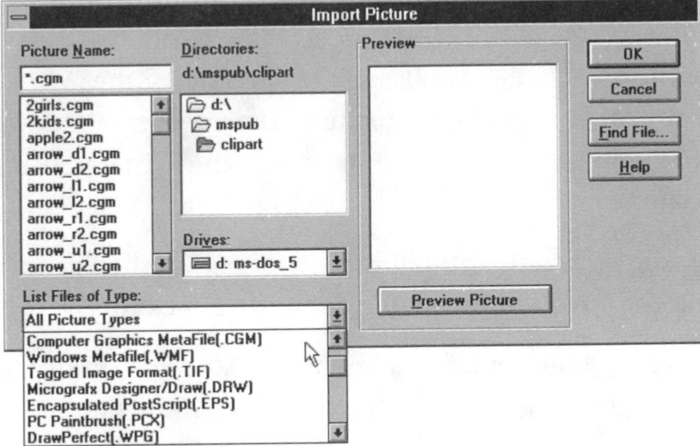

Fig. 8.6
Choosing a file type.

6. Change the drive and directory, if necessary, to find the file you want.

7. Highlight the name of the file you want to import in the Picture Name list box

8. Click on the **P**review Picture button to see the file (see fig. 8.7). If the picture is too large to fit in memory, Publisher displays a warning screen telling you that the picture cannot be previewed from within Publisher.

9. Click OK to add the file to the publication.

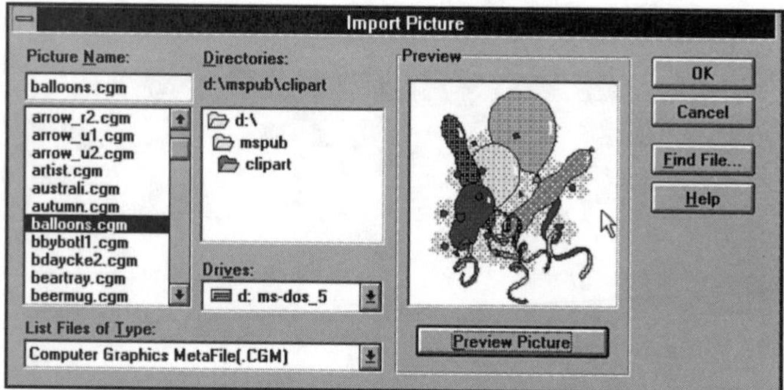

Fig. 8.7
Previewing the art file.

Copying a File by Using the Windows Clipboard. You also can use the Windows clipboard to copy a picture from one application to another. That's one of the great things about Windows—files you create in one application can usually be used in another Windows program. If you want to copy a picture from another Windows program into Publisher, follow these steps (you use Windows Paintbrush in this example):

1. Save the publication in Publisher by opening the **F**ile menu, choosing **S**ave, entering a file name, and clicking OK.

2. Minimize Publisher by clicking on the Minimize button (the triangle pointing down) in the right side of the Publisher title bar.

3. If the Program Manager is minimized, double-click the Program Manager icon.

4. Open the Accessories window by double-clicking on the icon. ***Note:*** If you are using a different graphics program, your program may be in a different window.

5. Select Paintbrush by double-clicking the icon (see fig. 8.8).

6. Create the picture you want. Figure 8.9 shows an example of a picture created in Paintbrush.

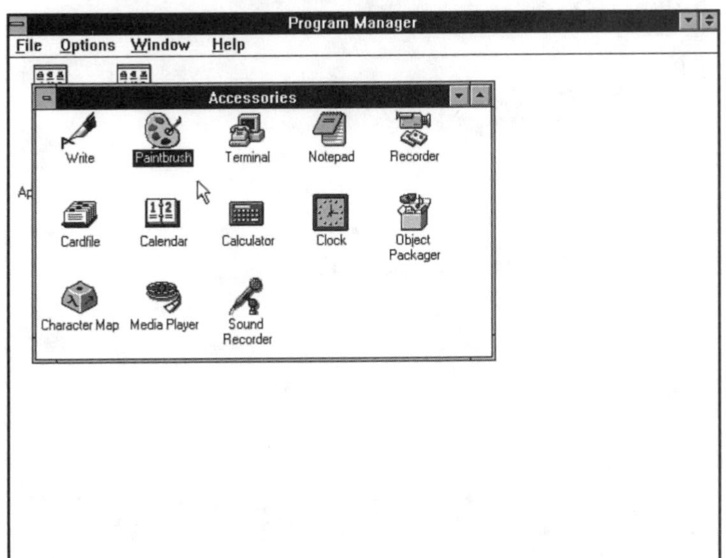

Fig. 8.8
Starting Paintbrush.

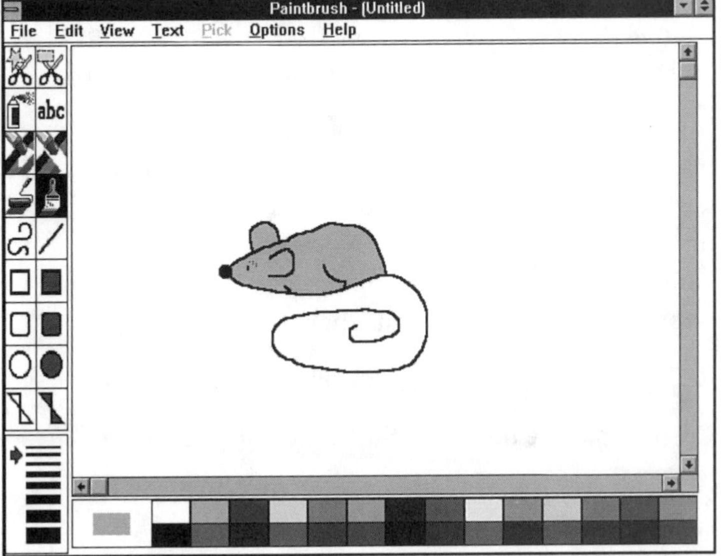

Fig. 8.9
The art created in Paintbrush.

7. Select the picture. In Paintbrush, you use one of the selection tools—the buttons showing the scissors—in the top of the tools row.

8. Open the **E**dit menu and choose the **C**opy command (see fig. 8.10). Now the picture has been copied to the Windows clipboard.

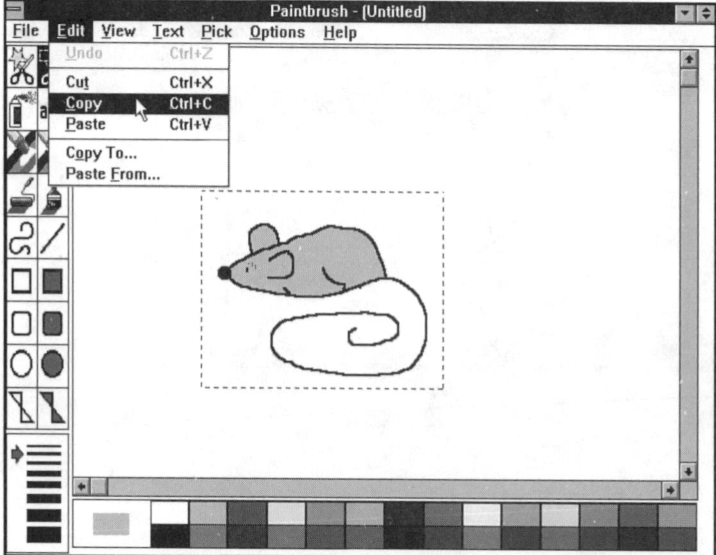

Fig. 8.10
Copying the art.

9. To save the picture, open the **F**ile menu and choose the **S**ave command. When the Paintbrush Save dialog box appears, enter a file name for the picture, and click OK or press Enter.

10. If you are finished using Paintbrush, you can exit the program by opening the **F**ile menu and choosing E**x**it. If you want to continue working in Paintbrush after you place the picture you just created in your Publisher document, you can minimize the Paintbrush program by clicking on the Minimize button in the upper right corner of the Title bar.

11. Restore Publisher by double-clicking on the Publisher icon.

12. Create a picture frame for the picture, if you haven't already done so.

13. Make sure that the picture frame is selected.

14. Open the **E**dit menu.

15. Choose the **P**aste Object command. The picture is placed in the publication (see fig. 8.11).

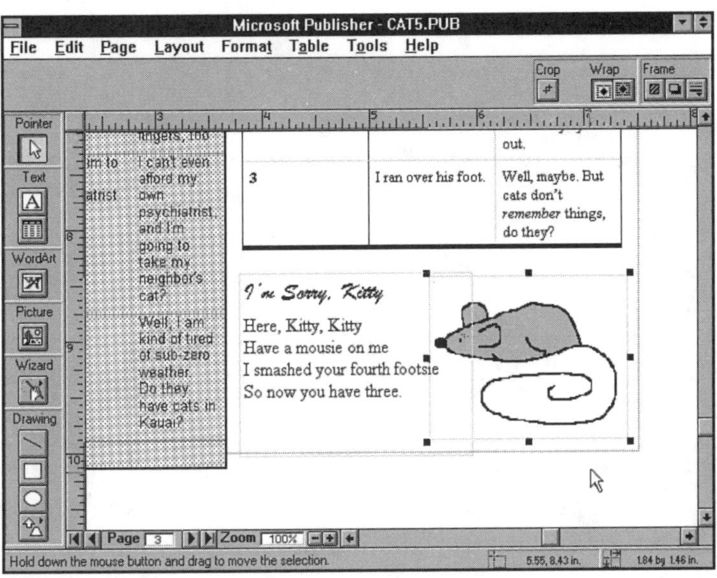

Fig. 8.11
Adding art to your Publisher document.

As you can see from figure 8.11, when the picture is placed in the publication, the handles still appear along the edges of the picture. You can resize or move the picture as necessary. When you have the picture where you want it, click outside the picture to remove the handles.

Tip
If you need to edit an image you created in Paintbrush or Draw, just double-click it. Publisher takes you right to the program in which you created the image so you can make the necessary changes.

Note

Publisher also supports OLE (pronounced O-lay), which stands for object linking and embedding. This feature allows you to link objects you create in other files to your Publisher document so that they are updated automatically anytime the original file changes. Suppose that you create a chart in Excel and want to incorporate it in your Publisher newsletter. You can copy the chart in Excel, return to Publisher, and choose Paste **S**pecial in the **E**dit menu. Publisher places the chart in your publication and whenever you make changes to the chart in Excel, the changes are reflected in the Publisher document too.

Creating Your Own Pictures

Although the Drawing tools in Microsoft Publisher 1.0 won't enable you to create any truly sophisticated graphics, Publisher 2.0 builds in a feature that will: Microsoft Draw. In addition to Publisher's four Drawing tools—Line, Box, Rounded Box, and Oval—you can create your own graphics, or edit those you acquire elsewhere, using Microsoft Draw. This section explores both options.

Trying Out the Drawing Tools

You might be surprised how much you can improve the look of your publication by using the simplest of drawing utensils. Even though Publisher's built-in tools don't appear to pack a lot of punch, they can add some pretty cool touches to your publications.

You don't have to make a frame to store the art you create with the Drawing tools. You can just place the images right into your publication.

Using the Line Tool. The Line tool is a little different from the other tools because it provides you with a few more options. When you click on the Line tool, a few options appear in the right end of the Top Toolbar (see fig. 8.12). Table 8.2 explains the Line tool options.

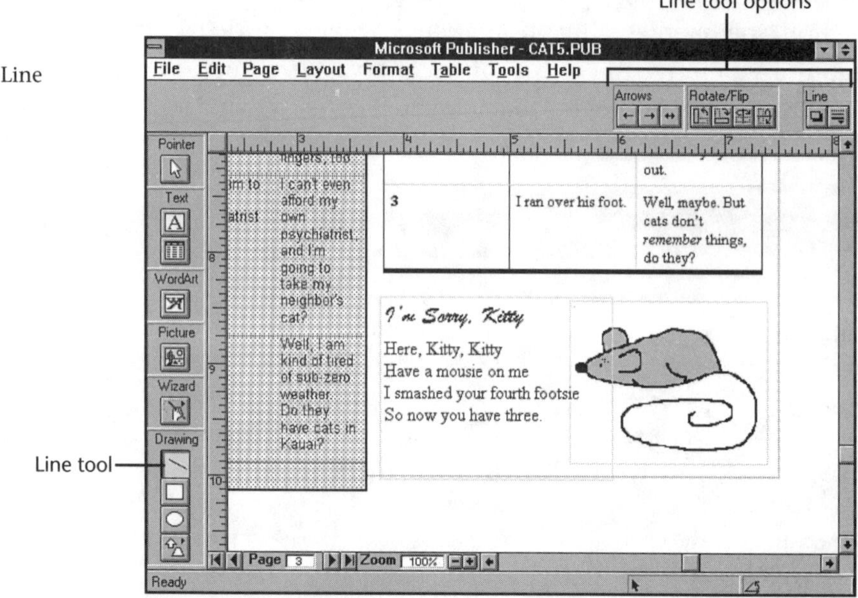

Fig. 8.12
Choosing the Line tool.

Table 8.2 Line Tool Options

Option	Description
	Creates a line with an arrow at the left end
	Creates a line with an arrow at the right end
	Creates a line with arrows at both ends
	Buttons allowing you to flip the line you draw
	Click to add a line shadow
	Click to choose line thickness

Using the Line tool requires relatively few steps:

1. Click on the Line tool (under Drawing) in the Left toolbar.
2. Select the Line tool options you want, if any, from the Top toolbar.
3. Move the pointer to the place in the publication where you want to begin drawing the line.
4. Press and hold the mouse button. ***Note:*** If you want to make sure that your line is straight, press and hold Shift while you draw the line.
5. Drag the mouse in the direction you want to draw the line.
6. When the line is the length you want, release the mouse button. The line appears on your publication. As you can see, the line has two handles—one at each end (see fig. 8.13).

Tip

You can create a publication without ever using the Line tool. With the Border command, available in the **L**ayout menu, Publisher can add lines around selected frames for you. For more information on borders, see Chapter 9, "Modifying Pictures."

You can move, cut, copy, delete, paste, and resize lines, as you can any other picture in Publisher.

Here are a few ways in which you may want to use lines in your publication:

- To separate the banner or masthead of your publication and the main article area
- Vertically, to visually divide columns on the page
- To underline a subhead, to help separate it from the main headline
- Across the bottom of the publication, to set off a footer
- At the beginning of a new text section in a report. This line helps show the reader where the new information begins.
- To connect text known as a *callout* to an item in a picture or figure

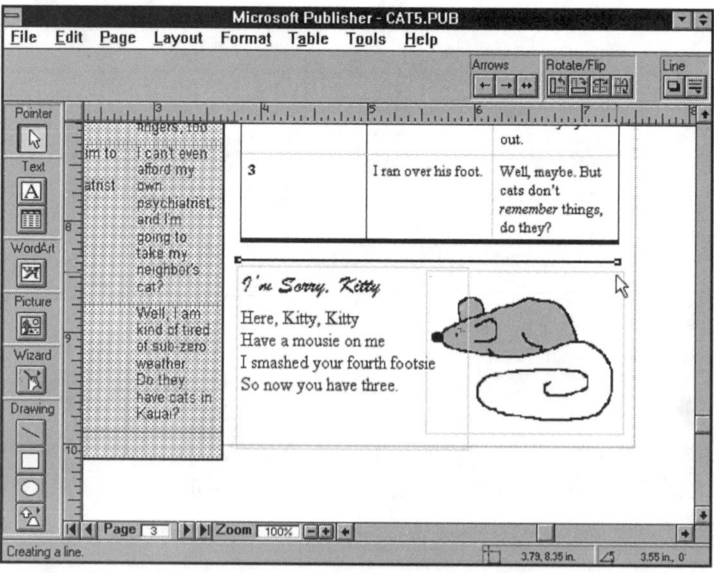

Fig. 8.13
The added line.

Which line thickness should you choose? The choice depends on you and the design of your publication. As you make decisions regarding line thickness, however, remember these tips:

- *The thicker the line, the more dramatic the effect.* As with many elements in desktop publishing, a little goes a long way. If you use a heavy line, use the line sparingly. You may want a heavy underline to set off the title of your table of contents box, for example, but don't use it for every headline on the page.

- *Be consistent with the line thickness you use.* Use lines of the same thickness to set off the same element. If you use a certain line thickness to underline the main headings in your paper, stick to that scheme and treat all other main headings similarly. Don't underline the heading on page 1 and forget about the rest. And be careful not to use different line thicknesses if you want the elements to look alike. This consistency helps readers recognize different elements in your publication and gives the document a more cohesive look.

- *Don't use lines when a box will do.* If you're planning to border your publication with lines, you may want to rethink your strategy. Do you mean for all lines to meet exactly at the corners? This will be harder to do with individual lines. You may want to consider using a box or a border to enclose the publication. Although you can draw straight lines easily by pressing Shift while you draw the line, matching the lines up so that they meet exactly at the corners can be a tricky business.

- *Use the rulers when positioning lines.* Sometimes what you see onscreen can be a little deceiving. If you're working with multiple lines, open the **P**age menu and choose **A**ctual Size or 200% Size to make sure that you're placing the lines accurately. Watch the ruler as you move the lines. Make sure that the same amount of space separates each pair of lines, and that each line begins and ends at the same point.

In the next section, you learn to work with the Box tool to add rectangles to your publication.

Using the Box Tool. The Box drawing tool is located beneath the Line tool in the Left Toolbar. At first glance, it may not look like you'll be using the Box tool a lot—why should you draw boxes when Publisher adds borders and frame outlines for you? In some instances, however, you'll be glad you have a box tool:

- When you want to add a box as part of a background design
- When you need to add a square as part of a larger object
- When you want to put a colored background behind a clear text frame

Suppose that you want to add a simple box as part of a design for your business cards. Here are the steps:

1. Click on the Box tool.
2. Select the Box tool options in the right side of the Top Toolbar (see fig. 8.14). These options are the same options that appear when you create frames. You can choose to add a shade or shadow, or you can control the line thickness used to draw the box. Click on the options you want. For this example, a light shade and the thinnest line were selected.
3. Move the mouse pointer to the place on-screen where you want to begin drawing the box.
4. Press and hold the mouse button and drag the mouse down and to the right.
5. When the box is the size you want, release the mouse button.

Tip
You can draw a perfect square box by pressing and holding Shift while you drag the mouse to draw the box.

The finished box appears with handles, which means that the box is still selected. You can use the pointer to move or resize the box. You also can cut, copy, or delete the box. You can change the line thickness of the box by clicking on different Line buttons. You also can do away with the line altogether by clicking the currently selected line button so that all buttons are disabled.

Figure 8.14 shows an example of an added box. You don't see the outline of the box because in the Line thickness options (the last button in the Box options), None was chosen, so no outer line was used along the edges of the box. The horizontal lines come from choosing the Shading button and then selecting the line pattern.

When might you want to use boxes in your document? Granted, in some cases, using a traditional line border or special BorderArt may be your best bet. In other cases, however, you'll want to add a box that isn't part of a text or picture frame. Here are a few ideas:

- As part of a design element that will not contain text, such as color blocking, thumb tabs for pages, part of a logo, and so on.
- In graphs or figures you're creating in Publisher.
- To highlight titles or bylines in cases where you don't want to enclose the entire text frame in a border.

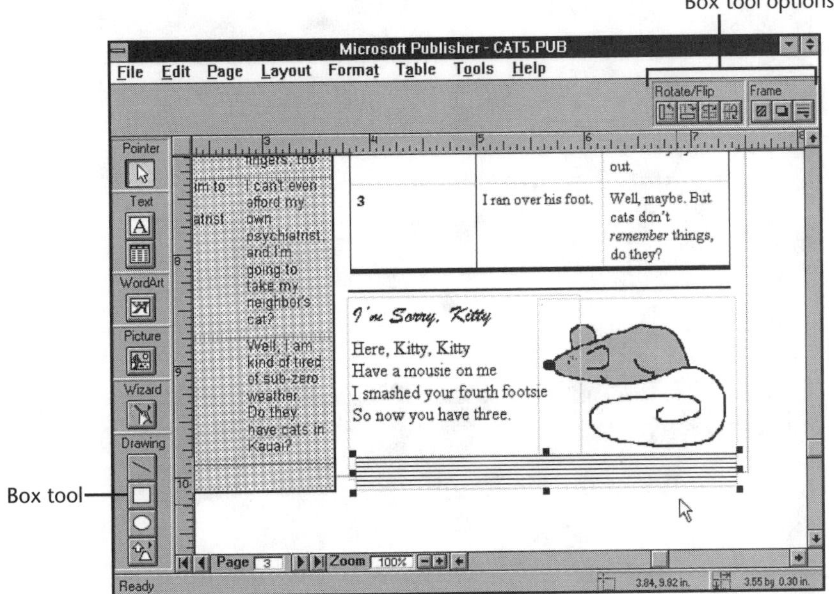

Fig. 8.14 The created box.

Remember, when you add boxes to your publication, a few boxes go a long way. Add boxes only when they will help the design of your publication, and make sure that you're consistent with the way you use the boxes.

Using the Shape Palette. Publisher 2.0 includes another nifty change. Instead of that little rounded Box tool, there's a huge palette with a bunch of different art tools. At the bottom of the Left Toolbar, you see a tool that hints at the possibilities. Click it and watch what happens (see fig. 8.15).

See—the rounded Box tool is still there, in the upper right corner of the palette. But so are a score of others. To use one of these tools, simply click on the one you want, move the pointer to the publication, press the mouse button, and drag to draw the shape. Figure 8.16 shows the L-shape after other design elements have been added.

Fig. 8.15
The shape palette.

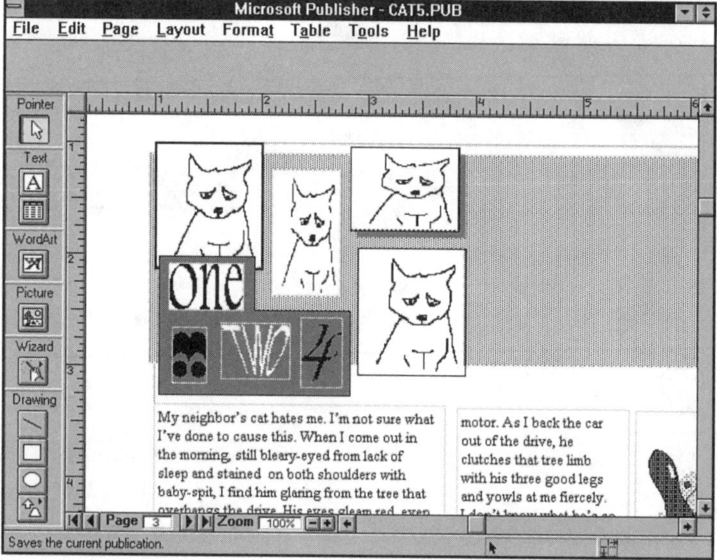

Fig. 8.16
The resulting shape.

After you release the mouse button, the shape remains selected. You can remove the handles by clicking outside the rectangle. Or, you can move, resize, copy, cut, change the shading or shadow, or change the line thickness used to draw the box. If you use a shade or a drop-shadow when you create the shape, you may notice that the shape "blocks out" text or pictures you have in that spot on your publication. As mentioned before, you cannot see the text or pictures behind the box because Publisher sees the different elements on the page in terms of layers. The rectangle you've just drawn has been placed on top of the existing layer of your publication. You can place the box behind the text or picture by opening the **L**ayout menu and choosing the Send to **B**ack command (or you can bypass the menu selections by pressing Ctrl+Z).

Using the Oval Tool. The last tool to discuss in the Drawing tools set is the Oval tool, located just beneath the Box tool. This is another tool you may not use often, but, sooner or later, you'll be glad you have it. To use the Oval tool, follow these steps:

1. Click on the Oval tool.
2. Select the Oval tool option(s) you want by clicking on the appropriate button(s) at the end of the tools row. You can choose from shaded or shadowed ovals, and you can select the line thickness.
3. Move the pointer to the page.
4. Position the pointer where you want to begin drawing the oval.
5. Press and hold the mouse button.
6. Drag the mouse down and to the right.
7. When the oval is the size you want, release the mouse button.

Tip
If you're in the mood to create perfect circles, select the Oval tool and press and hold the Shift key while dragging the mouse to create the circle.

After you release the mouse button, the oval is still selected. You can now make any necessary changes, such as moving, resizing, changing the shading or shadow, or altering the line thickness of the oval.

You may not have many opportunities to use the Oval tool because most publications tend to be linear in nature and a circular object can really shake up the design. For fun newsletters, invitations, fliers, and other promotional pieces, you can test your creativity and play around with the Oval tool. Here are a few suggestions of ways you can use the Oval tool:

- As part of a company logo
- To call attention to a special text item
- To draw round checkboxes on a business-reply card.

Troubleshooting

I made a line, but it's not straight.

It's not easy to draw a straight line without using the Shift key. If your line has a crimp in it, you can move the pointer to a handle. When you see the resize cursor, press the mouse button and drag the line until it straightens out. When you release the mouse button, you should have a straight line. For best results, zoom up to actual size or 200% size to make sure the line is straight. When all else fails, select the line and press Delete; then draw the line again—this time, pressing Shift while you drag the mouse to draw the line.

Using Microsoft Draw

When you installed Microsoft Publisher Version 2.0, the installation routine also installed another program, Microsoft Draw. This popular graphics program has been around a long time and has developed a loyal group of followers. Why? Because Draw is easy to learn, easy to use, and it can produce art that is usable for almost any application.

You can create artwork in Microsoft Draw or you can edit pieces of art you already have. To start working in Draw, follow these steps:

1. Start, of course, with your publication displayed on-screen.
2. Do *not* (this is unusual, isn't it?) select a picture frame.
3. Open the **E**dit menu and choose the Insert O**b**ject command. The Insert Object dialog box shown in figure 8.17 appears.
4. Under Object **T**ype, click Microsoft Draw.
5. Click OK or press Enter.

The Microsoft Draw screen appears on your monitor (see fig. 8.18).

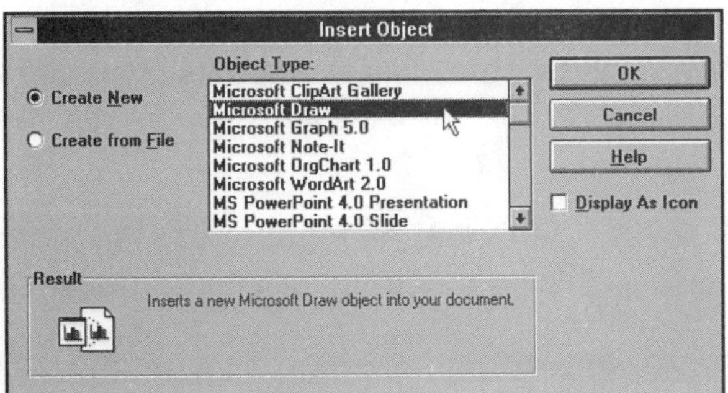

Fig. 8.17
The Insert Object dialog box.

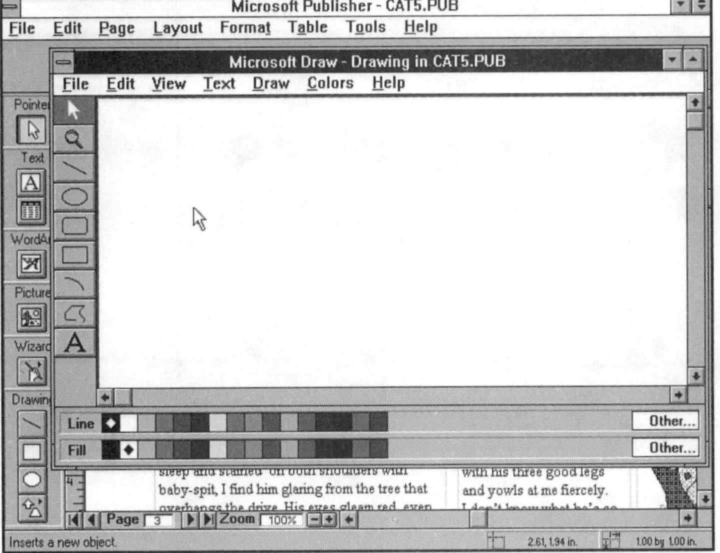

Fig. 8.18
The Microsoft Draw screen.

You can find your way around Microsoft Draw with no problem; it looks remarkably similar to Paintbrush. The tools are on the left side of the screen and the menus are at the top. Choose your colors from the palette at the bottom of the screen. When you are ready to paste the art into Publisher from Draw, select the art, and then open the **E**dit menu and choose **C**opy.

Using Logo Creator Plus

Another new feature of Publisher 2.0 is the addition of Logo Creator Plus. Actually a PageWizard design assistant, the Creator walks you through the process of creating a logo for your business or organization.

To start the Logo Creator, click the Wizard button in the Left Toolbar. Next, choose Logo Creator Plus from the pop-up box (see fig. 8.19).

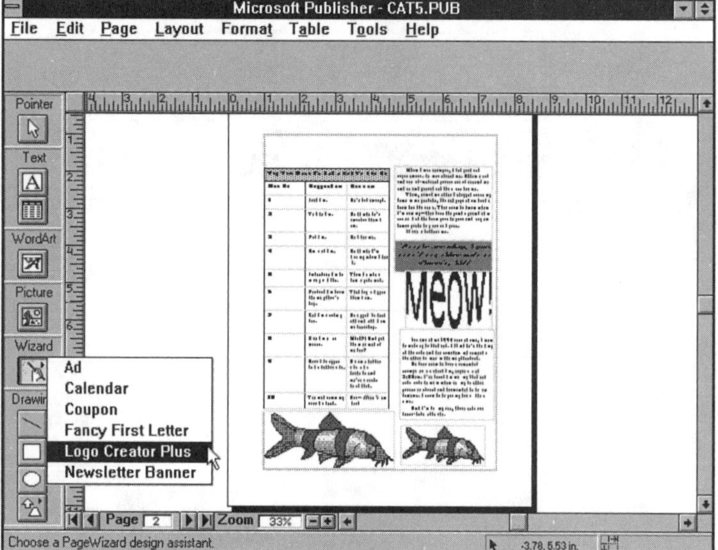

Fig. 8.19
Choosing the Logo Creator Plus Wizard.

Next, draw a box on-screen where you want the Wizard to put the logo. After you draw the box, Publisher takes you through a series of questions designed to help you choose the right elements for your logo (see fig. 8.20).

When the Logo Creator Plus is finished, the Wizard starts assembling the logo according to the selections you made. This may take a couple of minutes. When it's finished, the logo is positioned in the box you selected on the publication (see fig. 8.21).

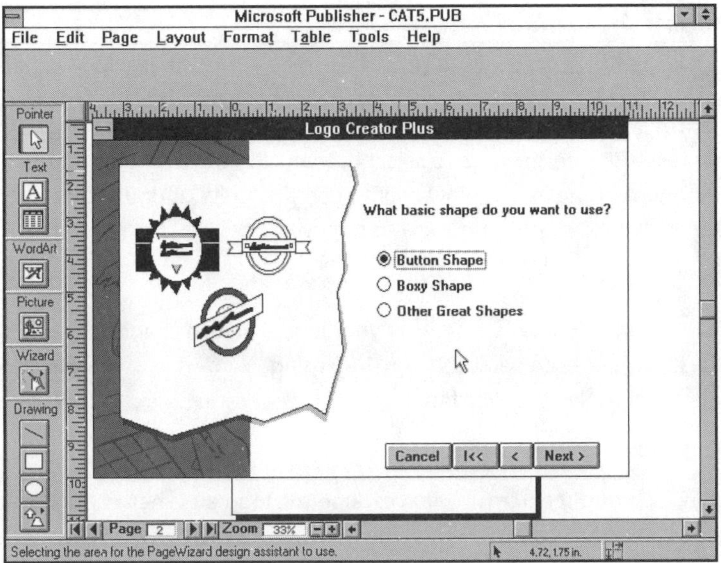

Fig. 8.20
Using the Logo Creator.

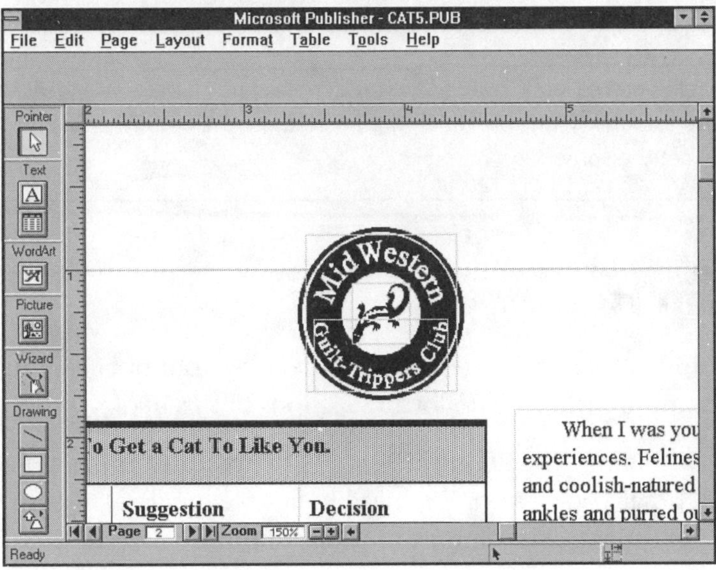

Fig. 8.21
The finished logo.

Troubleshooting

There are white dots on my letters.

Chances are, one of the design elements on the logo is overlapping some of your text. Click on the logo to select it; then click the Ungroup button in the bottom of the frame. Now zoom in on the white dots and click one. After you've selected it, press Del to remove it.

I don't like the way the letters look.

After you ungroup the elements in your logo, you can change the way the letters look—or even what they say—by using WordArt. Just double-click the text to display the WordArt box.

I want to turn the art the other way.

Again, ungroup the items by first clicking the logo and then clicking the Ungroup button. Zoom in on the picture and click it. Now use one of the Rotate/Flip options in the Top Toolbar to change the way the art is displayed.

The logo is too big.

Just click on the logo, grab one of the corners, and resize. If you want to make the logo thinner or wider, drag the side or the bottom of the frame and not the corner.

From Here...

For information directly related to enhancing your publication, you may want to review the following sections of this book:

- Chapter 9, "Modifying Pictures." The next step is to change the art that you created. You need to be able to move, resize, copy, paste, flip, rotate, and do all kinds of other things to the art objects that you added.

- Chapter 10, "Finishing the Layout." If you added your art and everything is just the way you want it, you can skip right ahead to the fine-tuning chapter, Chapter 10. In this chapter, you learn to add some special features, like BorderArt, and use new utilities, like the Layout Checker. Fun stuff.

Chapter 9

Modifying Pictures

In this chapter, you learn to do the following tasks:

- Select pictures
- Resize pictures
- Move, crop, copy, and paste pictures
- Use borders
- Add BorderArt

In Chapter 8, "Adding Pictures," you learned the basics of getting artwork into your Publisher documents. This chapter goes a little further by showing you how to modify—resize, move, copy, cut, paste, crop, place, border, and delete—the pictures you choose to illustrate your publications.

The figures in this chapter use the example from the preceding chapter to demonstrate the many changes you can make to your pictures. Figure 9.1 shows a sample document in Two Page view. To display your own document in Two Page view, open the **P**age menu and choose the **V**iew Two Page Spread command.

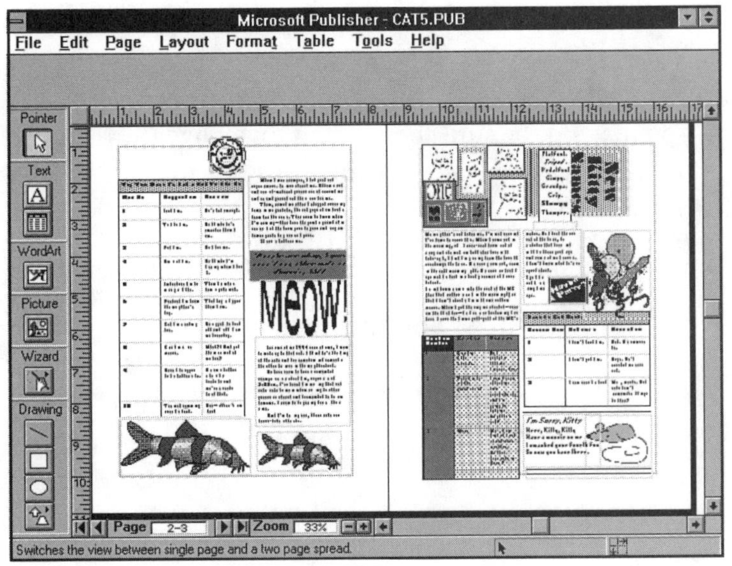

Fig. 9.1
The document in Two Page view.

Editing Pictures

The first course of business is to get your pictures the way you want them. Are they too large? Too small? Do they look different from the way you intended them to look? Publisher gives you a number of options for dealing with your pictures. In this section, you learn to perform the following operations:

- Select pictures
- Resize pictures
- Move pictures
- Copy pictures
- Cut pictures
- Paste pictures
- Crop pictures
- Position pictures in your publications
- Add borders
- Use Undo
- Delete pictures

Changing Pictures

At first, you may not be sure about when to change the pictures in your publication. Here are a few suggestions of when you will want to modify pictures:

- When you import a picture that's too large
- When you want to use only a portion of a picture
- When a picture interrupts the flow of the text
- When you want to add a border or shading to a picture to set it off from the text

- When you add a picture that you want to delete
- When you delete a picture you want to keep
- When you want to include the same picture, such as a company logo or product picture, on every page of your publication

When you work with Publisher to modify the pictures in your publication, you can copy, move, resize, cut, paste, and otherwise enhance your pictures. You can even edit the individual dots in a bit-mapped picture if you copy the picture into Windows Paintbrush, make your changes, and then copy the changed picture back to Publisher. If you work with draw-type graphics, you can ungroup, or separate, the individual elements and make changes to them. The best advice when you work with graphics—especially when editing—is to get close. Zoom in as close as you can on the item you're working with. This will avoid the frustration of repeatedly selecting the wrong item or making changes you don't mean to make.

Selecting Pictures

The first step toward modifying a picture is selecting it. The way in which you select a picture depends on whether you select a single picture or several pictures:

- To select a single picture, move the mouse pointer to the picture you want and click the mouse button. Handles appear on the picture, indicating that it's selected.
- To select more than one picture, press and hold the Shift key while you click the pictures you want. All the pictures you click are selected. The handles in a multiple selection appear in gray rather than black.
- To select multiple objects as a group, position the pointer in an area outside the group, press the mouse button, and drag the mouse until all the items are enclosed in a box with a dotted outline (see fig. 9.2). When you release the mouse button, gray handles appear on all the items included in the box (see fig. 9.3).

Tip

After you select a frame or a picture, handles appear along the sides of the object. To deselect the object, move the pointer off the object and click the mouse button.

Fig. 9.2
Selecting multiple items.

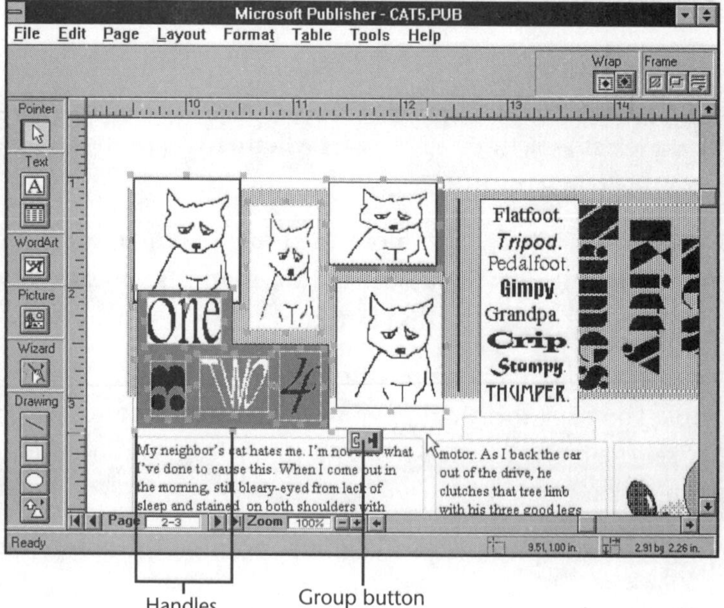

Fig. 9.3
The handles turn gray when a group is selected.

Grouping and Ungrouping Objects

Publisher likes for its objects to be grouped. When you highlight a bunch of items—a group—a puzzle-piece-like button appears along the bottom of the dotted selection box (refer to fig. 9.3). That's the Group button.

When you click the Group button, Publisher lumps all those items into one group (there's just no way to avoid saying it). What are the benefits of lumping these things together?

- When you move one object, you move them all.
- When you click to resize a corner, the whole group is resized in proportion.
- If you want to delete the group, everything goes at once.

Especially when you work with layers, the group option is a real life-saver. If you don't feel like clicking the Group button, you can choose the **G**roup Objects command from the **L**ayout menu (see fig. 9.4).

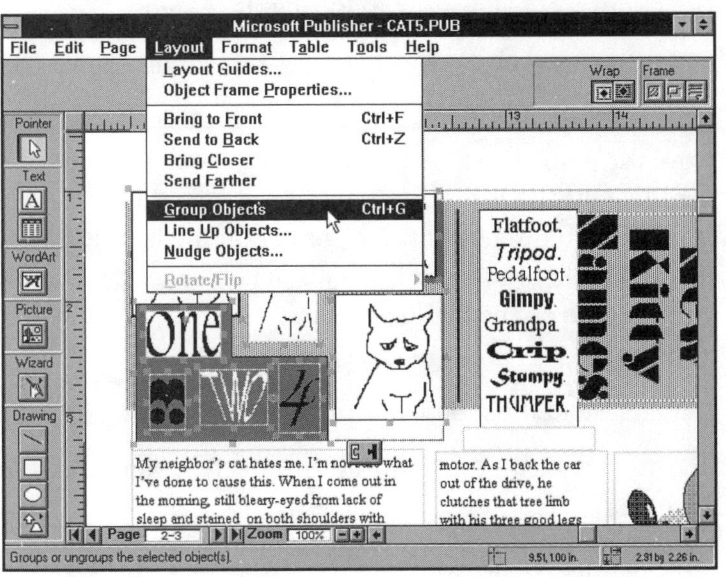

Fig. 9.4
Grouping objects with the conventional command.

After you group the objects, you can ungroup them at any time. When you click on a group, the button changes to reflect the "Ungroup" look. Similarly, the option in the **L**ayout menu changes to let you Un**g**roup, rather than Group, after the items have been bunched together.

Project Tip

Groups within groups can make your life easier. For example, if you have several layers of objects, such as a logo that has a circle on top of a triangle and then another layer of text, you may first want to group the shapes and then the entire object. That way, if you ever need to change the text, you can ungroup the first level while leaving the shapes still grouped so that you can't accidentally change them while you work on the text.

Resizing Pictures

If you plan to resize a picture, you need to select only one picture at a time. If you plan to resize several items in proportion to each other, however, group them all first by following these steps:

Tip
You can edit the logo created in Chapter 8. Just click it and ungroup it if necessary. The text is added in WordArt and the rest of the logo is an assembly of shapes and art elements.

1. Select the picture you want to resize. The handles appear on the picture frame.
2. Move the pointer to a handle on the side of the picture you want to adjust. If you want to make a picture shorter, for example, you can position the pointer on the handle in the bottom center of the frame. Notice that as soon as you move the pointer over the handle, the arrow pointer changes to the resize pointer.
3. Press and hold the mouse button.
4. Drag the handle of the frame in the direction you want to resize the picture.
5. When the picture is the size you want, release the mouse button. If you make the picture smaller, the rest of your page will not change. If you enlarge the picture so that it now overlaps text, the text reflows to make room for the picture.

Project Tip

Remember that the best layout designs are effective because they are balanced. Try not to tip the scales with items that are too big or too small. When in doubt, try something different; but remember to make a backup copy of the file first in case you like your original version better.

Moving Pictures

When moving a picture, you can move one or more objects at the same time. To move pictures, follow these steps:

1. Select the picture(s) you want to move.
2. Place the pointer on the picture. The pointer changes from an arrow to the move pointer.
3. Press and hold the mouse button.
4. Drag the picture to the new position.
5. When you have the picture where you want it, release the mouse button.

If you move the picture so that it overlaps another text frame on the page, the text in that frame will move to make room for the picture. If you place the picture on top of another picture or WordArt frame, the other picture or piece of WordArt is hidden behind the picture you just moved.

Tip
If you are unhappy with the position of the picture you just moved, you can repeat the move procedure or open the **E**dit menu and choose **U**ndo Move Object(s).

Copying, Cutting, and Pasting Pictures

The copy, cut, and paste procedures for pictures are similar to the same commands you use when you work with text. When you copy or cut a picture, Publisher places the copy of the original on the clipboard. You then can use the paste procedure to place the picture back in the document.

To copy a picture, follow these steps:

1. Select the picture you want to copy.
2. Open the **E**dit menu.

3. Choose **C**opy Picture Frame. You can bypass the menu selections by pressing Ctrl+C.

Publisher then makes a copy of the picture and places the copy on the clipboard.

> **Note**
>
> You can copy more than one item at a time. Simply select all the pictures you want to copy (by pressing and holding Shift while you click the pictures) before you choose the **C**opy Object(s) command. When you paste the items back into the publication, all pictures appear the way they were copied; that is, they are placed in relation to each other the same way they appeared in the original document.

Cutting a picture is similar to copying one, except that instead of making a duplicate of a picture, you remove it from the publication. Use the cut procedure when you want to move a picture from one page to another or from one part of a publication to another part.

To cut a picture out of your publication, follow these steps:

1. Select the picture (or pictures) you want to cut.
2. Open the **E**dit menu.
3. Choose the Cu**t** Picture Frame command. If you select more than one picture, the command is shown as Cu**t** Object(s).

The picture then is removed from your publication and placed on the unseen clipboard. If the picture overlapped another frame, the text may reflow after the picture is removed.

Note

When you copy or cut a picture to the clipboard, the picture is still taking up a portion of your computer's memory. Because pictures can use such large portions of memory, you should avoid leaving a picture on the clipboard any longer than needed. You can remove the picture by copying something small (the letter *a*, for example) to replace the picture on the clipboard.

Caution

The clipboard retains only your most recent cut or copy. If you cut a picture of an apple and then copy a picture of a bear, for example, you cannot paste the apple back into the publication. The bear replaces the apple. Each time you move something new onto the clipboard, the old item is replaced.

Pasting involves placing whatever item is on the clipboard back into the publication. Pasting is another kind of copy operation because the item on the clipboard is not removed when you paste it in the document. A copy still remains on the clipboard until you replace it with something else. If you copy a picture of a cat to the clipboard and then paste it on another page, for example, the cat isn't gone from the clipboard. You can paste cats until the cows come home, or at least until you copy something else to the clipboard.

To paste items into your publication, follow these steps:

1. Open the **E**dit menu.

2. Choose **P**aste Object(s).

The object is placed on the publication beside the original item (see fig. 9.5). After you paste the picture, you can move or resize it if necessary to fit the spot in your publication. You also can delete the picture by pressing Delete. Figure 9.6 shows the art after it is flipped and moved to its new location.

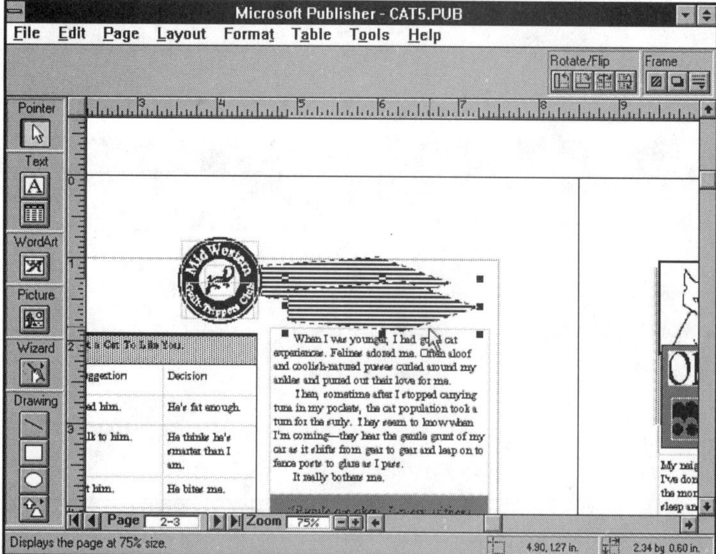

Fig. 9.5
Pasting the copied item.

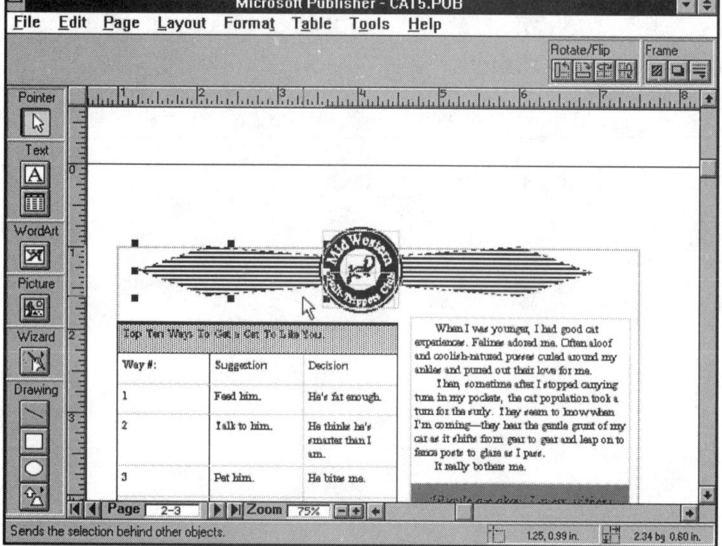

Fig. 9.6
The object placed in the publication.

> **Note**
>
> Remember that you can use **U**ndo for any of the procedures described in this section—as long as you try to undo your *last* operation. Of course, if you use Copy, you have no reason to undo anything; you can simply copy something else to the clipboard. If you use Cut, however, and wish you hadn't, select **U**ndo Cut Objects from the **E**dit menu, and everything returns to normal, at least as far as your publication is concerned.

Cropping Pictures

Another editing feature that comes in handy when you work with pictures is cropping. *Cropping* is the publishing term for trimming the edges off a picture. Like traditional manual layout, when you crop a picture by taking it to the paper cutter and cutting off the parts you don't want, the Crop tool in Publisher enables you to remove the unnecessary parts of a picture in your publication. Unlike manual layout, however, electronic cropping preserves the edges you have "cut." If you want to enlarge the picture later, it's all there, just beyond the cropped edges.

To crop a picture, follow these steps:

1. Select the picture you want to crop.

2. Click the Crop tool in the Top Toolbar. The Crop tool is to the left of the Wrap tools.

3. Move the pointer to the side of the picture frame you want to crop. Notice that when you move the pointer to a place that otherwise would display the resize pointer, the pointer changes to the cropping pointer, which resembles two pairs of scissors.

4. Move the side of the frame inward (by pressing and holding the mouse) as though you were resizing it. Instead of changing size, however, the picture stays the same size, and the space surrounding the picture is cropped (see fig. 9.7).

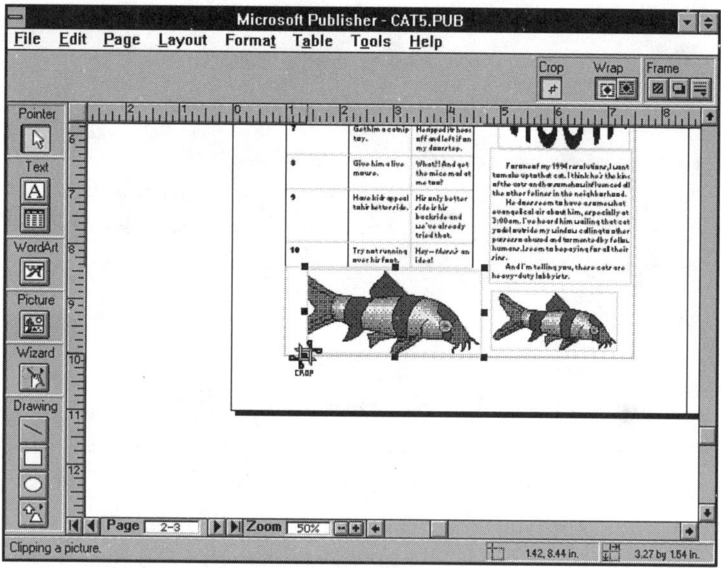

Fig. 9.7
Cropping a picture.

Now that you've cropped the picture, anytime you move the pointer to a corner of the selected picture, the cropping pointer appears, where the resize pointer would appear in an uncropped picture.

To restore a cropped picture with the cropping pointer, follow these steps:

1. Select the cropped picture by clicking it.
2. Move the pointer to the picture edge you want to restore.
3. When the Cropping tool appears, press and hold the mouse button.
4. Drag the picture to its full size.

The cropped picture is returned to its original display. You can crop pictures as many times as you want. You also can restore them as often as is necessary. If at any time during the process you're not happy with the results, use the **U**ndo Crop Picture command to return to the preceding version of the picture.

Positioning Pictures

One technique for positioning pictures in your publication requires that you understand how the layers of your publication work. At first glance, you may think that everything is positioned on one flat layer, like a two-dimensional piece of paper. However, you can overlap items to create a certain effect (see fig. 9.8).

In figure 9.8, the picture at the beginning of the publication is a layered object. The circle, in the middle, was done with Logo Creator Plus. It consists of several circles, one on top of another, with writing on the topmost layer. The two banners are positioned behind the circle, giving the impression that they come from behind it.

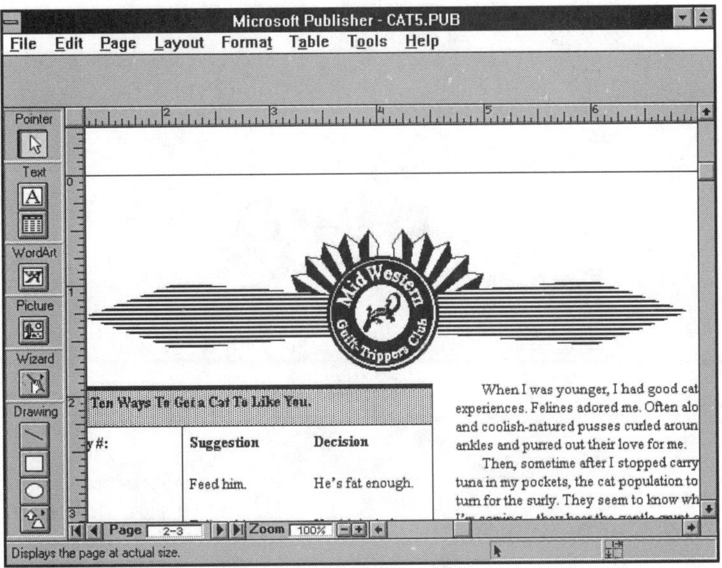

Fig. 9.8
A layering example.

Understanding Layering. When you bring a picture into a publication or, for that matter, position another text frame over any existing frame, the text in the publication moves to accommodate the picture. In this case, when the picture and the text overlap, the picture is inserted and the text reflows. You can prevent this readjustment of text by placing one item in front of the other item. You use four commands for this task, all from the Layout menu:

- *Bring to Front.* Brings the selected item to the front of other items.
- *Send to Back.* Sends the selected item behind other items.
- *Send Farther.* Moves the item one layer back.
- *Bring Closer.* Brings the item one layer closer.

To create the effect of the banner coming from behind the logo, you select the banner and select the Send To **B**ack command (see fig. 9.9). Consider what happens when you select the banner again and choose Bring to **F**ront (see fig. 9.10).

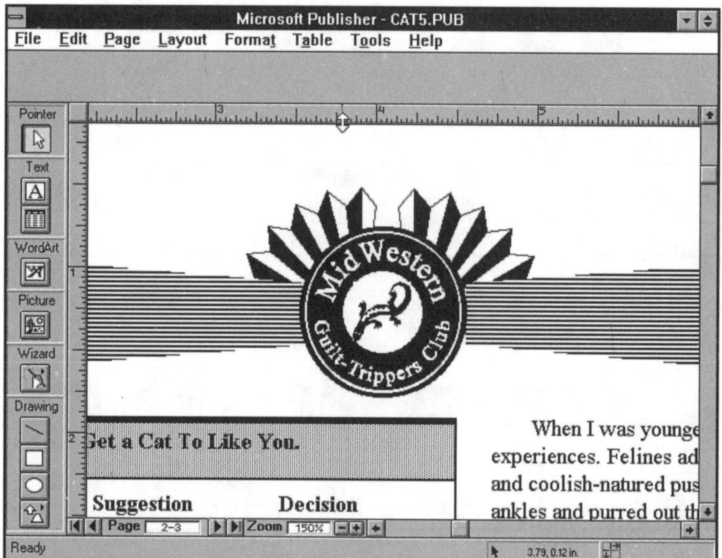

Fig. 9.9
The banner is behind the logo.

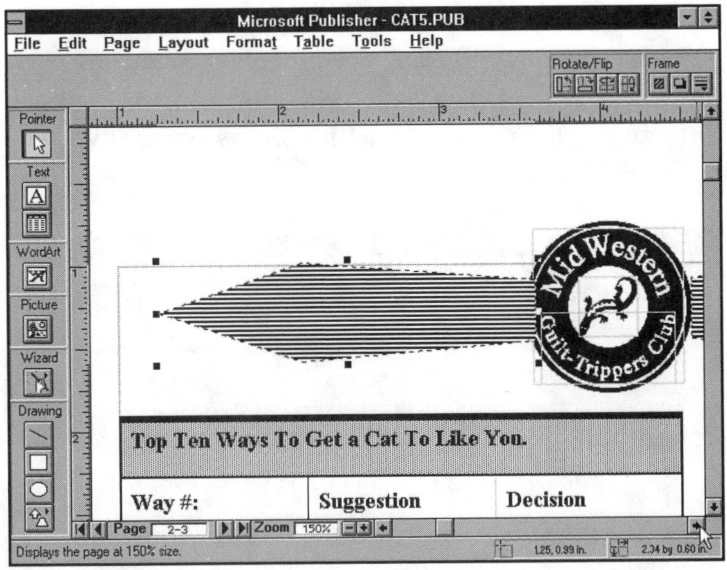

Fig. 9.10
Bringing the banner up front.

Placing a Picture on the Background Page. Another option for controlling the way items appear on the page involves the use of the *background page*. Publisher gives you the option of using a background page to hold items that are to appear on every page of your publication. Some items you may want to add to a background page include the following:

- Page numbers
- Name of publication
- Company name or logo
- Date
- Volume number

You add items to the background page by first moving to that page. To display the background page, open the **P**age menu and choose G**o** to Background. A blank page appears (see fig. 9.11). A small symbol in the bottom left corner of the status line shows you that you are on the background page.

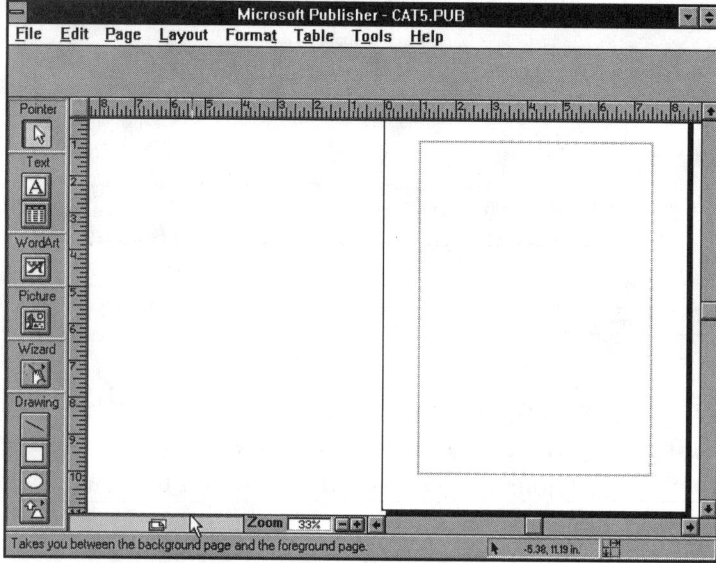

Fig. 9.11
Working on the background page.

You can add items to the background page just as you would to any regular Publisher page. Figure 9.12 shows a small picture added to the background page.

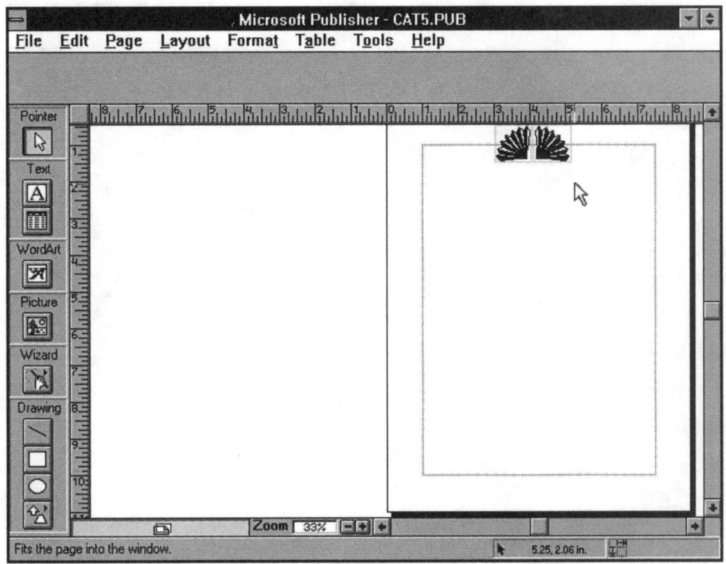

Figure 9.12
Adding an item on the background page.

Simply because you add something on the background page, however, doesn't mean that the item will appear on your publication page no matter what. If you cover up the spot where the background item is placed, the item on the "real" page blocks the background item from being printed.

When you are ready to return to the publication page from the background page, open the **P**age menu and choose G**o** to Foreground. As you can see in figure 9.13, the picture on the background page is displayed on the publication page. You cannot select the background picture frame from the publication page. You have to move to the background page in order to do that.

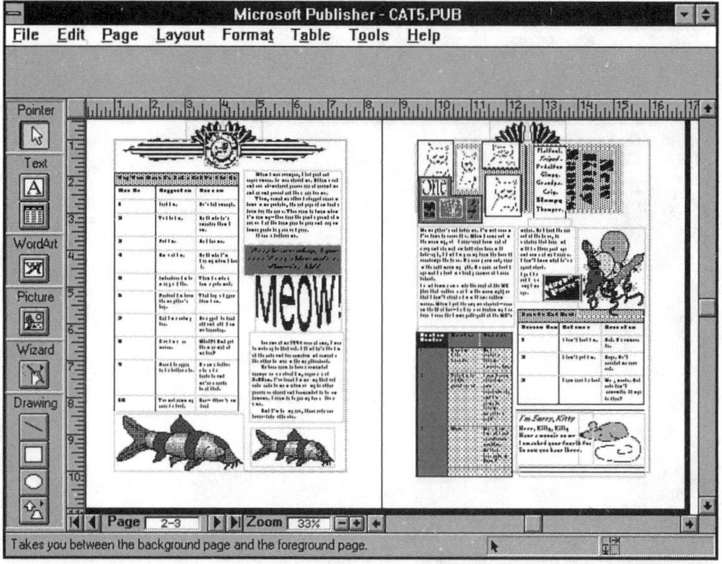

Fig. 9.13
Returning to the publication page.

After you add items to the background page, you aren't committed to showing these items on every page of your publication. You can use the Igno**r**e Background command, on the **P**age menu, to suppress the display of the background items for a particular page.

> **Project Tip**
>
> You can add a watermark logo to your publication page. In the case of a corporate report, scanning and then placing the corporate logo right in the center of the page (perhaps in a light gray shade, so it won't detract from the text) can be very effective. If you want the logo to show through, make sure that the text boxes are set to a clear background.

Adding Borders to Pictures

Borders represent another way you can improve the look of your pictures. Sometimes, you want the picture to stand out from the text; at other times, setting the picture off with some kind of border is effective. By default, Publisher does not enclose pictures in a border. There are two methods to add borders.

You can add a border when you first create the frame for your picture. When you select the Picture Frame tool, the options are shown on the right side of the Top Toolbar. You can click one of the line width settings to choose the width of border you want for the frame. You also can choose to use a shaded frame or a shadowed frame.

Or, after you have imported a picture into an unbordered frame, you can add a border of your choosing. You also can vary the way the border is displayed. If you want to add border lines only at the top and bottom of the picture (not the sides), you can use the Forma**t** menu's **B**order command to customize the border. To add a border to an existing picture, follow these steps:

1. Select the picture to which you want to add a border.
2. Open the Forma**t** menu.
3. Choose Bord**e**r. The Border dialog box appears (see fig. 9.14).

   It may not be readily apparent from the box, but the border currently chosen in the Select A **S**ide box is all sides, with a thickness setting of None. This default essentially means that you have no border on all sides. In the Border dialog box, you can choose the sides on which you want the border to appear, the thickness of the line, and the color of the border.

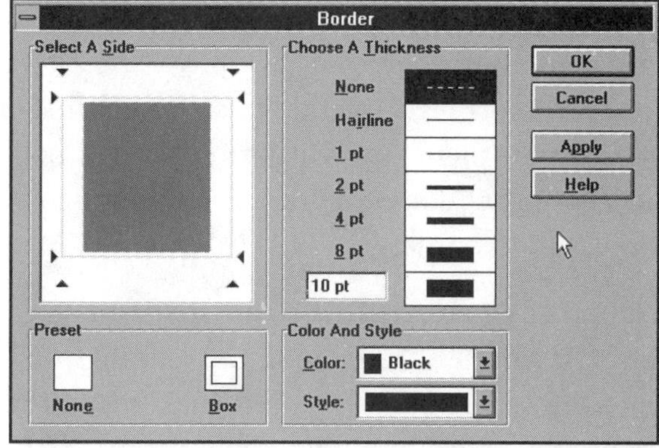

Fig. 9.14
Choosing borders.

4. To choose a border that does not surround all sides (for example, if you want a border on only the top and bottom), position the mouse pointer on the side of the frame you want to border in the Select A **S**ide box and click the mouse button.

5. Click the thickness setting you want. You can choose a 1-point, 2-point, 4-point, or 8-point border; or, you can specify, in the text box, a border thickness of your own choosing. The Select A **S**ide window shows the border and side you have selected. Figure 9.15 shows the bottom border selected.

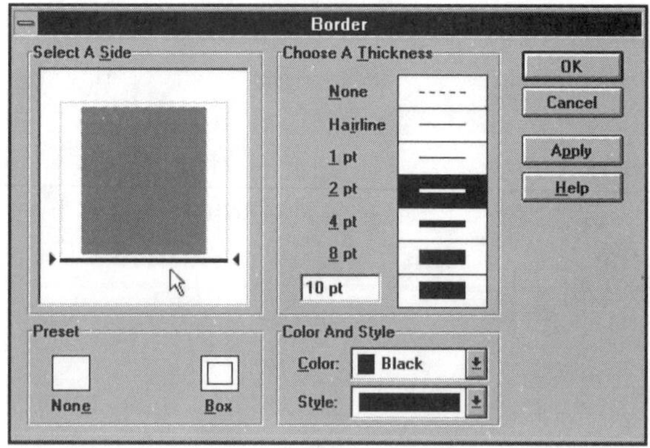

Fig. 9.15
Specifying which border to add.

6. Add borders to any other sides as needed.
7. If you want to change the color of your border, you can click the down arrow to the right of the **C**olor box. A list of available colors appears. If you have a color monitor, you can choose the color you want and Publisher will display the border in that color. Remember, however, that unless you have a printer with color capabilities, the border will be printed in black and white.
8. When you're finished, click OK to return to the publication. Publisher adds the border.

Project Tip

Instead of adding lines before and after art or text, use a border above and below. Lines can get "bumped" accidentally and moved out of place. Borders stay attached to the text box.

Deleting Pictures

Undoubtedly, at times you may need to delete pictures in your publications. You can use one of two methods:

- Select the picture you want to delete and press Delete.
- Select the picture, open the **E**dit menu, and choose **D**elete Picture Frame.

After you delete a picture, you can restore it by selecting **U**ndo Delete Object(s)—if you do it right away. If you perform other operations after deleting a picture, it's gone; so be sure you want to delete an item before you blow it away. If you are unsure whether you will need the picture later, you may want to cut the picture to the clipboard or move the picture to the desktop area (outside the sides of the page). Items on the desktop do not print, but they are there if you need them later.

Troubleshooting

This picture looks awful.

After you resize the picture, you may decide that you made a mistake. Don't panic—you can easily return the picture to its previous size. Open the **E**dit menu and choose **U**ndo Resize Object before you do anything else. The picture returns instantly to its previous size.

I don't like the way my picture is cropped.

Open the **E**dit menu and choose **U**ndo Crop Picture to return the picture to its precropped state, or you can use the Crop tool to restore the cropped picture.

I can't find the item I want!

At times it's difficult to select a specific element in an object that has numerous layers, but be patient. Zoom in as close as you can and then cycle through the layers by clicking the topmost item and choosing Send To **B**ack. Sooner or later, you're going to hit the item you're looking for.

Using BorderArt To Enhance Pictures

The final enhancement option discussed in this chapter is a spiffy feature Publisher offers that other desktop publishers do not: BorderArt. You can add creative borders—beyond your basic 1- or 2-point line—to give your publications an extra spark.

To add a BorderArt border to a picture, follow these steps:

1. Select the picture to which you want to add the BorderArt.
2. Open the Forma**t** menu.
3. Choose the Border**A**rt command. The BorderArt dialog box appears (see fig. 9.16). A list of **A**vailable Borders is displayed on the left side of the window.

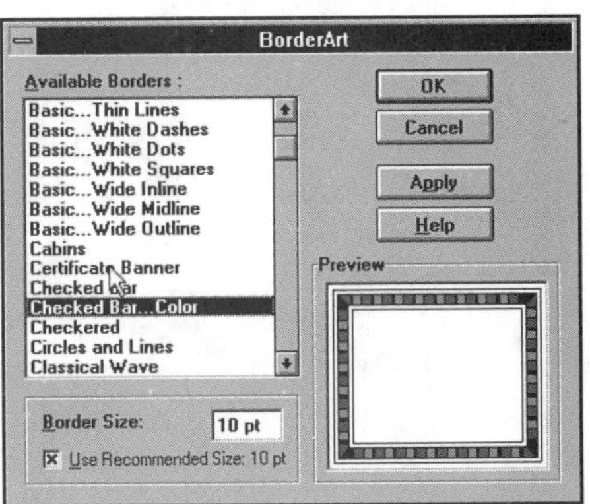

Fig. 9.16
Choosing a BorderArt border.

4. Move the pointer to a border you want to see. The Preview window shows you what that border looks like.

5. When you have found the border you want, click OK. Publisher then adds the border to your publication (see fig. 9.17).

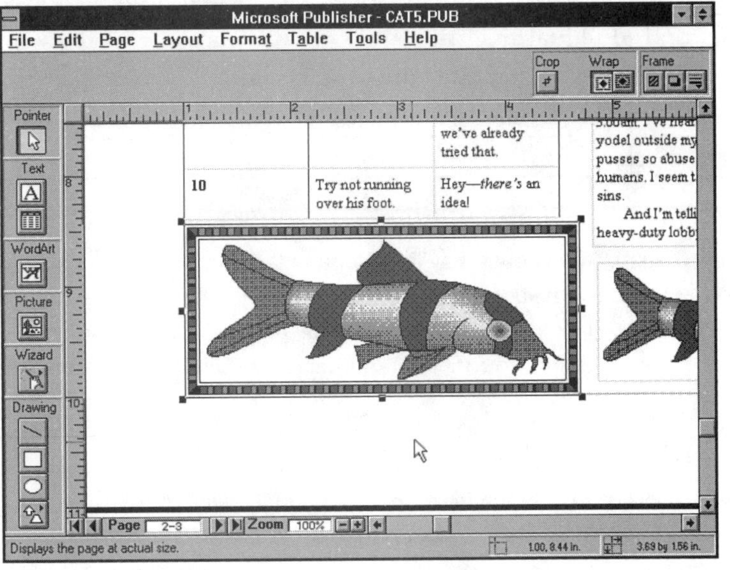

Fig. 9.17
Adding the BorderArt to your publication.

Again, if you decide that you don't like the border, you can open the **E**dit menu and choose **U**ndo BorderArt. If you want to replace the border later, you can select the picture and select a different BorderArt border.

BorderArt includes over 100 different borders, ranging from serious designs, such as dots and dashes, to humorous ones, such as fish and ice-cream cones. Undoubtedly, you'll be able to find a border that suits the tone of your publication somewhere in the list of available borders.

Because the list of borders is so long, it can take you quite some time to scroll from one end of the list to the other. You can move through the list quickly by typing the first letter of the border you want. Publisher then takes you directly to the group of borders that begins with the letter you typed. To move to the Light Bulb selection, for example, press **L** when the BorderArt dialog box is displayed. You can use this procedure to move backward or forward through the list.

One other thing you should remember when using BorderArt is that the options in the Border dialog box, which you display by selecting the frame, opening the Forma**t** menu, and choosing Bord**e**r, are also available for BorderArt borders. You can choose to use the BorderArt border on individual sides of the frame, you can change the width of the border, and you can alter the border's color.

Troubleshooting

My borders are too loud.

The BorderArt you choose may look good in the BorderArt dialog box, but once you place it in your publication, the result may be overwhelming. You can choose a different piece of BorderArt by redisplaying the BorderArt dialog box and selecting a different border. Make sure that the frame is still selected.

I have too many borders.

Use BorderArt like you use fancy fonts—sparingly. One or two artistically bordered frames should be enough for a page. If you want to remove the border on a frame, first select the frame and then open the Forma**t** menu, and choose Border**A**rt. When the BorderArt dialog box appears, select None and click OK. When you return to the publication, the BorderArt on the selected frame is gone.

From Here...

For information directly related to enhancing your publication, you may want to review the following sections of this book:

- Chapter 10, "Finishing the Layout." You've been through almost everything there is to do on your Publisher project. The next chapter shows you how to do some last-minute layout checking and add a few finishing touches to your publication.
- Chapter 11, "Printing the Publication." If you just can't wait, go ahead and print. But check out Chapter 11 first, so you know the routine.
- Chapter 12, "Publisher Design Tips." Before you close the door on that publication, take a look at some of the design tips in Chapter 12 to see whether there's anything you'd like to add to your Publisher project.

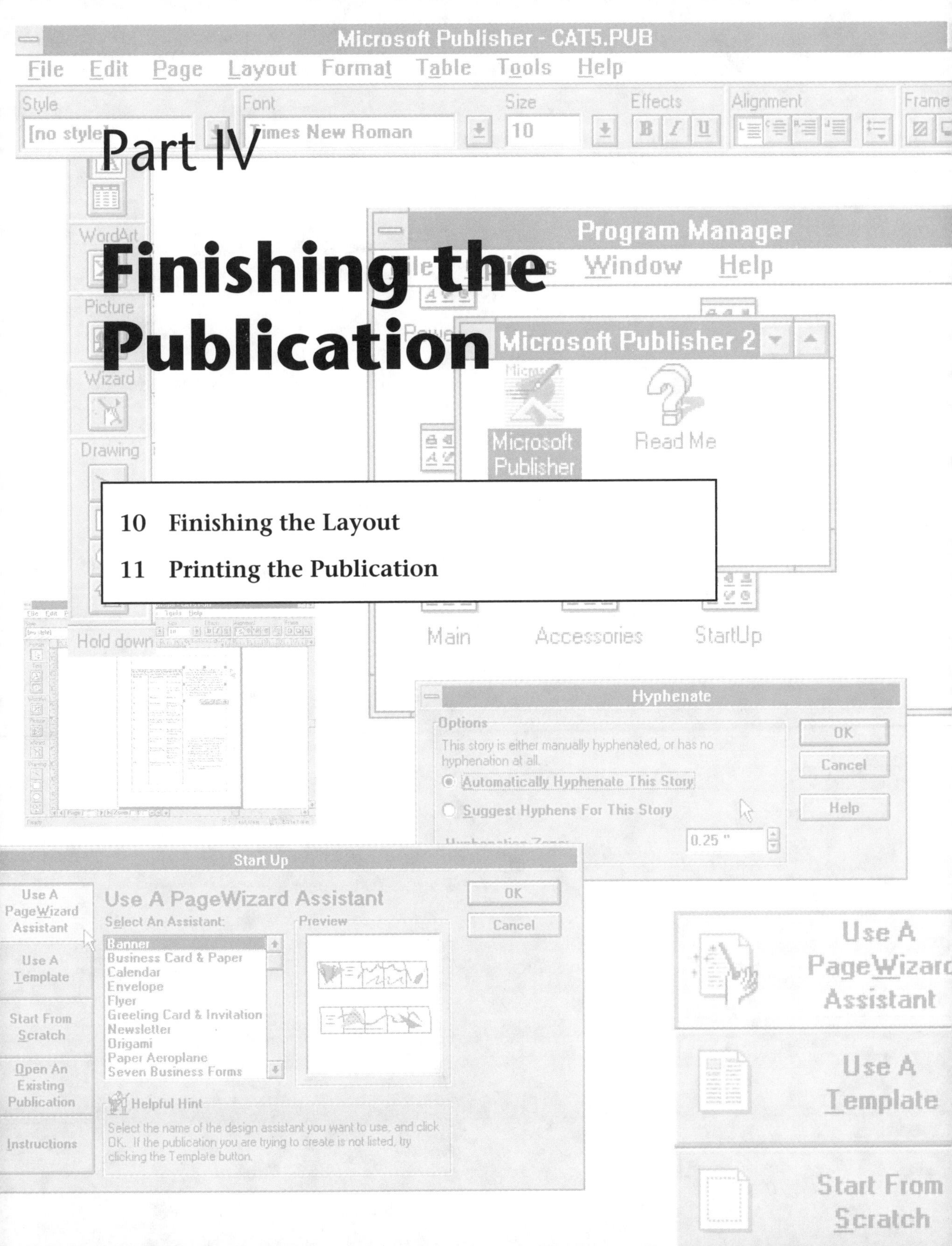

Part IV

Finishing the Publication

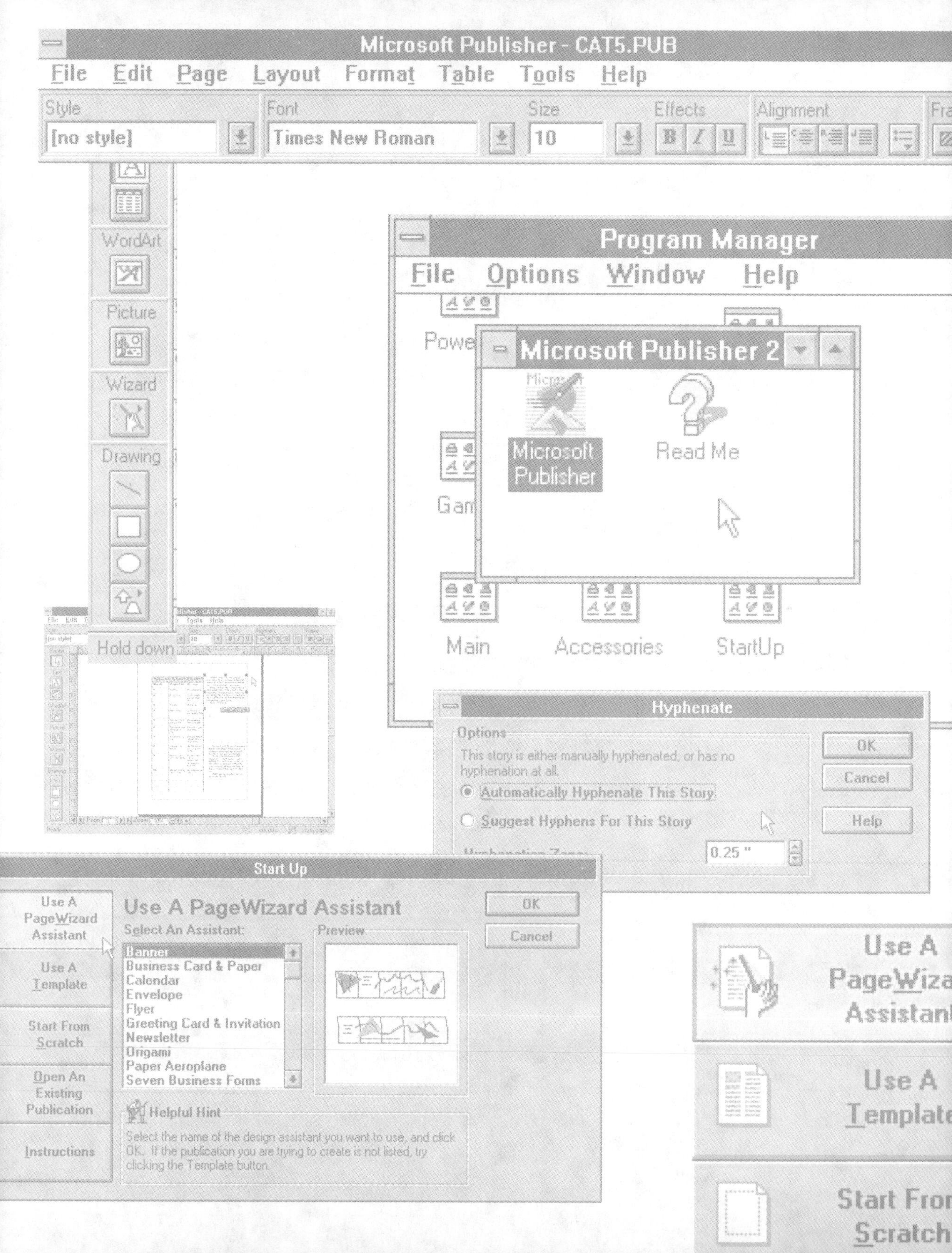
Microsoft Publisher - CAT5.PUB
File Edit Page Layout Format Table Tools Help
Style
[no style]
Font
Times New Roman
Size
10
Effects
Alignment
WordArt
Picture
Wizard
Drawing
Hold down
Program Manager
File Options Window Help
Microsoft Publisher 2
Microsoft Publisher
Read Me
Main
Accessories
StartUp
Hyphenate
Options
This story is either manually hyphenated, or has no hyphenation at all.
Automatically Hyphenate This Story
Suggest Hyphens For This Story
0.25 "
OK
Cancel
Help
Start Up
Use A PageWizard Assistant
Use A Template
Start From Scratch
Open An Existing Publication
Instructions
Use A PageWizard Assistant
Select An Assistant:
Banner
Business Card & Paper
Calendar
Envelope
Flyer
Greeting Card & Invitation
Newsletter
Origami
Paper Aeroplane
Seven Business Forms
Preview
OK
Cancel
Helpful Hint
Select the name of the design assistant you want to use, and click OK. If the publication you are trying to create is not listed, try clicking the Template button.
Use A Template
Start From Scratch

Chapter 10

Finishing the Layout

By now, you have learned how to open new publications, design pages, add text and pictures, and create frames with text and pictures. You also have learned how to use PageWizards, templates, WordArt, and BorderArt to enhance your publications and make your publishing tasks easier. This chapter takes you through a review process in which you evaluate what you've done so far and fine-tune the publication by changing the spacing and alignment in your layout. At the end of this chapter, you find a design library that helps you add special design elements to your publications.

Publisher 2.0 includes a special feature that enables you to make the most of this evaluation step. The Layout Checker, available in the T**o**ols menu when you select the Check **L**ayout command, looks for layout problems in your publication.

In this chapter, you learn to do the following tasks:

- Review your layout
- Use the Layout Checker
- Fine-tune spacing
- Add special design elements

Why Should You Check the Layout?

Nobody likes to be surprised at printing time. Yet it happens to everyone sooner or later: you're standing by the printer, waiting to see the publication you've been working on for hours. When the printer finally spits it out, at first glance everything looks okay. But then you notice the following flaws:

- Cramped lines
- Overlapping text and graphics
- Text boxes that are too close together
- A missing border where you thought you added one

- Text that didn't wrap where you thought it would

But wait, you say, isn't Publisher a WYSIWYG program? Isn't what you see on the screen what you get in print?

Ideally, the publication you see on-screen is supposed to be the same as the one that appears in print. In reality, however, things tend to look much different when they are printed. One immediate difference is that the background guides are visible on-screen and not in the printed version. Also, depending on the type of text and graphic frames you create, you may not print the outlines for the frames.

The Way It Used to Be

In conventional publishing, the layout of a document is completed in stages. In a traditional publishing project that doesn't have the benefit of desktop publishing, for example, the completion of your project may involve the following steps:

1. Writing and editing the text.
2. Typesetting the text.
3. Creating the artwork.
4. Reproducing the artwork in final form.
5. Laying out the text on a page, leaving space for the art.
6. Adding the art.
7. Taking the finished layout to be reproduced.

One of the biggest problems with this method is that you have no flexibility in the layout. After a column of text is typeset in a certain column width, changing the width of that column is a big deal. You have to return to the typesetting stage and start over. With Publisher, you can modify and create as you go. You can try a variety of column widths and layouts, and you can add pictures here or there and then move them to different places in your publication with no trouble at all.

To get the best results, you need to look objectively at your publication in each stage of development. After you add text frames, sit back and imagine how the publication will look after you add pictures, headlines, and a banner. If you're not completely happy with what you see, try a few changes—Publisher doesn't mind. The surest way to find a truly effective layout for your document is through trial and error. Experiment and find out how the publication looks best to you. And don't be afraid to rely on the expertise of the Layout Checker—that's what it's there for.

Using the Layout Checker

Now, with Publisher 2.0, you can use an automated feature to check the layout of your documents for you. Similar to the way the Spelling Checker functions, the Layout Checker goes through the publication, element by element, and makes sure that boxes are used the way they're supposed to be, that all the text has been placed, and that there is no text remaining on the Clipboard.

Starting the Layout Checker

You need to begin by opening the publication you want to check. If you want to check only a couple of pages, move to those pages before you begin. Then, to start the Layout Checker, open the T**o**ols menu and choose Check Layout. The Check Layout dialog box appears (see fig. 10.1).

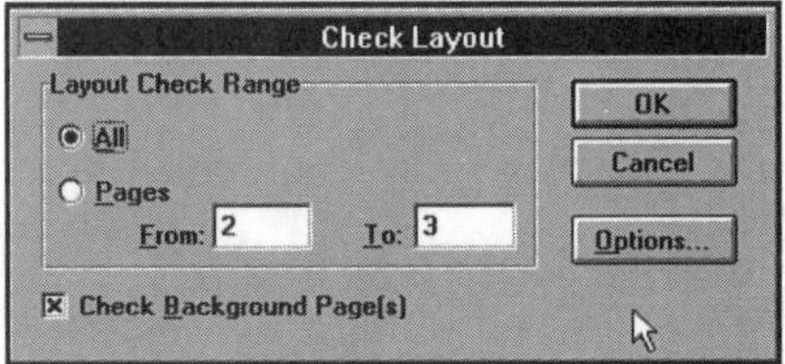

Fig. 10.1
The Check Layout Dialog Box.

When the Check Layout dialog box appears, choose which pages you want the Layout Checker to scan. If you want the entire publication checked, click the **A**ll button (this button is selected by default). If you want to select specific pages, enter the page numbers in the **P**ages **F**rom and **T**o boxes.

> **Project Tip**
>
> If you know which pages you want to check before you start the Layout Checker, display those pages on-screen before you choose Check **L**ayout from the T**o**ols menu. The page numbers will be entered automatically in the **P**ages **F**rom and **T**o boxes.

If you want Publisher to check the background pages, make sure that the Check **B**ackground Page(s) box is checked. If you haven't placed anything on those pages, there's no need to check them.

If you're ready to start checking the layout, click OK. If you want to see what other options you can set, read on.

Setting Layout Options

To display the options you can set for the Layout Checker, click the **O**ptions button in the Check Layout dialog box. The Options dialog box appears (see fig. 10.2).

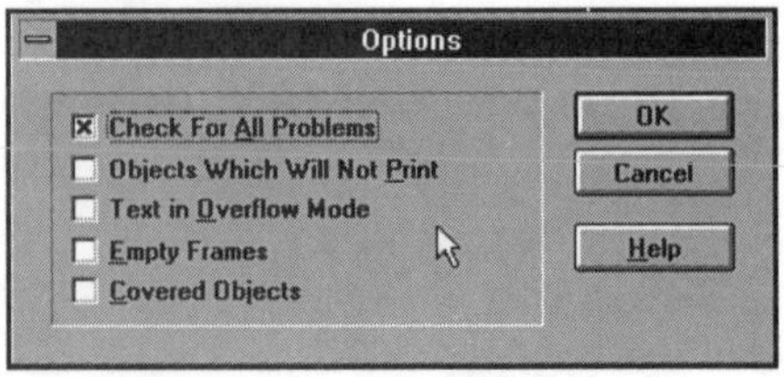

Fig. 10.2
The Options dialog box.

Publisher's Layout Checker searches for four different layout problems:

- *Objects Which Will Not **P**rint.* You won't know, of course, about the objects that refuse to print until you print the publication at least once. It's a good idea to have this option selected any time you do a layout check—just in case.

- *Text in **O**verflow Mode.* Selecting this option causes the checker to look for text frames in which not all the text is displayed. In other words, there's still some text waiting in the overflow area to be placed.

- ***E**mpty Frames.* Publisher catches frames that don't need to be there. In the best case, all they do is use up memory; in the worst case, the frames print where you don't want them to or they cover up other items in your publication.

- ***C**overed Objects.* This problem may sound obvious, but it may not be so obvious on-screen. If text or graphics overlap on the page, only the top layer will appear on the printed page. The checker will alert you to any problems with overlapping items and will suggest possible solutions.

You can choose any or all of these items before you start the layout check. If you want to look for all of these problems, leave Check For All Problems (the option chosen by default) selected.

After you set all the options you want, click OK to return to the Check Layout dialog box.

Go Checker Go

After returning to the Check Layout dialog box, click OK to start the Layout Checker. Publisher starts going through your publication item by item, just looking for trouble. When a trouble spot is found, the Check Layout screen appears (see fig. 10.3).

Fig. 10.3
The Layout Checker screen.

In this case, the Layout Checker has found a frame that is empty (the frame is a text frame, and it is positioned behind the Maybe a Party? WordArt object) and suggests deleting the frame. Each Layout Checker screen contains the same basic elements:

Element	Description
Problem	A statement of the layout error
Suggestions	Instructions for solving the problem
Ignore	A button that allows you to ignore the found problem
Ignore **A**ll	A button that enables you to ignore all similar problems in this publication
Con**t**inue	A button that you use to tell the checker to continue checking the publication. The button changes to Stop while the checker is looking for the next layout problem.
Close	A button you click to stop the layout checker
Explain	A button that brings up a CueCard, which gives you more information about the problem and explains how you can fix it

If you're not sure what the Layout Checker is telling you, click the **E**xplain button. For example, the problem found in figure 10.4 is a bit more confusing than the "empty frame" problem in figure 10.3. In this case, click the **E**xplain button to see what Publisher tells you to do. A Layout Checker Explanation screen appears, giving step-by-step instructions on how to correct the problem (see fig. 10.5).

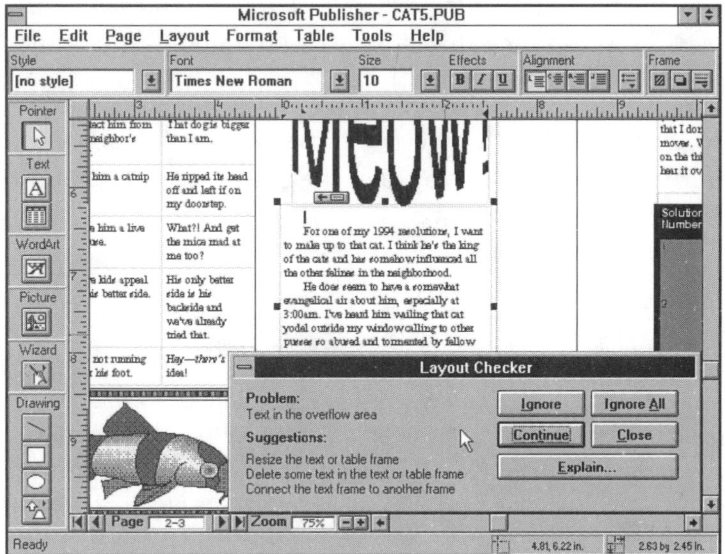

Fig. 10.4
A new problem.

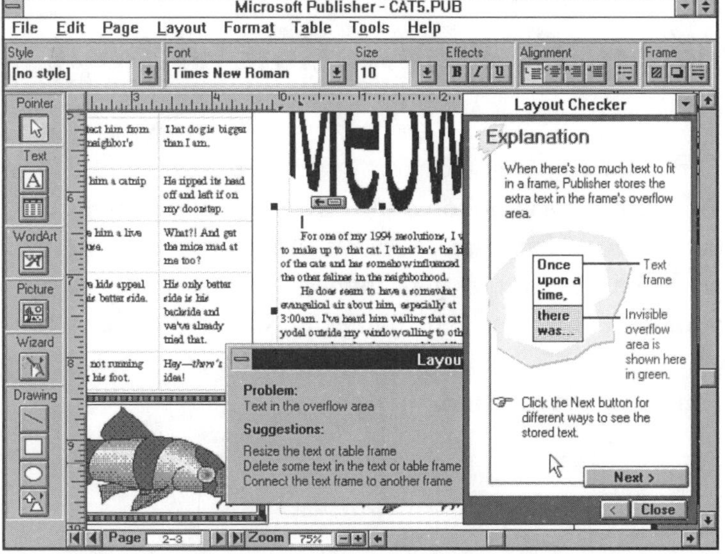

Fig. 10.5
Displaying an explanation of the problem.

Some Explanation screens, like the one shown in figure 10.5, include more than one screen of text. Click the Next button to move to the second screen.

Stopping the Layout Checker

Although the Layout Checker finds the problems in your publication, it's up to you to fix them. When the checker is finished, it displays a screen asking whether you'd like to check the layout again. For now, choose No. You can then make the necessary modifications and run the checker again.

Or, if you want to stop the checker in the middle of the process, you can click Stop when it's displayed or the Close button after a problem has been found.

Troubleshooting

I can't remember what the Layout Checker told me to do.

It's a good idea to keep a notepad beside your computer to jot down the steps you can take for fixing the error in your layout. Short of that, however, you can redisplay CueCards related to the task at hand by opening the **H**elp menu, choosing C**u**eCards, and selecting the procedure you need help with.

Viewing the Publication without Frames

One of the first things you can do, as you try to get an idea of what your finished publication looks like, is to display the publication without the frames that store pictures and text. Unless you specify a border or a background for your frames, the frames don't show when you print the publication. The frames are shown on-screen, however, so that you can see what you have created and get a general picture of how things are put together.

To hide the frames, follow these steps:

1. Open the publication.
2. Zoom the display up to Full Page view.
3. Open the T**o**ols menu. Choose the Hide **B**oundaries and Guides command (see fig. 10.6). The items on the publication disappear (see fig. 10.7).

Tip
To redisplay frames, open the T**o**ols menu and choose Show **B**oundaries and Guides (or press Ctrl+O). The frames and guides reappear.

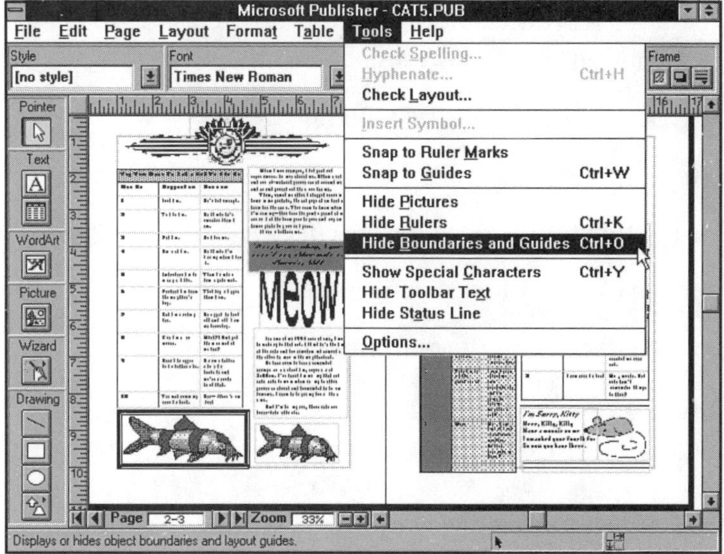

Fig. 10.6
Hiding the frame boundaries.

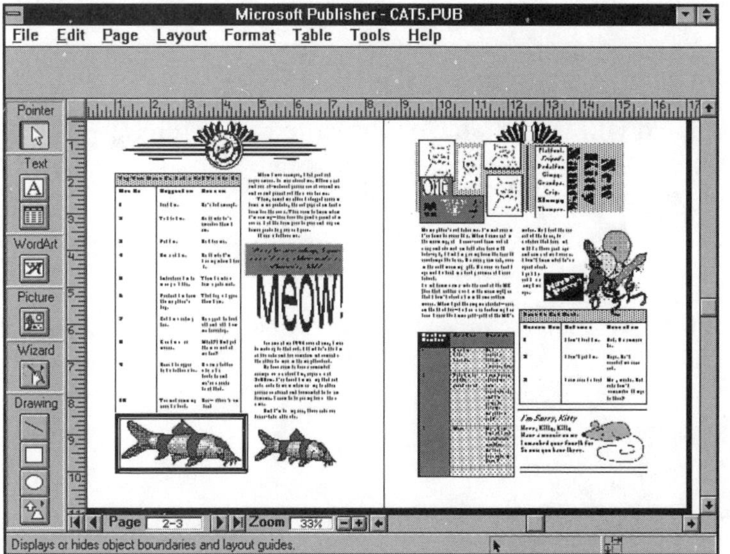

Fig. 10.7
The publication after guides and boundaries are hidden.

Now you can see the publication as it will appear in print. Do you like what you see? Does more white space show than you had expected? The following sections explain various ways in which you can fine-tune the layout of your document.

Evaluating Your Publication

The basic steps for evaluating your publication echo the process you use to create it. As you sit there contemplating changes to your document, ask yourself these questions:

- Are you happy with the text alignment?
- Is the text too crowded?
- Are the text font, size, and style effective?
- Is the margin of the text sufficient?
- Does the banner fit the publication?
- Is the style of headlines consistent?
- Is the text readable?
- Does the layout lead the reader's eyes through the publication?
- Do the pictures you have chosen fit the publication?
- Are the pictures arranged effectively?
- Should the pictures be cropped?
- Should you add a frame or border to the pictures?
- Is your publication consistent?

In the sections that follow, you look at several of these publication concerns.

Checking Text Frames

Start with the first step you completed when you created the document: the text frames. Ask yourself the following questions:

- *Is there enough space between the margin of the text and the frames edge?* If you haven't used a border or a pattern for the frame, you may not have this concern. If the edges of the frame will not show when you print, the amount of space between the text margin and the sides of the frame becomes a moot point. If you do want to change the margin around the text, first select the frame so that the handles appear, and then open the **L**ayout menu and choose the Text Frame Properties command. The Text Frame **P**roperties dialog box appears (see fig. 10.8). You then can change the amount of space used for **L**eft, **R**ight, **T**op, and **B**ottom margins. After you change the settings, click OK.

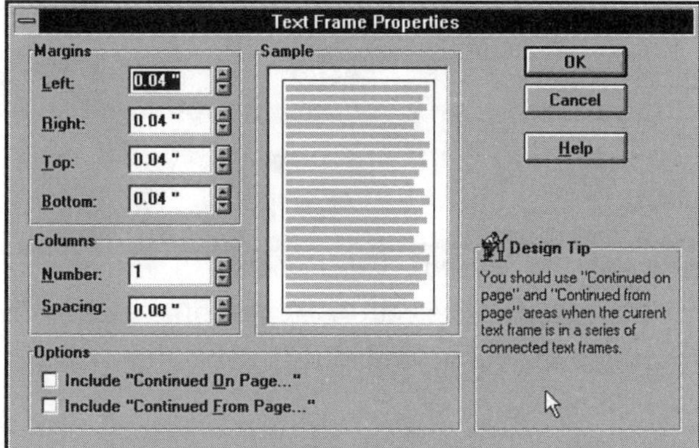

Fig. 10.8
The Text Frame Properties dialog box.

- *Are the frames the right size and shape?* If not, click the frame and use the resize pointer to move the frame as necessary. After you resize the frame, Publisher rewraps the text to fit around the other elements on your page.

- *Are there overlapping text frames?* Does the text jump from one box to another when you don't want it to? You may be able to solve this problem by resizing the box or by using the Send To **B**ack command in the **L**ayout menu to layer one frame behind the other. If that doesn't work, try moving the frames manually so that they don't overlap as much as they previously did.

- *Do you like the way the text is aligned?* After you remove the frame display in your document, the layout may not look as organized as you had hoped. Are you sorry that you chose a left alignment rather than justified text? You easily can change the alignment by highlighting the text you want to change and clicking the appropriate alignment button.

- *Is the text too crowded?* After viewing the document, you may be concerned that you tried to cram too much text into too small a space. You can remedy this problem by using the **L**ine Spacing command in the Forma**t** menu to change the spacing between lines and before and after paragraphs. You can also choose a larger font. In other cases, you may want to use the Spacing **B**etween Characters command from the Forma**t** menu to change the kerning of the individual characters.

- *Are you happy with the text font, size, and style you have chosen?* You can change these selections at any time by highlighting the text you want to change and clicking the appropriate buttons in the Top Toolbar.

- *Is the banner effective?* The banner is an especially important part of your publication because it's what most people see first. Be sure that your banner represents the tone of your document: bold, serious type for formal publications; lighter, friendlier type for informal documents. You can change the banner at any time by clicking the frame and making the necessary changes. If you used WordArt to create the banner, simply double-click on the frame.

- *Are the headlines consistent?* As mentioned in Chapter 7, "Enhancing Text," using a variety of typefaces may be tempting, but you do need to maintain some sort of consistency in your publications. You may, for example, want to keep all headlines in one certain typeface and size. This pattern helps readers identify where one story ends and another begins.

Evaluating Picture Frames

Now consider the pictures in the publication. Publisher moves the text whenever you place a picture in your publication, so after you move a picture around, you may need to go back and check what the move has done to your text. Ask yourself the following questions about each picture:

- *Is the picture positioned effectively?* Does the picture appear at a logical place in the publication? If necessary, you can select the picture frame and move the picture to another point in your document. Remember that the text rewraps after you make the move.

- *Did you vary the picture placement?* If you have a multipage document, placing a picture at exactly the same place on every page can be tedious. Vary the placement to give your readers a little diversity. On one page, for example, you may place a picture in the lower left corner; on the next page, place the picture in the lower right corner.

- *Did you crop the picture?* In Chapter 9, "Modifying Pictures," you learned how to crop the pictures in your publication. Are you happy with the way you cropped the art? Would the page look better if you used the entire picture? You can crop or uncrop a picture by clicking the picture frame, selecting the cropping tool, and resizing the picture frame. Remember that your entire picture is always available, even if the picture is cropped down to a fraction of its former self.

- *Is the picture positioned well in relation to the text?* Publisher wraps text around the picture frames in your publication. At times, perhaps because you moved a picture, the text wrap may not look good.

- *Are the pictures aligned with the text?* You don't have to rely solely on your eyes to help you align pictures with text. You can also use Publishers Snap to **G**uides and Snap to Ruler **M**arks commands, both found on the T**o**ols menu. Snap to **G**uides causes the objects you create or move to align with the layout guides in your publication (see fig. 10.9). Snap to Ruler **M**arks causes objects to align with the ruler marks. When you select either option, the option appears with a check mark beside it.

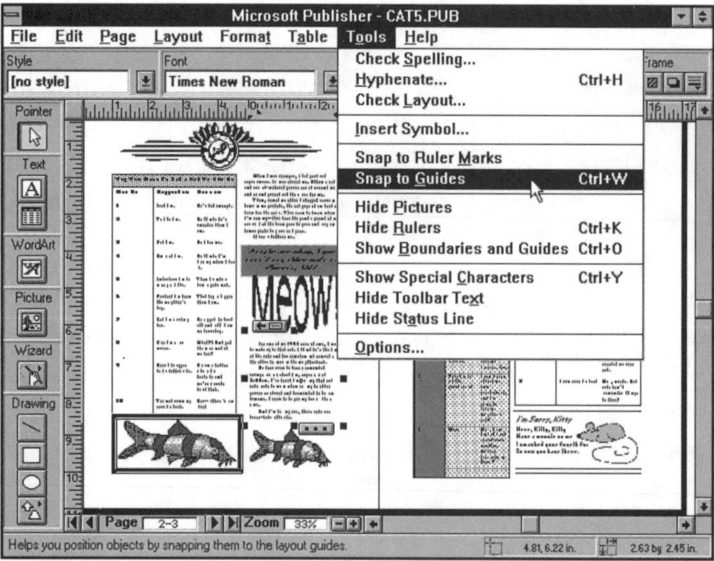

Fig. 10.9
Selecting the Snap to Guides command.

- *Should you add patterns or borders to your pictures?* You have the option of specifying borders or patterns for your picture frames. You can do so before you create a frame by clicking the appropriate frame option on the right side of the Top tool bar. Or you can use the S**h**ading and Borders commands from the Forma**t** menu to add the items you want to existing frames.

Checking WordArt Frames

Another element you may have used in your Publisher documents is WordArt. *WordArt* is a special feature that enables you to be creative with your text. You can choose from a number of graphic fonts and then display the text in a variety of ways not available for regular text. As you consider the WordArt you have created, ask yourself these questions:

- *Do you like the font you have selected?* WordArt presents you with many graphic fonts—from sophisticated to artsy; you can choose several different kinds of type. You can experiment with the font you have selected by double-clicking the WordArt frame.

- *Is the style effective?* WordArt enables you to stretch, slant, flip, curve, and perform other operations on your text. Do you have a reason for using slanted text? Have you used too many styles? Does the style help carry the tone and convey a message to your audience?

- *Should you add a colored background or shadow the text?* WordArt gives you additional options for the way that your text is displayed. You can add a shaded background to the characters or have WordArt shadow the text. Do so by clicking the appropriate options in the WordArt Top Toolbar (see fig. 10.10).

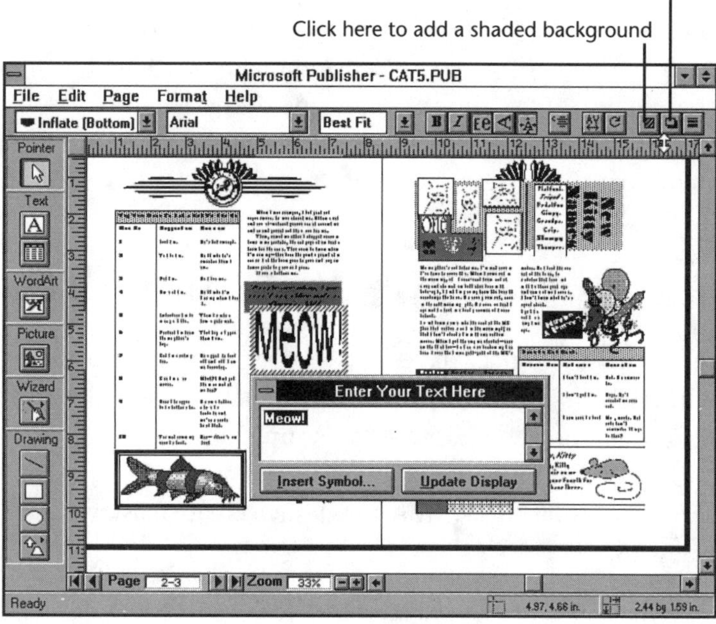

Fig. 10.10
Selecting WordArt options.

Now you have read through a wide range of questions that help you analyze the way you have put your document together. The next section introduces you to some special design elements you may want to add to your Publisher projects.

Adding Special Design Elements

Up to this point in the book, you have found out about all the aspects that go into publishing a document with Microsoft Publisher. This section introduces you to a few special elements that are not mandatory but that can add extra spice to your publications.

Adding Pull-Quotes

Pull-quotes are text frames that you use within an article to highlight a particularly relevant sentence or phrase. You use text larger than the size used for the body of your article but smaller than the size used for headlines. Place the pull-quotes strategically so that they add to, rather than detract from, the flow of the text. Pull-quotes can enhance your publication in the following ways:

- Reinforce main points in your article
- Break up the design of the page
- Give the reader's eyes a rest
- Interest readers who are flipping through your publication

To create a pull-quote, follow these steps:

1. Select the Text tool in the Left Toolbar.
2. Choose any frame options. You may want to shade the background of the pull-quote or add a border (refer to Chapter 7 for more information).
3. Draw the text frame.
4. Select the text font, size, and style that you want.
5. Type the text.
6. Choose the alignment in the Top Toolbar. The alignment in a pull-quote can be important for the look of your publication. Experiment with different alignments to see what looks best.

Figure 10.11 shows a pull-quote printed in Times Roman 12-point bold italic. The text is centered in the selected text frame.

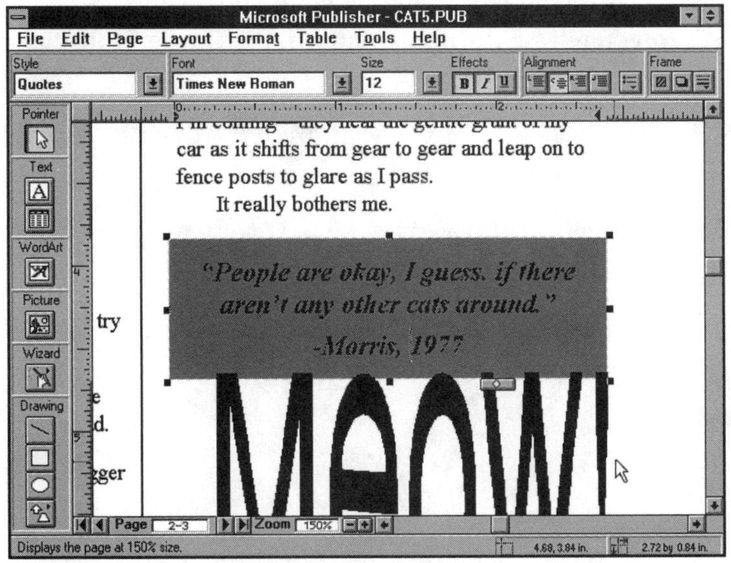

Fig. 10.11
A sample pull-quote.

Adding a Table of Contents

Does your publication require a table of contents? In a publication of more than a few pages, a table of contents tells readers how to quickly find the articles they need and also provides readers with an overview of what they can find in your publication. A table of contents can give your document the following benefits:

- Lets readers know what is covered in your publication
- Shows readers where to turn for more information
- Gives your publication a professional look
- Helps break up long text passages on the page by giving the reader something else to look at
- Varies the text font and style

With Publisher 2.0, you don't have to rely on tabbing this and tabbing that to make your table of contents line up. You have a table feature right at your fingertips that allows you to create three different kinds of tables of contents. Just follow these steps:

1. Click the Table tool in the Left Toolbar. (The Table tool is directly under the Text tool.)
2. Draw the table frame on the page by pressing and holding the mouse button and dragging the mouse down and to the right. When you release the mouse button, the Create Table dialog box appears.
3. Select the Table **F**ormat you want from the Create Table dialog box (see fig. 10.12).
4. Click OK. Publisher places the table of contents in the table frame with a flashing cursor, ready to receive data.
5. Type the heading **Table of Contents** at the top, or whatever heading you want for the table of contents.

6. Press Tab. Fill in the data as necessary, pressing Tab after each entry.

7. When you finish entering data, click outside the table. Figure 10.13 shows the finished table of contents.

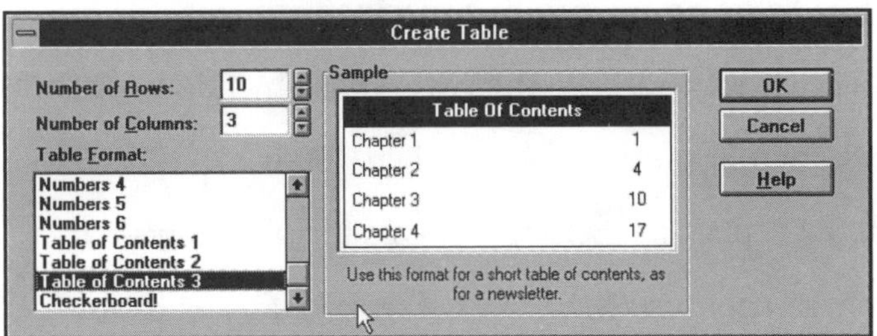

Fig. 10.12 Choosing a Table Format.

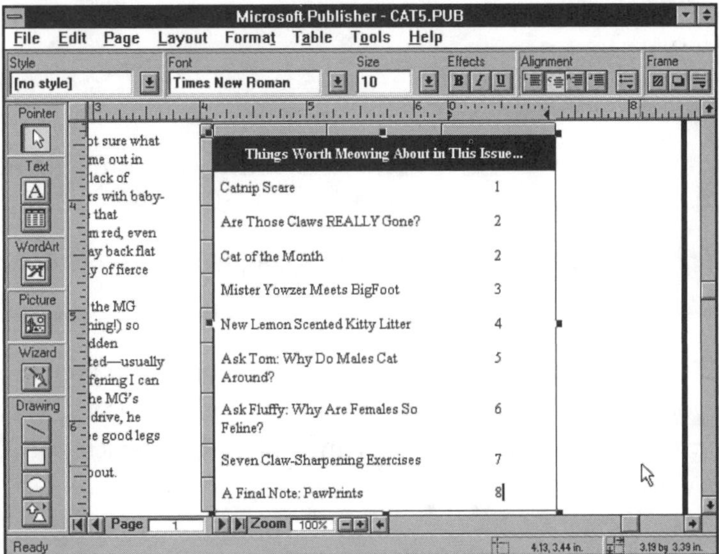

Fig. 10.13 The completed table of contents.

Using Fancy First Letters

Ah, those PageWizards have done it again. Have you ever seen those cool publications in which the layout person has decided to start the article with a dramatic or funky first letter? If used sparingly, it can be quite effective.

Creating a fancy first letter in Publisher is a snap. The simplest method—and that's always the best way anyway—is to let the PageWizard do it for you. If you prefer, you can take the long road and try to create the letter manually by highlighting the character and choosing the **C**haracter command from the Forma**t** menu. But then you're going to run into line-spacing problems.

Go for the easy way out. Use the PageWizard by following these steps:

1. Click the Wizard button in the Left Toolbar.
2. Choose Fancy First Letter. A crosshair cursor appears.
3. Move the pointer to the work area, and drag a box for the letter you want to create.
4. Follow the PageWizard instructions, and choose the style, border, and background.
5. Type the first letter.
6. Click Create It. You can watch as Publisher creates the frame, adds the art, and uses WordArt to create the letter.
7. At the closing screen of the PageWizard, click OK to return to the publication.

Figure 10.14 shows a sample of a fancy first letter. If you prefer to create your own, you can use the **C**haracter command in the Forma**t** menu mentioned earlier or enter a single WordArt character of your own.

Fig. 10.14
A sample of a fancy first letter.

Adding Captions

Captions are lines of text that explain pictures, graphs, or tables in your publication. You add captions in the same way you add any other traditional text frame, by following these steps:

1. Select the Text tool.
2. Choose the frame options you want.
3. Draw the text frame.
4. Type the text for the caption; then click outside the frame.

> **Project Tip**
>
> You can create a background box for a caption and then place the caption overlapping the photo or picture. This way, readers can tell that the caption is a separate element, yet it's still linked to the text.

Note

Most publications include captions that are set off from the text. You may want to choose a smaller font, an italic typeface, or a different alignment to help readers distinguish between the caption and the text. If the graph, picture, or table and the caption are surrounded by text, extra spacing after the caption helps the reader understand that it's different from the body text of your article.

Adding a Bulleted List

The last special feature covered in this chapter is the creation of a bulleted list. A *bulleted list* is a list of text items in your text. Each line of the text begins with a bullet character that "hangs out" to grab the reader's attention.

To add a bulleted list, follow these steps:

1. Highlight the text you want to turn into a bulleted list (see fig. 10.15).

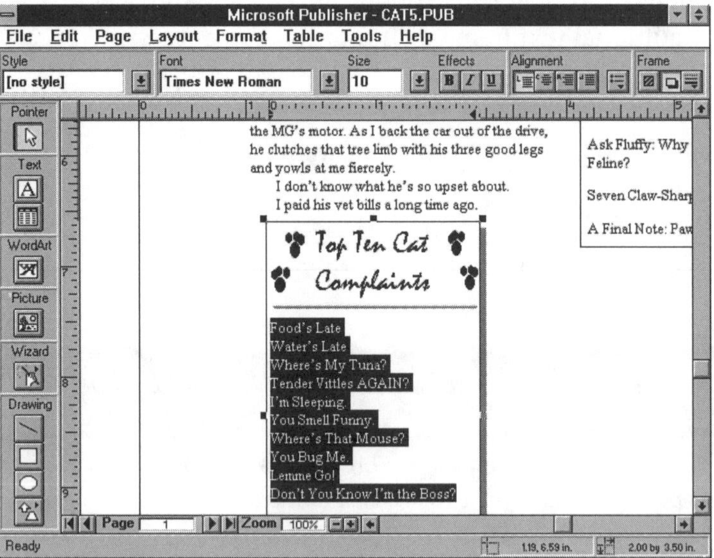

Fig. 10.15
Selecting text for the bullets.

2. Choose **I**ndents and Lists from the Forma**t** menu. The Indents and Lists dialog box appears.

3. Click the **B**ulleted List option. Instantly the Indents settings that were in place before you selected Bulleted list disappear and change to Bullet Type choices (see fig. 10.16).

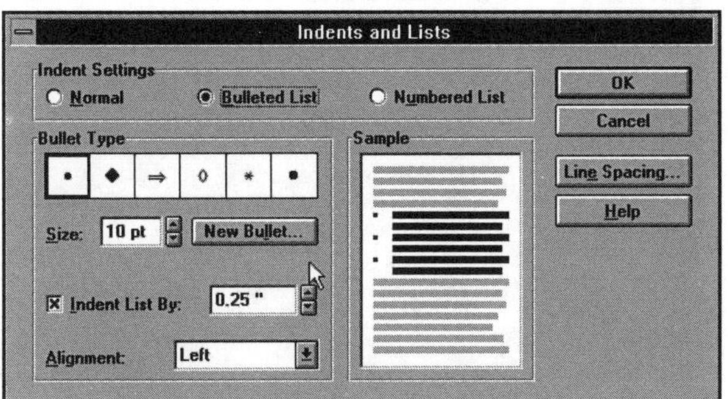

Fig. 10.16
Selecting the Bulleted List option.

4. Click on the Bullet Type you want. Then choose the **S**ize, how much to **I**ndent [the] List By, and the **A**lignment.

5. Click OK.

Project Tip

Bulleted lists are an effective way of communicating a few points in a concise format. Lists allow you to introduce the ideas quickly.

After you click OK, the Indents and Lists dialog box disappears and you return to the publication. There are the bullets, right where you expected them to be (see fig. 10.17).

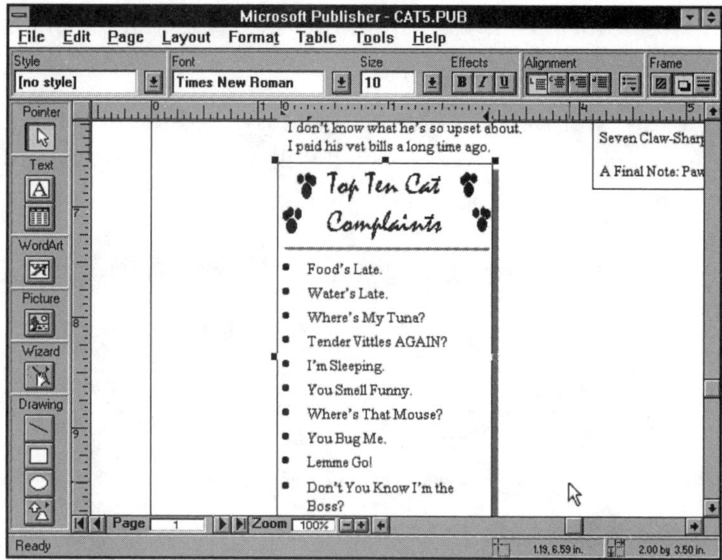

Fig. 10.17
The new bullets.

From Here...

For information directly related to finishing your publication, you may want to review the following sections of this book:

- Chapter 11, "Printing the Publication." Now that you've run the Layout Checker and made sure that all is well, you can print your publication in confidence.

- Chapter 12, "Publisher Design Tips." If you're in the mood for improvements, you may want to consider tips on how to make your publication better.

Chapter 11

Printing the Publication

In this chapter, you learn to do the following tasks:

- Make sure the printer is set up to work with Publisher
- Choose print options
- Print the publication
- Use the Print Troubleshooter
- Assemble the document

At this point, you have almost completed the publishing process. After you enter text and pictures and fine-tune your layout, you undoubtedly will want to see what the document looks like on the printed page.

Publisher is a WYSIWYG, or *what you see is what you get,* program so you shouldn't notice any major surprises when you print your document. It should look basically the same way it appears on-screen. Depending on the type of monitor and printer you use, however, you may see a slight variance. If even a slight difference is too much, you can safeguard your project by using the rulers and the Snap to Ruler **M**arks command in the T**o**ols menu to help you place frames and other items accurately.

In this chapter, you learn to print your Publisher publications. First, you review some history of printing with desktop publishing programs and learn how to make all the necessary preparations for printing your work. You then learn to control printing options. Finally, you learn how to assemble your document after its printed and handle possible printing problems.

The Basics of Printer Types

When the first affordable desktop publishing programs appeared on the market, the choice of usable printers was small. Most programs worked only with dot-matrix printers. Few supported laser printers; in fact, not many laser printers were available at that time. Since those days, the number of available printers—and printer types—has grown incredibly. Not too long ago, color output was impossible for anyone but the elite well-funded few. Today, regular folks can print colored newsletters to their heart's content, assuming, of course, they have a color printer.

Here's a quick overview of the popular printer types that work with Publisher 2.0:

- A *dot-matrix printer* prints your publication in a series of dots. This type of printer offers relatively low quality; if you look closely enough, you can see the patterns of dots that comprise individual characters. Dot-matrix printers use ribbons, similar to typewriter ribbons, to place the characters and pictures on the page. For in-house publications and nonbusiness use, dot-matrix printers are sufficient.

- An *ink-jet printer* offers a quality somewhere between that of a dot-matrix and a laser printer. Ink-jets are very popular, especially as an inexpensive option for color printing. The ink-jet printer works by squirting dots of ink on the page. You purchase ink cartridges instead of print ribbons to keep these printers in the black (and blue, and green, and red).

- A *laser printer* uses laser technology to produce output. The process is similar to that of a photocopying machine: a cartridge with toner (the substance used to place the information on the page) is used to print the output.

Note

Resolution refers to the quality of the printed publication. Publisher prints your documents at the resolution best for your printer. Typically, the term *resolution* is used to refer to the number of dots per inch (dpi) in a printed or on-screen item. The more dots, the higher the resolution. Text or pictures printed at high resolution (such as 300 dpi) look much smoother and less jagged than images printed at 72 or 120 dpi, which are the resolutions of most dot-matrix printers.

- A *PostScript laser printer* is a printer that uses the PostScript page description language to put images on the page. PostScript is a type of programming language that your printer reads in order to print output. Because the page description language tells the printer how to create the characters and pictures, the characters are not formed in a pattern of dots like they are with a dot-matrix printer. As a result, the output is smooth and clear. PostScript printers are currently among the highest-quality desktop printers available.

Publisher can produce output on any printer supported by Microsoft Windows. Chances are, you can use any IBM-compatible printer with Publisher.

Note

With Windows 3.1 came the introduction of TrueType fonts, a new font that looks good on virtually any type of printer. So, if you have a less-than-the-coolest printer, don't despair—with Publisher's TrueType fonts, your publication will still look good.

Preparing to Print

Before you print your publication, you need to make sure that everything is set up properly. The first step is to check your print options. These settings affect how Publisher sees the page, what the orientation of the page is at printing time, and what paper size and source you are using. If you change the print options after you create the document, you may change how things look on the page.

Checking the Printer Setup

To check the print options, follow these steps:

1. Open the document you want to print.
2. Open the **F**ile menu.

3. Choose the Print Setup command. The Print Setup dialog box appears (see fig. 11.1). In this figure, a PostScript printer is selected.

4. Check the Printer, Orientation, and Paper settings.

5. Make any necessary changes. Remember, changes may affect the way the document appears. If you choose **L**andscape for the Orientation setting after you have created the document based on Po**r**trait orientation, for example, the text and picture frames no longer fit the page.

6. Click OK.

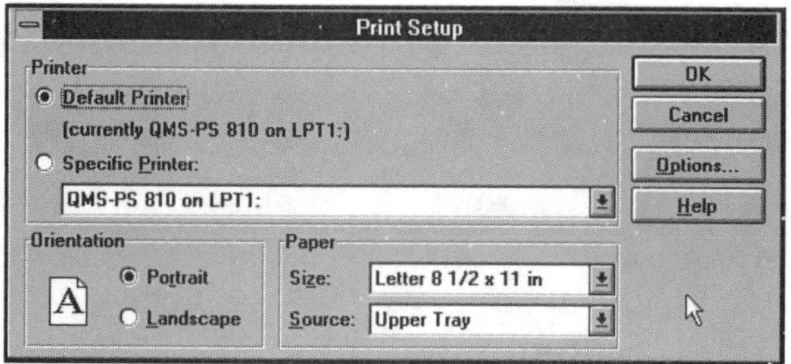

Fig. 11.1
Checking the printer setup.

Checking Printer Connections

The next step is to check the physical setup. Ask yourself the following questions:

1. Is the printer turned on?

2. If you're using a laser printer, is the paper cartridge full?

3. If you're using a dot-matrix printer, is the paper fed through the printer?

4. Is the printer on-line?

5. Is the printer cable fastened securely to both your printer and the port on the back of your computer?

Troubleshooting

My printer isn't listed in the Print Setup dialog box.

You need to install the driver for your printer in the Windows Control Panel. Display the Control Panel by double-clicking the Main group icon and choosing the Control Panel icon. Next, double-click **P**rinters. Choose the **A**dd button and select your printer from the list. Have your Windows disks handy, because Windows will need to copy the printer driver from the original disks.

Printing the Publication

After checking the setup and print options and previewing the publication, you're ready to print. Follow these steps:

1. Open the **F**ile menu.
2. Choose the **P**rint command. The Print dialog box appears (see fig. 11.2).

As you can see, you have a number of items to consider in the Print dialog box. The following sections explain each of these settings.

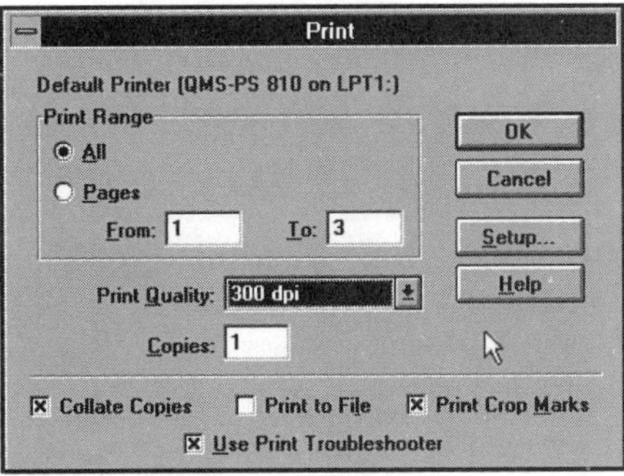

Fig. 11.2
The Print dialog box.

Selecting a Print Range

Publisher enables you to specify the range of pages you want to print. Instead of printing the entire document each time you print, you can elect to print only a few selected pages.

If you want to print the entire publication, leave the **A**ll button selected. This setting is the default. If you want to print a smaller range of pages, click the **P**ages button. In the **F**rom box, type the first page number of the range you want to print. In the **T**o box, enter the last page that you want printed. If you want to print pages 4 through 7, for example, enter 4 in the **F**rom box and 7 in the **T**o box. These entries tell Publisher to print pages 4, 5, 6, and 7. You cannot, however, specify pages that are not in the same range. You cannot tell Publisher to print, for example, pages 4, 6, and 7. To print these pages, you need to use two separate print procedures, printing page 4 first by entering 4 in both the **F**rom and **T**o boxes, and then printing pages 6 and 7.

Choosing Print Quality

Depending on the type of printer you select, Publisher may give you options for choosing the quality or resolution of your printout. In the Print **Q**uality box, you can choose the resolution you want.

The actual choices you see in the Print Quality box depend on the type of printer you are using. You may see Low, Medium, and High as the options for the quality of your printout. You may see numbers instead, such as 75, 150, or 300.

Here are a few guidelines for when you may want to use these different resolutions:

- Choose Draft or Low when you print a first draft of a publication.
- Choose Medium when you need to circulate a first or second draft of a publication for approval.
- Choose High when you need professional-quality printouts or, at least, the best quality your printer is capable of producing.

High quality generally prints more slowly than medium or low quality. The text and pictures printed at high quality, however, are much clearer. When a few extra moments don't matter much, high quality is worth the wait.

To choose a quality different from the one shown, click the arrow beside the Print **Q**uality box. A drop-down list of options then appears. Click the quality setting of your choice.

Project Tip

If you're doing a first copy just to see how the publication looks, choose the lowest quality setting. You'll get your printout quicker and you'll get an idea of how everything looks together on the page.

Specifying the Number of Copies

Publisher enables you to print as many copies of the publication as you want. Generally, however, the best approach is to print only one copy the first time you print the publication because you never know what the results may be. No matter how carefully you placed items on the page, a line may be misplaced. Printing 10 copies and then finding a small mistake would be awful. Print one copy first, check it carefully, then print a larger amount.

Tip
Always do a test print of one copy before you print multiple copies.

To specify the number of copies you want, click the **C**opies box in the Print dialog box and enter the number.

Setting Additional Print Options

Four more options are shown at the bottom of the Print box: Collate Cop**i**es, Print to Fi**l**e, Print Crop **M**arks, and **U**se Print Troubleshooter. Three of these options (Collate Cop**i**es, Print Crop **M**arks, and **U**se Print Troubleshooter) are selected by default. The following list explains each of the four options:

Option	Description
Collate Copies	If you print more than one copy, you can choose the Collate Copies option to have Publisher order the copies as the publication is printed. That way, you don't have to sort through the pages and separate them to assemble your publications. Collate Copies is selected by default.
Print to File	This option enables you to print your Publisher publication to a file on disk. You may want to print to a disk file, for example, when you create the publication on your computer, but you want to print the publication on another computer. When you use Print to File, you can print your publication from another computer even if it does not have Publisher installed.
Print Crop Marks	*Crop marks* are small lines printed in the corners of your publication. Typically, commercial printers use crop marks to make sure that your pages line up during the printing process. Print Crop Marks is selected by default.
Use Print Troubleshooter	The Print Troubleshooter is a new feature of Version 2.0 that helps you figure out what went wrong if your publication doesn't print the way it should. The Use Print Troubleshooter option is selected by default.

Starting and Canceling Printing

Tip
Always make sure that the Print Troubleshooter is on before you print.

After you complete all options in the Print dialog box, you are ready to print. To start printing, simply click OK. Publisher displays a message that it is printing your publication. If your publication is longer than one page, Publisher displays a print status line that tells you which page is being printed (see fig. 11.3).

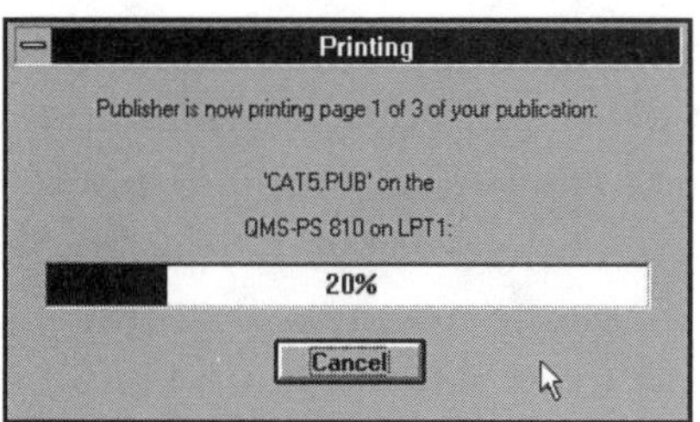

Fig. 11.3
Checking the status of your printing.

You can cancel printing at any time by clicking the Cancel button at the bottom of the message box.

When Publisher is finished sending your publication to the printer, the dialog box disappears, and Publisher redraws your publication on-screen. Then a pop-up window appears—the Print Troubleshooter—asking whether everything printed okay (see fig. 11.4).

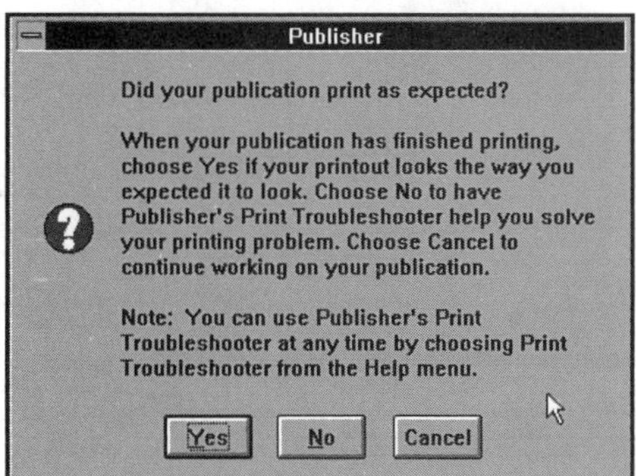

Fig. 11.4
The Print Trouble-shooter pop-up screen.

Be prepared to wait a minute or two (depending on the type of printer you have) while Publisher prints your document. If you use a laser printer, you may worry that nothing is happening. Check your printer's Active light. It should be flashing, indicating that the printer is putting the page together. With a dot-matrix printer, the process should be more apparent; soon after you click OK, your dot-matrix printer should begin working.

Letting the Print Troubleshooter Figure Out the Problem

If your publication didn't print or something went wrong, you'll be glad to have the Print Troubleshooter there to sort things out. If your document didn't turn out the way you expected it to, click **N**o when the pop-up Print Troubleshooter message appears. A CueCard-size window then appears to ask you questions that will narrow down the amount of possible problems (see fig. 11.5). Did your publication print at all? Did it start printing and then stop?

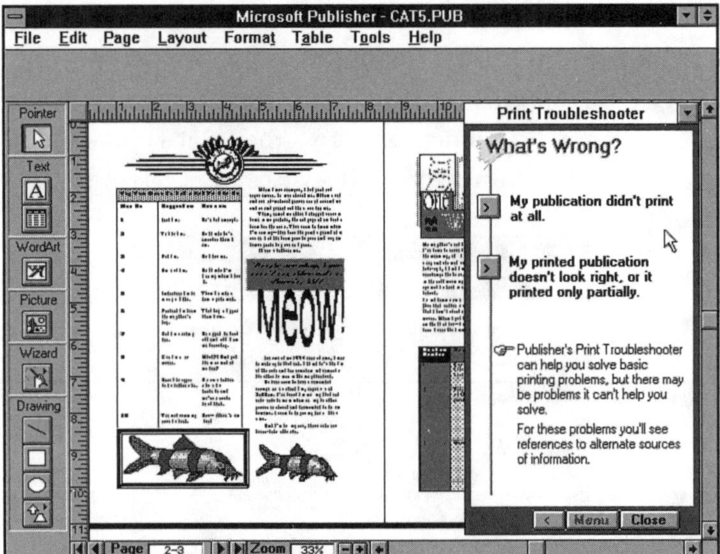

Fig. 11.5
The Print Troubleshooter.

Some questions provide a button so that you can get a quick rundown of procedures you can use to fix the problem (see fig. 11.6). Follow the questions through and when you finish, try to print again. Chances are, you'll get your printout without a hitch.

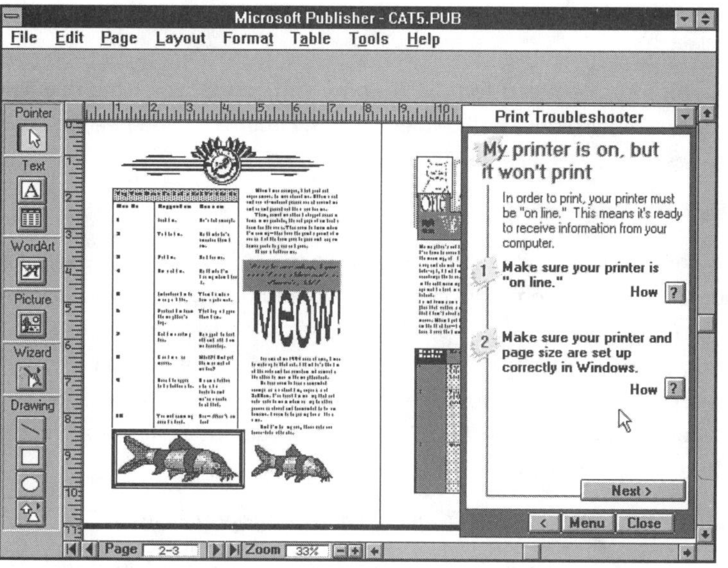

Fig. 11.6
For more information, click the How? button.

That's all there is to it. After you see your publication in print, you may have some additional fine-tuning to do. Or, if you have created a book, brochure, or card, you may be a bit confused about the order in which Publisher has printed your pages. The next section shows you the tricks on how to assemble your new Publisher document.

Troubleshooting

Help! My publication still doesn't print!

You've gone through all this trouble to create a publication, and your printer isn't doing a thing. What's the problem? First, check all the hardware connections—make sure that cables are connected securely, the printer is on-line, and the paper is in place. Next, open the **F**ile menu and choose P**r**int Setup to make sure that you have selected the right printer.

I have selected Print Crop Marks, but the crop marks don't print.

The crop marks print only when enough room exists between your page margins and the printable area of the page. Most printers have a certain area on the page where they stop printing usually a fraction of an inch from the edge of the page. If you set your page margin so that it extends almost all the way to the edge of the print area, then you didn't leave enough

(continues)

(continued)

room for the crop marks to print. To print crop marks, you need to enlarge the page size or reduce your page margins. Either way, you need to make changes to your publication.

The edges of the publication are cut off.

This problem can be caused by one of two things: you may have specified page margins that come too close to the print boundaries of your page, or you may be trying to print a publication that is too large for your printer's memory. Check the page margins and try to reduce the margin amounts by selecting Page Se**t**up from the **P**age menu. If the document is too large for your printer's memory, try printing the document a page at a time, reducing the number of graphics, or using fewer fonts.

I can get my printer to print one page, but then the printer stops.

Your publication file may be too large to fit in your printer's memory. Try to use different pictures that require less memory, such as substituting a shaded background box for a complex BMP picture you had used as a background, or try dividing the publication into smaller chunks that your printer can handle.

The publication starts out OK, but the page is cut off halfway down the page.

Again, the publication is too large for your printer's memory. You may need to reduce the number of elements on your page or make some of the items smaller. Look for elements that you may not need, such as sophisticated graphics behind a text box or an element that employs a number of items where just a few would suffice.

Publisher uses a different font than the one I specified.

Check the printer setup options to make sure that you haven't changed the printer from the one you originally chose. You may have created the publication while the first printer was chosen and now you're trying to print on a different printer.

Assembling Your Publication

How much trouble is involved in assembling a publication? The answer depends on the type of publication you produce. If you create a newsletter that is simply a three-page document that you staple in one corner, the assembly is minimal. If you create a flyer—a one-page advertisement—you don't need to do anything except copy the publication.

If you create a book or a card, however, the assembly process takes a little more thought. In fact, if you print a book or card without first investigating the process, you may be shocked to see pages 6 and 3 printed on the same piece of paper. On your card, some of the information is upside down. How do you put something like that together? The next paragraphs give you a clearer picture of the assembly process.

Printing Books

If you're not expecting it, seeing the order in which Publisher prints your book or card may alarm you. *What did I do wrong?* you may ask yourself. Don't worry—things are supposed to print out of sequence.

You need to know a little about publishing before this printing scheme makes any sense. In book publishing, books are not printed sequentially—from page 1 to 100, in order. Rather, the pages are printed in *signatures* (16 pages) that are put together in the binding stage to form your book. With this scheme in mind, the makers of Publisher organized the printing process in such a way that the book fits together correctly when you staple or bind it. The pages, therefore, do not follow a traditional sequence.

When you create a book, Publisher assumes the following things:

- The number of pages you have created is a multiple of 4. Your book, for example, should be 4, 8, 12, 16, or 20 pages. If the total number of pages is *not* divisible by 4, add blank pages at the end of the publication to get to a number that is. This step is essential so that all of your pages work out evenly.
- You're going to print or copy pages on the front and back of each sheet of paper.
- Each printed sheet of paper contains two separate pages.

When you print a book, it's best to print one page at a time. Even though you may specify in the Print dialog box that you want to print only page 1, you wind up with pages 1 and 8 (the first and last pages of an 8-page publication). Likewise, you may plan to tell Publisher to print page 2, but you will get pages 2 and 7. So, before you print page 2, take the first printout (pages 1 and 8) and turn it over. You can feed page 2 (and 7) manually on the back of pages 1 and 8.

If you aren't doing the assembly yourself, you can take all the pages to your printer and have the assembly and binding done there. If you take the book to a commercial printer, be sure to print the pages with crop marks so that the printer can line up your pages correctly.

Printing Cards

As you know, Publisher gives you a choice of three kinds of card layouts:

Tent card	Two pages printed on each sheet of paper, with the fold on the top
Side-fold card	Four pages printed on each sheet of paper, with the fold on the left
Top-fold card	Four pages printed on each sheet of paper, with the fold along the top

When you print cards, some of your text and pictures may appear upside down because of the way your card will be folded.

To assemble a tent card, simply fold the card in half from top to bottom, so the fold is along the top. To assemble a side-fold card, fold the top half of the sheet down. Then bring the left side over to the right, with the fold on the left. To assemble a top-fold card, fold the page in half vertically. Then bring the top down to meet the bottom edge of the page, with the fold along the top.

Tip
If you have trouble with this folding business, let Publisher's PageWizard help you out. The Greeting Card PageWizard will help you create the card you want and provides instructions for folding it after it's printed.

Troubleshooting

The publication started to print and never did anything.

When you print, remember that some printers take an unusually long time to print cards because the printers have trouble printing upside down. If you find that your printer "goes away" and never comes back, the makers of Publisher suggest that you use WordArt to create the text that you need printed upside down.

I have only one Print Quality setting available in the Print dialog box.

Don't sweat it. If your Print Quality box shows only one setting (such as 300 dpi), that's the best setting for your particular printer. Go ahead and print as usual.

My printer won't let me insert pages manually.

If you are trying to do two-sided printing and your printer doesn't allow you to manually insert paper, first print the two pages on separate pieces of paper and then use a copy machine to copy page 2 onto the back of page 1.

The Print Troubleshooter didn't solve my problem.

Printing can be a mysterious business. If your publication isn't printing and the Print Troubleshooter isn't helping, try turning your printer off and then on again. If you're using a laser printer, wait a few seconds after turning the machine off before you turn it back on again. Also, make sure the printer is on-line, ready to receive the file, and is equipped with paper.

From Here...

For information directly related to finishing your publication, you may want to review the following sections of this book:

- Chapter 12, "Publisher Design Tips." Learn some of the basics for trying a new look. What's important for newsletters? What about flyers?
- Chapter 13, "Turning Your Publication into a Finished Product." What's next? Once you have the basic article printed, you're ready for the next step in finishing the publication.
- Chapter 15, "Publication Ideas." Ready for something new? Take a look at the designs in Chapter 15 to get some ideas.

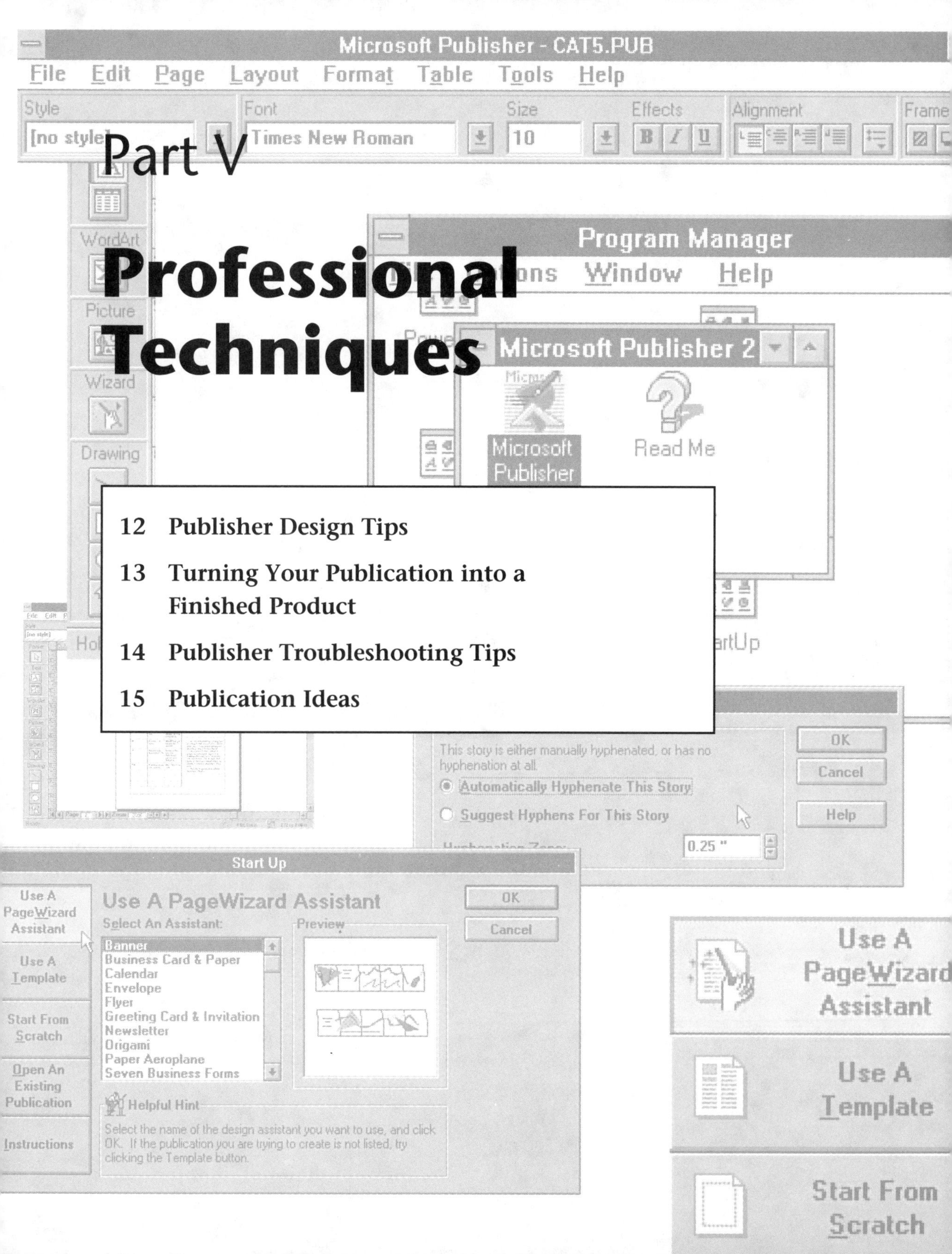

Part V

Professional Techniques

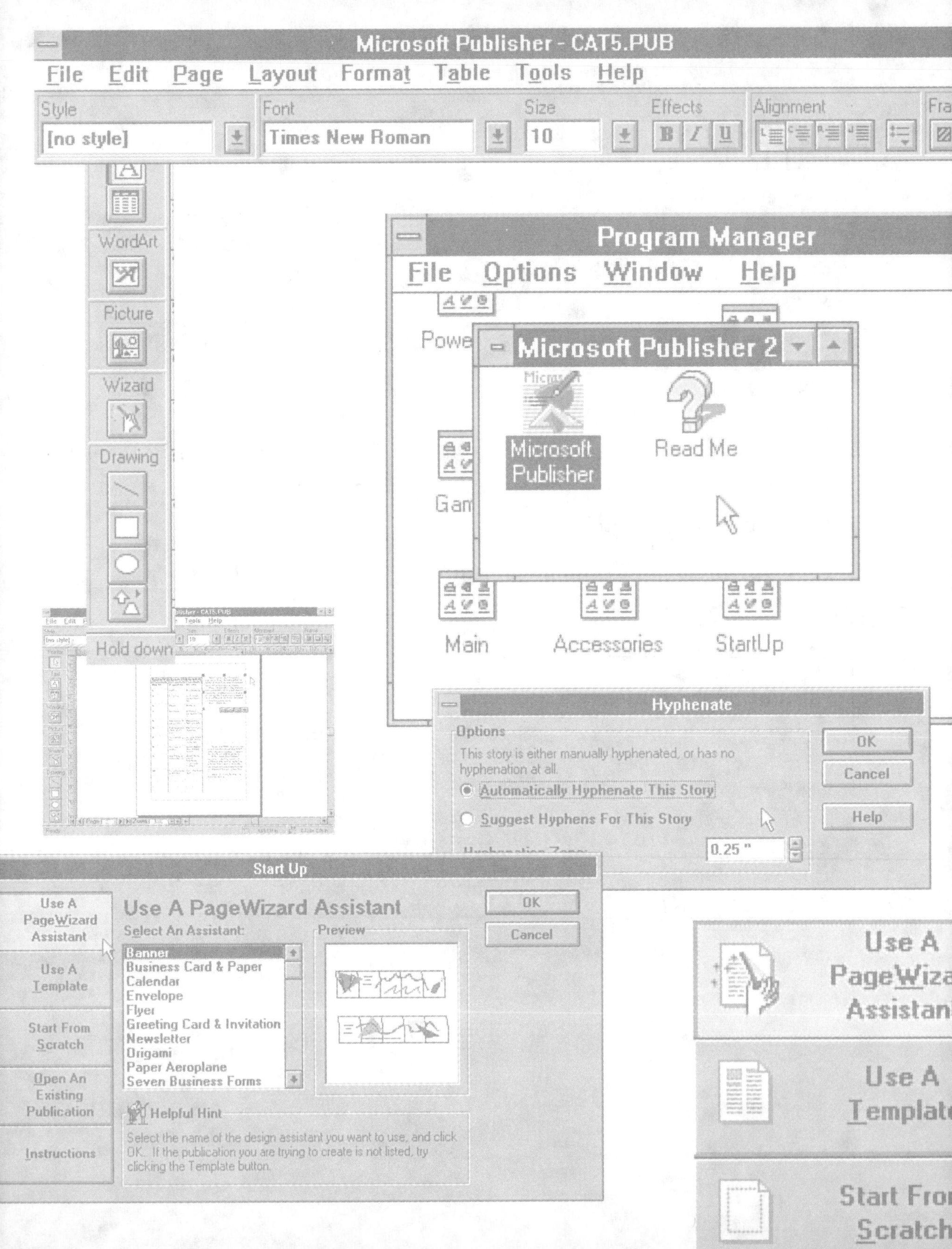

Microsoft Publisher - CAT5.PUB
File Edit Page Layout Format Table Tools Help
Style
[no style]
Font
Times New Roman
Size
10
Effects
Alignment
WordArt
Picture
Wizard
Drawing
Hold down
Program Manager
File Options Window Help
Microsoft Publisher 2
Microsoft Publisher
Read Me
Main
Accessories
StartUp
Hyphenate
Options
This story is either manually hyphenated, or has no hyphenation at all.
Automatically Hyphenate This Story
Suggest Hyphens For This Story
0.25 "
OK
Cancel
Help
Start Up
Use A PageWizard Assistant
Use A Template
Start From Scratch
Open An Existing Publication
Instructions
Use A PageWizard Assistant
Select An Assistant:
Banner
Business Card & Paper
Calendar
Envelope
Flyer
Greeting Card & Invitation
Newsletter
Origami
Paper Aeroplane
Seven Business Forms
Preview
OK
Cancel
Helpful Hint
Select the name of the design assistant you want to use, and click OK. If the publication you are trying to create is not listed, try clicking the Template button.
Use A PageWiza
Assistan
Use A Template
Start Fro
Scratch

Chapter 12

Publisher Design Tips

For some people, desktop publishing is an electronic excuse to let their creative spirits fly. For others, the freedom and responsibility of designing an effective document is a fearsome task. Whether you are excited or intimidated at the prospect of becoming a desktop publisher, a little education goes a long way. Look at current books and magazines on graphic design and find out about the latest trends in publishing. The tips in this chapter provide you with some suggestions as you create your publications.

This chapter includes some basic design considerations for the following elements:

- Overall design
- Newsletters
- Business stationery
- Flyers
- Training materials
- Graphics

Overall Design Tips

Consider what you want to accomplish with your publication. Are you trying to enlighten, amuse, inspire, or inform people? Do you simply want to get your business name out in front of the largest amount of people possible?

Think about the tone of your publication. Plan everything—from the design to the content—to correspond with the tone your audience is expecting. Figure 12.1 shows a banner that was created for a not-so-serious audience.

Fig. 12.1
An informal banner.

Picture your audience. Are they business people or members of the Parent Teacher Organization? Do they sell stocks and bonds, or roses and daffodils? Think about what type of publication your audience expects to see. Sketch a rough draft of the publication before you begin. If you will be using more than one page, sketch out additional pages as well. Decide where to position different elements.

After you have created some of the basic elements on the page, print a copy, using draft mode. This printout will give you a paper guide—something you can continue to sketch ideas on or use to decide what to do or *not* do as you continue developing your design.

Think about the way a reader's eyes scan text. Choose columns and place graphics in such a way that they won't interrupt the reading flow.

Use rules and boxes sparingly. If not overdone, these items help to enhance the organization of the publication and guide the reader's eye.

Keep a folder of styles you like. You can pick and choose among design elements to create the effects you want in your own publication.

Newsletter Tips

What does your banner say about the publication? Make sure that the banner is appropriate for your audience. Should it be dramatic? Try inverting the banner so that it's white text on a black background. Is it lighthearted? Use a clip art item as a side graphic and work that into the banner.

Avoid bad breaks. A *bad break* in a publication is a word or character that wraps to the next line or next column, causing your document to look confusing and unbalanced. Additionally, watch out for too many hyphenated words in one paragraph.

Don't overdo pictures. Remember that pictures are meant to support the text, not the other way around. Use one or two pictures on each page. Unless you're creating a catalog, you may distract your readers by placing too many pictures on a page.

Use only a few fonts in each publication. Don't run the risk of cluttering your publication by trying to include too many fonts. Select one or two typefaces that you like and stick with them throughout the document.

Align your text columns. If you have two or three columns on a page, use the ruler lines to make sure that the columns line up.

Use pull-quotes to emphasize key points. Used sparingly, pull-quotes add strength to your publication and help readers recognize important topics.

Use templates for publications you create often. If you use the same newsletter month after month, create a template of the newsletter file so that you don't have to start from scratch every time you begin the publication.

Don't be afraid to experiment. If you have been given a green light to be a little creative with your publication, don't be afraid to try formats you haven't tried before. If you're producing a one-of-a-kind publication (something that won't be repeated from month to month), you can afford to try something a little different. You could try using four columns instead of three, centering a photo in the middle of the page and flowing text around it, or placing two or more uneven columns next to each other.

Figure 12.2 shows the sample layout created throughout the course of this book. Not exactly conventional, is it? With the heavy use of tables, uneven text columns, and numerous graphic elements, this layout is not one you would use for a typical monthly publication.

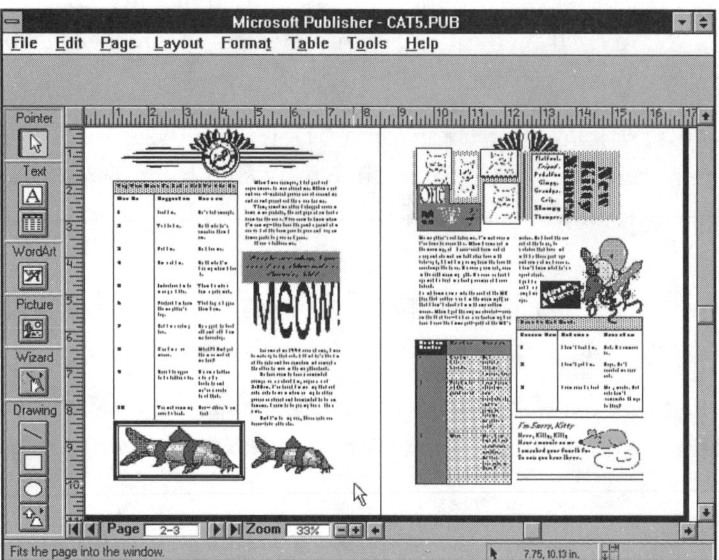

Fig. 12.2
Experimenting with layout.

Remember the importance of white space. Fight the temptation to fill up every bit of available space. Leave some white space to give the reader's eye a rest. White space also helps to set off important elements on your page and lead readers to the sections you want them to see the most.

Make sure your typeface reflects your newsletter's personality. If you create a light-hearted, fun publication, choose a typeface that shows a bit of humor, like Vivaldi, Mistral, or Playbill. If your newsletter is more serious, use a more formal typeface like New Century Schoolbook or Times Roman.

Include a footer or header line with the page number and document name. By numbering your pages and including the publication name, you help the reader identify your publication.

Use lines to separate columns. If you are using multiple columns in a publication, you may want to add vertical lines between columns. This helps to guide the reader's eye and to contribute to the linear layout of the page.

If you use photos in a newsletter, crop the photos effectively. If the main focus of a photograph is the CEO of your company, for example, you don't need to use the entire photo of her sitting at her desk; you could crop the picture to show only her face (this is known as a *mug* shot). You then could enlarge the picture to fit the space in your publication. This keeps the readers from focusing on the less important parts of the picture.

If you will be printing your publication on a high-end output device, like a Linotronic, do a test run first. Sometimes items that print on a laser printer (such as a 0.5 line) will look washed out when printed on a high-quality printer. When you have decided on your design, create a sample that you can output on the Linotronic to make sure that you don't need to make any design adjustments before printing.

Business Stationery Tips

Keep a collection of stationery and logos you like. This selection will give you ideas for your business stationery.

Create a logo that reflects your business. Make sure that you choose a picture or design that is in some way connected to the business you're involved in. This helps readers identify with your business and recognize it later (see fig. 12.3).

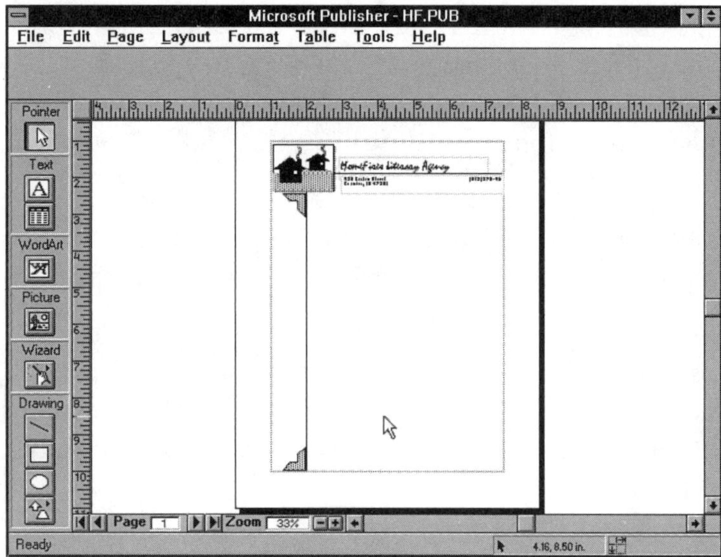

Fig. 12.3
A sample home-drawn logo.

Create a subtle but effective letterhead. Don't let the letterhead of your stationery overwhelm the page. In publishing, understated is usually best.

Be consistent by using the same design on all business forms. Keep your company in your readers' minds by using the same logo and company identification information on all of your business forms and cards. The more that readers see the same design, the more they'll remember your company.

Don't underestimate white space. Remember that the white space on your publication is as important as the text and pictures. Use white space effectively to draw the reader's eyes to the most important elements on the page.

Spotlight your company name. Use the items on the page to lead the reader's eyes to your company name. You may want to use lines, boxes, pictures, or simply the placement of text to remind the reader of your business.

Flyer Tips

The fewer words, the better. Because flyers are meant to be quick-impact items that usually promote a new product, advertise a sale, and so on, too many words can detract from your overall message.

Use pictures to help reinforce the text. One large picture in a flyer is much better than several smaller pictures. Remember that a flyer is a "hit-'em-fast" kind of publication that should communicate its message as fast as possible.

Include your company logo. Be sure to have your company logo and address information in the same place on all of the flyers that your company produces.

Use more white space than text. Flyers need even more white space than newsletters or brochures. Remember that your readers want to understand your intent quickly—so use the white space to your advantage (see fig. 12.4).

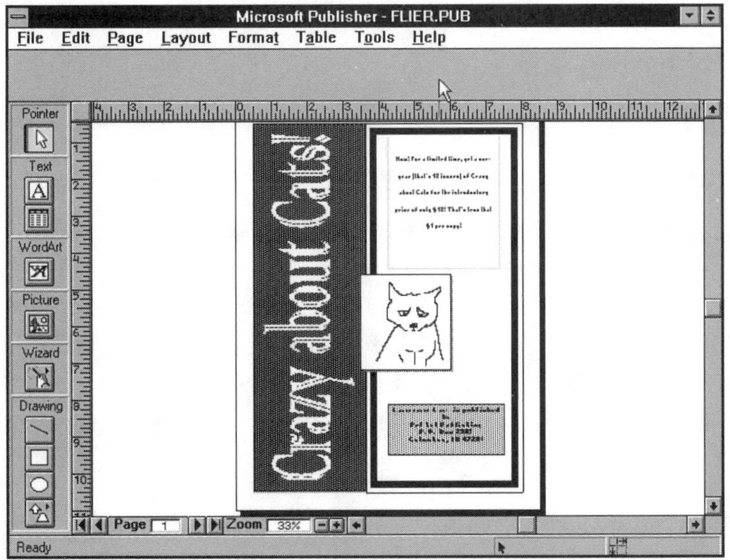

Fig. 12.4
A flyer with plenty of white space.

Use a larger text size in flyers. Because you have less text in a flyer than you would in a brochure or newsletter, you can use a larger text size, such as 14-point.

Use bulleted lists. In the "hit-'em-fast" world of flyers, bullets are an effective means of leading the reader's eye through the publication.

Training Material Tips

Be short and sweet. Keep your handout brief. Include only enough information to refresh the reader's memory later.

Leave room for notes. Leaving space for notes can be a great service to your readers, especially if your class is in a seminar format.

Make a point. Make sure that your training materials include an agenda box that lets readers know what to expect from the course. You may want to use WordArt to create the box.

Identify figures and graphs. Be sure to use captions for all the figures and graphs in your publication. Readers may not remember later what the pictures represent.

Graphics

Decide what graphics you need. Today, graphics are a big business. Just a few years ago, adding special art files to your document, or drawing them yourself, was unthinkable. Before you start adding graphics, consider the tone of your publication and choose a graphics style. Would line art look right, or perhaps a more traditional approach using photos? Be aware of the personality of your publication when you choose the graphics style.

Determine what graphics you have. You may already have graphics files you can use. Many programs—especially Windows programs—can share clip art and other art files. Check the subdirectories of other programs like Microsoft Works or PowerPoint to see whether there are any files you can use.

Are you a draw-it-yourself publisher? You can always use Windows Paintbrush to draw sketches on-the-fly. However, for high-quality art, you'll need to use a more specialized drawing program like Micrografx Designer or Adobe Illustrator. Remember, you can do simple shapes and lines in Publisher, then move into Draw for basic additions.

Do you need to scan images? Scanning photos is still considered a relatively high-end desktop publishing task because not many people have full-time access to a high-quality scanner. But, if you need to add photos to your newsletter or brochure, call around to local printing places. Often, printers who offer desktop publishing have a scanner on-site.

For best results, be consistent when placing photos together on a page. If you create a catalog, for example, try to use a uniform size for all the photos. The same goes for the content of the photos. If you're including photos of cars, for example, make sure the central focus—the individual car—in each photo is close to the size of the cars in the other photos. If you have one huge car and a bunch of tiny cars, your photo layout will look imbalanced.

Get a good graphics conversion program. Even if you just dabble in graphics work, you need a graphics conversion program like GIFConverter or Paint Shop Pro for Windows. These programs enable you to change from one graphics file to another format easily, thereby eliminating the headache of trying to open a piece of art that Publisher can't recognize.

Add art items you create to the Clip Art Gallery. Whenever you create something, add it to the library so it'll be there if you need to use it again.

Chapter 13

Turning Your Publication into a Finished Product

Many new desktop publishers feel out of their element when they walk into a print shop. They think they don't know what questions to ask, what the "normal" choices are as far as paper weight, size, ink, and so on, or what price range to expect.

If you create a newsletter for a small group or publish pamphlets for a grassroots organization, you may feel at even more of a disadvantage. Today, with the corporate world striving for more control of its published products, desktop publishing and final printing are not nearly as foreign as they once were. Whether you feel threatened by this final step in the publishing process or you're more comfortable with printing decisions, this chapter helps answer some basic printing questions.

In this chapter, you learn the following:

- How the publication should look
- What kind of paper to choose
- How to reproduce your publication
- What to say to the commercial printer

How Should You Finish Your Publication?

Just a few years ago, your choices in deciding how to reproduce your publication were very limited. You either photocopied it (or had it done) or had it professionally printed. There were several factors that figured into that decision:

- Desktop printers weren't of the quality that they are today.
- Desktop printers couldn't handle much more than simple text with a couple of graphics.
- Most desktop printers could not do things like rotate text, resize text, and print special effects without losing quality.
- Photocopiers in the home or the office were not the same quality as those offered by quick-press printers.

Today, however, you have a wider range of options. In fact, when you're deciding whether to print the publication yourself or have it professionally done, ask yourself these questions:

1. How many copies do you want? If you're printing 100 copies of a report, doing it yourself is incredibly time-consuming and is a heavy duty task for your printer, as well.
2. Do you need special print services? In other words, do you need color that your printer can't supply, special resizing, or bleed effect, and so on?
3. Do you have access to the paper that you want to use?

Today, many companies offer custom papers. In fact, Microsoft Publisher 2.0 includes in the **P**age menu a Special **P**aper command that enables you to choose a template with a preset paper design. This helps you lay out the page based on how the page will look when printed on a special paper. To choose this feature, select the Special **P**aper command (see fig. 13.1). The Special Paper dialog box then appears so that you can select the paper style you want (see fig. 13.2). If you want to order the exact paper type shown in the template, contact the paper manufacturers that are listed in your Publisher manual.

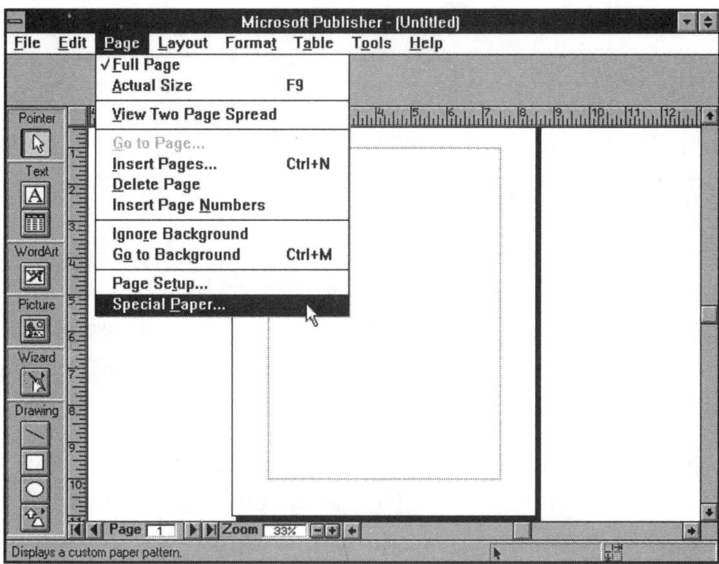

Fig. 13.1 Choosing the Special Paper option.

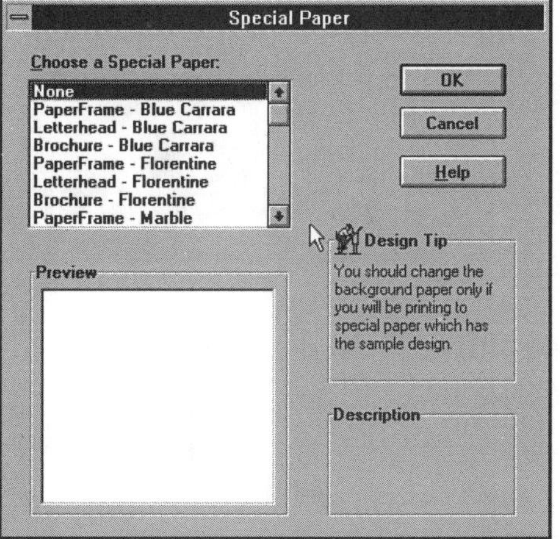

Fig. 13.2 The Special Paper dialog box.

How Do You Choose a Printer?

Finding a good printer isn't always an easy task. Here are some ideas for finding a printing service that will work for you:

- Ask friends or coworkers who have produced projects similar to yours.

- Check with associations that represent the kind of work you do.
- Call local printers and ask about their rates and services.
- Look at brochures, newsletters, or other printed work similar to yours and see whether the printing company is listed.

Remember that old established companies are usually reliable, but they also may not be up-to-date in terms of technology. This means that if you want to take in Publisher files for printing instead of hard copy, they may not be able to accommodate you. For best results, call and ask before you go in.

Many professional printers who do large jobs, such as corporate reports, books, and more, now have the capability of taking files over the phone. In some cases, the printer will want you to print the publication to a file that they can then print at their agency. In many cases, the files are transmitted by modem over the phone lines. If you work with one of these printers, be sure to call them to find out how they want files saved before you send your publication for printing.

What Makes a Good Printer Good?

The best printers

- Are willing to answer your questions
- Take the time to work with you personally
- Advise you about design issues
- Help solve layout problems
- Give you a guaranteed print date
- Work with you if the result is unsatisfactory

The best advice for working with printers, however, is to find a printer who is willing to advise you, shows creative judgment you can trust, and gives you a reasonable price. If you're satisfied with the quality, turnaround time, and cost, stay with that printer. Developing a business relationship with one printer is good business sense for a budding desktop publisher, and this relationship will work toward your company's best interest in the future.

How Should the Publication Look When You Take It to the Printer?

Most of the time, when people finish a publication, they simply don't want to look at it anymore. Part of the reason is that they're tired of reworking and revising it; the other part is that they're afraid they will see something else they want to change.

Generally, when you consider yourself "finished" with a publication, you should take one last careful look. Make sure that the lines are where you want them to be, read it over for grammatical and punctuation errors, and check your graphics to make sure that they printed correctly.

Basic rules for letting go of a finished publication:

- Put the publication in your desk drawer for 24 hours.
- Look at the publication again after you've been away from it.
- Allow coworkers or friends to look at the publication one last time.
- If you see a glaring error, change it.
- If you are tempted to change something just to change it, restrain yourself.

You need to think about how you're delivering this publication, as well. If you print the publication and take it or send it to the printer, make sure that

- If you've had to paste anything manually, it is secure and neatly done (big wads of rubber cement don't look very professional).
- You print the original on high-quality paper with the highest quality print setting for your printer.

- When you print, the toner or print ribbon is new, or relatively new, so that you get a dark printout.
- The originals are put in an envelope or folder to keep them neat.
- There are no smudges, spills, or folds in the corners (pet peeve).
- All your pages are in the right order.

If you send the publication somewhere in file form, make sure that

- You call the receiving printers to make sure they know it's coming.
- You save the file in the right format.
- You put the file on a disk all by itself.
- You include any necessary clip-art files on the same disk as the submitted publication.
- You send a printout by fax or overnight service.
- You make arrangements about deadlines, correction costs, and printer transmission prices.

Typical Newsletter Orders

Today's businesses are using a more polished, sophisticated newsletter style. Gone are the days of the typed-and-photocopied company newsletter. Now, newsletters from both large and small businesses use eye-catching color, customized art, and laser or typeset-quality type to create dramatic effects for their publications.

The publication typically is a four-page newsletter, which is actually one sheet of a fairly heavy-stock paper, printed front and back and folded in the middle. One-half of the last page is reserved for the mailing panel, to which mailing labels are affixed. The bulk mailing permit number also may be printed in the top right corner of the panel. A print run of a publication of this type may be anywhere from 2,000 to 4,000.

Although that type of high-investment "typical" order may be the norm for the corporate world, there are plenty of people still producing informational newsletters for nonprofit organizations, parent-teacher organizations, and businesses. These types of businesses rely on Publisher the most, making good use of the program's clip art, flexibility, and wealth of features.

Paper

What paper weight do you want? This is one of the first questions your printer will ask you. For newsletters, a 60-pound offset paper is best. The coarseness of the paper can stand up to printing on both sides. If you're on a low budget, you can use a 50-pound offset paper, but you run the risk of the ink bleeding through when you print on both sides of the page.

If you are producing a brochure for mailing, you should use a different type of paper. You can select from a flat finish, enamel text stock (with high gloss to strengthen the paper), text stock, or card stock. *Text stock* is a relatively lightweight paper that folds easily. *Card stock* is heavier paper, often used for producing materials such as business reply cards.

Unless you are including a business reply card that will be detached and mailed separately by the recipient, an enamel text stock is a good choice for a mailer. It folds neatly, it doesn't need to be scored like card stock does, and it costs less in postage. (The term *scored* refers to the process of cutting lines at the folds of the publication so the heavy stock can be folded neatly.)

What size should the paper be? For a typical four-page newsletter, printers most often use one 11-by-17-inch sheet. The sheet is folded vertically in the center, so it ends up having four pages. If you stay within the Publisher margins set in the program, your printer will be able to print the pages on 11-by-17-inch paper.

If you modify the margins and extend the graphics to the edge of the page, or if you want a graphic image, such as a rule or border, to bleed off the page, the printer must print the publication on larger sized paper and then cut the pages back to an 11-by-17-inch size.

For publications other than the standard 8 1/2-by-11-inch size, keep in mind that the process may require cutting and/or printing on larger or smaller sized paper. Naturally, the larger the paper size or the more work involved, the more you pay.

If you're producing business cards, be sure to create the publication card at actual size: 2 inches by 3 1/2 inches. Your best bet is to use the business card PageWizard to get the correct size. If the card is larger than standard business card size, the printer must photograph it, electronically reduce it, and print from the reduced copy. This process can detract from the readability of the card. It's best to create the card at the size you need; then you can simply print the card and let the printer do the rest.

What color paper should you use? You have a big range of choices in the color of paper you use for your publication. From fun colors like blue, pink, and yellow, to more business-like colors such as gray, off-white, and white, you can choose the paper color that best suits your publication.

Remember that you want a paper color that will complement the ink color you use on the publication. So if you're using red ink as part of a company logo, a publication on pink paper may make your readers cringe. Before you decide, ask the printer to show you the color selection available.

How much will the paper cost? Several factors figure into the price of the paper you use: weight, size, finish, and quantity. Heavier paper costs more but often is a necessity; larger stock costs more than regular sizes.

Keep in mind that most printers offer a substantial price break for buying a large quantity. If you have taken on the responsibility of printing your organization's newsletter for 12 months, for example, and you expect to print at least 500 copies a month, you may want to buy your paper for the entire year at one time. Most printers will store the paper for you, and this gives you a significant price break on the paper.

Inks

What color ink should you use? As you may expect, black is the least expensive ink you can use. Most printers also have standard inks in several colors. (You'll pay an additional charge per color if you use more than one color.) If you are trying to match a specific color, or simply don't like the selection you see, you do have the option of requesting custom colors, possibly at an additional cost.

For custom ink color, you select the color from a chart much like the paint scales at your local hardware store, and the printer mixes it for you. Usually, there's an additional fee of $25 per ink used for standard ink (the price may be more or less, depending on your area), and an additional $10 to $15 charge for custom colors.

You can cut costs on printing in special ink and printing in quantities with one blow, if you prefer. Suppose that in addition to the mass amount of paper you purchased in the last example, you also want to print the company's masthead, in a custom royal blue ink, at the top of every page. The rest of the publication will be done in black ink.

In this instance, you can buy the paper in bulk and have the colored masthead printed for the whole amount at one time. This keeps you from having to buy the paper and pay the specialized ink fee every month when you print the publication. Then, when you take the monthly publication in to be printed, the cost will be minimal.

Copying

Is it cheaper to photocopy? Depending on your project, the type of audience you're aiming to reach, and the quantity you want, photocopying is probably not your best bet. Although most people think "I'll just take this flyer down and run off 50 copies," the quality they get for the price they pay may be pretty poor. Here again, think in terms of quantity. Is the flyer you're producing a one-time seasonal promotion that will have a limited shelf life? Or is it a flyer that you'll be able to use several times throughout the year, by circulating it to different client groups? If you can justify printing 100 or 150, have the printer reproduce it for you. The quality will be much better and the cost is still minimal—about $15 for 100 copies.

Additional Printing Tips

Let the printer make suggestions. The printer has worked with many clients, some of whom must have produced publications similar to yours. Rely on the printer's experience to tell you which paper, ink, and envelope weight works best for your particular project. Most printers keep samples of recent works, so you can feel the various paper weights, see the inks, and examine the layout.

Keep a folder of publications you like. It's important to identify the styles that catch your eye, as those styles will catch other readers' eyes, as well. If you like the paper, the ink, or the size, keep it with your publications file; then take it to the printer with you. The printer will be able to make suggestions based on your likes and dislikes.

Ask questions. If you don't understand something about the printing process or your responsibilities in preparing the material, don't be afraid to ask. An informed customer is much easier for the printer to deal with than a customer who doesn't understand the process.

Remember to get a guaranteed print date. Most printers will give you a target date, or a time by which they expect to finish the publication. Reputable printers stick to that deadline. However, bear in mind that sometimes, even in the best of situations, deadlines get bumped. So, if your chosen printer misses by a little bit, don't write them off—unless it becomes a pattern.

Chapter 14

Publisher Troubleshooting Tips

This chapter includes tips on dealing with problems in the following areas:

- Files
- Frames
- Text
- Pictures
- PageWizards and Templates

Files

The picture I imported came in looking squashed.

The picture frame you selected before importing the picture may be a strange size. You can resize the picture by clicking on the frame and using the resize pointer to drag the frame to a more appropriate shape.

When I try to import a text file I created in my word processor, Publisher says that it doesn't recognize the file.

You may not have saved the file with an extension Publisher understands. Publisher expects WordStar documents to have the extension DOC, for example, although the name you gave the file may be different. Look in the List Files of Type box, in the Import Text dialog box, to see what kinds of extensions Publisher expects to see. Then try renaming your text file with the appropriate extension.

I can't find the file I just created! I know it's here somewhere...

You're probably looking in the wrong directory. Double-click on the directory you want in the Directories box in the center of the dialog box. You may need to change to a different drive, as well.

Nope, it's not here.

Use the Find File command, in the File menu, to locate that stubborn file.

I tried to import a picture, but I didn't find any clip art files.

You aren't in the ClipArt subdirectory. To move to the ClipArt subdirectory, find the directory name in the Directories box of the Import Picture dialog box. Double-click on ClipArt. The clip art files should appear.

Frames

I tried to draw a frame, but nothing happened.

It could be that you didn't have the tool selected that you need. If you want to create a text frame, choose the Text Frame tool. For a picture frame, click on the Picture Frame tool. To draw a frame for WordArt, choose the WordArt tool. To add a frame for a Wizard section, choose the Wizard tool.

Whenever I change to Actual Size view, I have to use the scroll bars to find the frame I was working with.

You can solve this problem by first clicking on a frame before you choose Actual Size. Then, when you move to Actual Size, the screen will show the frame you selected.

When I try to select some of the commands in the menus, Publisher won't let me.

Some commands will be disabled depending on the operation you are performing. If you're working in a text frame, for example, some of the commands related to pictures are unavailable (they appear in gray). For some commands, you must select a picture frame or text before the command becomes available.

I want to move the frame, but I just keep getting the resize cursor.

Try zooming in on the display so that you can get closer to the item you're trying to select. When the cursor changes to the move symbol, drag the frame to the new location.

I'm trying to place the frame in a certain place, but it keeps jumping away.

Turn off Snap to **G**uides in the T**o**ols menu.

The text frame I've created overlaps a piece of art and blocks it out.

Click the shading button (the third button from the right in the Top Toolbar) and select Clear as the background color. You should now be able to see the art behind the text.

Text

I created a text frame, but when I tried to enter text, Publisher told me the frame was too small.

Although the frame may look big enough to store the text you want to enter, Publisher warns you when there's not enough room. Try resizing the frame just a bit. Or, if another frame is overlapping that frame, try using the Bring to **F**ront command in the **L**ayout menu to place that frame on top of any other layers.

Publisher only displays part of the text I type in the text frame.

The text frame isn't large enough to display all the text. Resize the text frame or create a connected frame. For more information about connected frames, see Chapter 5, "Entering Text."

When I place another text frame on top of the current frame, some of the text from the first frame disappears.

Try moving the text frame that overlaps the bottom frame. You also can change the spacing or text frame margins to position your text more accurately.

I tried to select the text frame, but Publisher won't let me.

The text frame may be on the background. You can find out by opening the **P**age menu and choosing G**o** to Background. Then simply click on the frame to select it and press Ctrl+Del to delete it.

I don't remember in what order I connected the text frames in my publication.

You can press Ctrl+Tab to move the highlight from one text frame to another to see the order in which the frames are linked.

I designed a header and footer line for the background page of my publication, but I don't want it to appear on the first page.

You can easily solve this by having Publisher hide the display of background page elements. To do this, move to the page on which you want to hide the background items (in this case, your first page), open the **P**age menu, and choose Igno**r**e Background. A check mark appears beside the option. If you want to redisplay the background items later, simply select the command again.

I accidentally created a text frame with a dark shade. Now I don't want it. How do I get rid of it?

You have two options for removing the shading: you can click the shading button in the Top Toolbar and change the shade options, or you can open the Forma**t** menu and choose S**h**ading. The Shading dialog box appears, giving you the option of selecting a different shade or a clear background. Click OK after you make your selection.

Pictures

I want to draw a perfectly round circle, but it comes out as an oval instead.

You can draw a perfect circle or a perfect square by pressing and holding Shift while you drag the mouse.

When I resize the picture frame I'm working with, the picture gets all out of whack.

It's another Shift trick; press and hold Shift while you drag the corner handle of the picture. This keeps the picture in proportion within the frame.

I used the drawing tools to create an item for my publication, and when I try to move the item, I can only select one line or one box at a time. I need to move the entire drawing.

You can select many different objects in several ways: You can choose the Pointer tool and drag a large box around all the items you want to select; you can press Ctrl while you click the mouse on the items you want; or you can press Shift while you select the items. Once you've selected the items, click the Group button to put them all together. Then you'll be able to move them together without leaving anything behind.

I'm having trouble lining up the pictures in my publication.

You can press Shift while you move the picture. The picture will move in a straight line. You can also turn on Snap to **G**uides or Snap to Ruler **M**arks to control the alignment of the picture.

I'm using the drawing tools to create an item for my page, and every time I draw a line I have to go back and reselect the line tool.

Rather than selecting the same tool time after time, you can lock the tool in place by clicking the right mouse button. When you finish, choose the Pointer tool to "unlock" the tool.

Layout

These layers are giving me a headache. I have three items, and I'm having trouble putting one item behind the next two.

You can select several items at once by pressing Shift and clicking on the items that you want. Then when you select Bring to **F**ront or Send to **B**ack, the items will move together.

I want to select a piece of a logo I just created with the Logo Creator Plus, but Publisher won't let me.

You may need to ungroup the items before you can select the one you want. Click the locked icon at the bottom of the frame. The handles for the individual items should appear. Zoom up close so that you can see what you're working with.

The layout looks okay on-screen, but when I print it, one of my text boxes is slightly out of alignment.

When in doubt, Zoom! Move in as close as you can stand—200 or 400 percent—to make sure that things are as they seem. You can move back out after you double-check the placement of the elements.

Pages

I specified the wrong page size for my document and everything is already placed on the page. What should I do?

Your only option at this point is to change the page margins and manually resize the text and picture frames to fit the new page dimensions.

I added a page number on the background page of my document, but it doesn't appear on the rest of the pages.

The background item will appear only if you don't have other elements obstructing it on the publication pages. If you have a text or picture box occupying the place where the page number should appear, the page number is hidden. Open the Page menu and make sure that you haven't selected Ignore Background. This option hides the display of background items for the current page. If that option is selected, click it again to deselect it.

Printing

Parts of my page are cut off when I print.

The document may be too large to fit in your printer's memory, or you may have created a document that extends beyond your printer's print margins. Try resizing the page or removing one or two complex pictures to lessen the demand for your printer's memory. As a print test, you can cover the entire page with a shaded frame to see where the print margin for your particular printer is found.

I don't see a choice for changing from portrait to landscape orientation in my Print options box.

Your type of printer is not capable of printing publications in landscape mode. All the documents you print will be in portrait mode.

I don't have any pictures in my publication, and my document still won't print.

Frustrating as it may be, you still may be facing a problem with your printer's memory. Do you have any WordArt items in your publication? If so, try removing these and printing the document without them. Be sure to make a backup copy of your document first.

I want to be able to use all of Publisher's special features, but the amount of memory in my printer limits what I can do.

With the increasing technology and lowering costs of laser printers, you probably can find a memory upgrade package for your type of laser printer. Call your printer dealer or consult popular computer magazines for current information on memory upgrades.

PageWizards and Templates

When I started typing text in the publication I created with a PageWizard, the text acted strange.

There may be preset text settings that you don't know about. Check out the text settings row. What alignment has been chosen? How's the text wrap feature look? Find out what settings are entered in Indents and Lists and Line Spacing (in the Forma**t** menu).

The text in my template is scrunched.

Highlight the text and change the font and/or the size. Some fonts—Gradl, for instance—look right only in a larger size. Also, whenever possible, make sure that you use TrueType fonts and not printer fonts (TrueType fonts have a small TT symbol beside the font name).

Chapter 15

Publication Ideas

Example 1: Business Card

This card was created by using the Business Card and Stationery PageWizard. The style is Classic, with initials used in place of an artistic logo.

The initials for the logo are created in WordArt.

Standard text frames are used for the card text.

RescueVP

295 Eggroll Lane
Columbus, IN 47201

RVP

George Snider

Ape Trainer

phone (812) 333-3333

Three different line thicknesses are used for the rules.

The smallest items are set in 8-point type.

This chapter features some sample publications with descriptions of their unique features. Samples include:

- Business card and stationery
- Calendar
- Flyer
- Newsletter
- Invoice
- Coupons
- Book table of contents

Example 2: The Business Stationery

The sample letterhead was also created by using the Business Card and Stationery PageWizard. The letterhead complements the business card, providing all the same information except employee name and job description.

Tip
Press Shift when drawing the lines to keep them straight.

Tip

To center the phone number perfectly, create a text box the width of the page margins, highlight the text, and choose Center alignment.

Example 3: The Calendar

The Calendar PageWizard was used to create this calendar. You can choose from a yearly or monthly calendar, in a variety of styles.

Tip

Add special arrows or shapes to highlight important days.

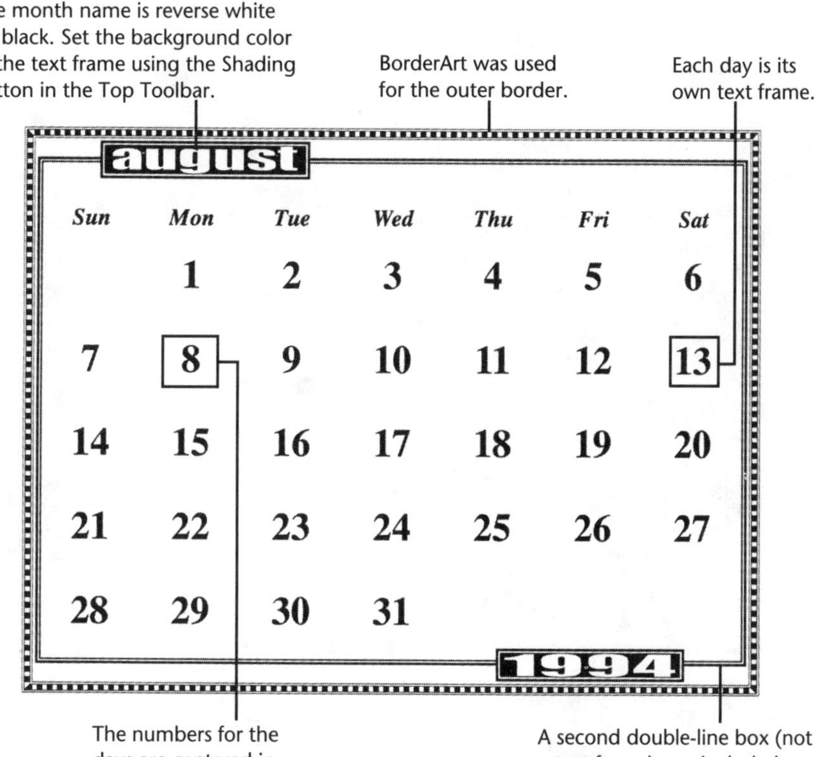

Tip
Don't add too much text to a flyer. The flyer is meant to communicate your company's name and message in as few words as possible.

Example 4: The Flyer

This flyer was created by using a PageWizard. The Modern style was selected for the small amount of text, WordArt was used to create the vertical banner, and the shaded rectangle on the left side of the page adds a special effect.

Example 5: Newsletter, Page 1

This is the first page of an off-the-wall newsletter. Several different fonts and design elements are used.

Tip

Remember to pay attention to your audience. A straight-laced corporate newsletter wouldn't fit this style, obviously. Before you take a chance on a design, run it past a few friends and coworkers.

Graphics elements are placed on the background page and show through.

The background shape is created by resizing a corner shape (selected from the AutoShapes palette).

In these trying times of separation and bigotry, it's important to pull in our claws and extended a helping paw when a fellow human asks for our sage advice. For that reason, our feature article this month is based on a recent letter from a man in Redmond, Washington:

"My neighbor's cat hates me. I'm not what I've done to cause this. When I come n the morning, still bleary-eyed from lack of ɔ and stained on both shoulders with baby- I find him glaring from the tree that hangs the drive. His eyes gleam red, even in soft morning light. His ears lay back flat nst his head in a dead giveaway of fierce ed.

I slink down slowy into the seat of the MG (boy that leather is cold in the morning!) so that I don't startle him with any sudden moves. When I get the engine started—usually on the third try—his hiss is so deafening I can hear it over the tinny putt-putt of the MG's motor. As I back the car out of the drive, he clutches that tree limb with his three good legs and yowls at me fiercely.

I don't know what he's so upset about.

Things Worth Meowing About in This Issue...	
Catnip Scare	1
Are Those Claws REALLY Gone?	2
Cat of the Month	2
Mister Yowzer Meets BigFoot	3
New Lemon Scented Kitty Litter	4
Ask Tom: Why Do Males Cat Around?	5
Ask Fluffy: Why Are Females So Feline?	6
Seven Claw-Sharpening Exercises	7
A Final Note: PawPrints	8

Background shading continues shape started above.

Next Month: The Trouble with Kittens : Don't Miss It!

BorderArt is used for a funky effect.

Top Ten Cat Complaints

- Food's Late.
- Water's Late.
- Where's My Tuna?
- Tender Vittles AGAIN?
- I'm Sleeping.
- You Smell Funny.
- Where's That Mouse?
- You Bug Me.

The Indents and List box was used to create this bulleted list.

Example 6: Newsletter, Page 2

The second page of the newsletter isn't much tamer. For this one, three predominant elements were used: a table, WordArt, and clipart.

The table tool was used to create this simple table.

The pull-quote is a regular text box oversized, shaded, and italicized.

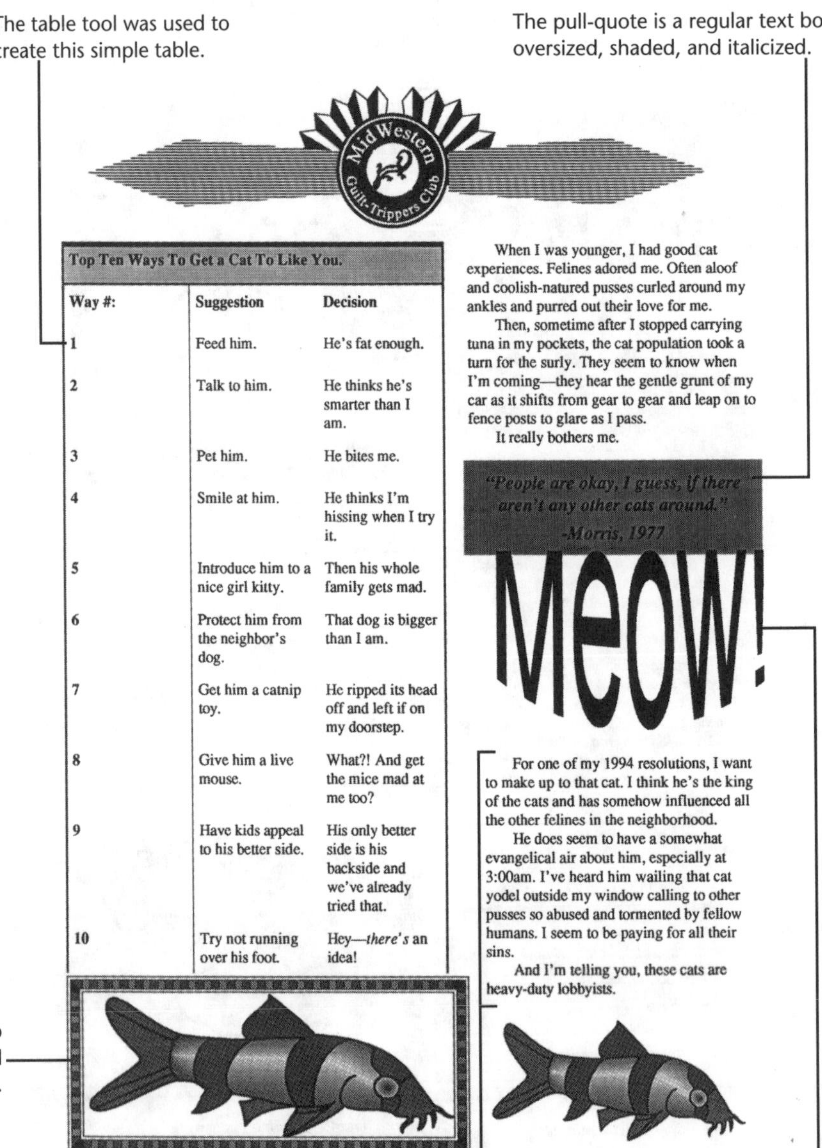

Top Ten Ways To Get a Cat To Like You.		
Way #:	**Suggestion**	**Decision**
1	Feed him.	He's fat enough.
2	Talk to him.	He thinks he's smarter than I am.
3	Pet him.	He bites me.
4	Smile at him.	He thinks I'm hissing when I try it.
5	Introduce him to a nice girl kitty.	Then his whole family gets mad.
6	Protect him from the neighbor's dog.	That dog is bigger than I am.
7	Get him a catnip toy.	He ripped its head off and left it on my doorstep.
8	Give him a live mouse.	What?! And get the mice mad at me too?
9	Have kids appeal to his better side.	His only better side is his backside and we've already tried that.
10	Try not running over his foot.	Hey—*there's* an idea!

When I was younger, I had good cat experiences. Felines adored me. Often aloof and coolish-natured pusses curled around my ankles and purred out their love for me.

Then, sometime after I stopped carrying tuna in my pockets, the cat population took a turn for the surly. They seem to know when I'm coming—they hear the gentle grunt of my car as it shifts from gear to gear and leap on to fence posts to glare as I pass.

It really bothers me.

"People are okay, I guess, if there aren't any other cats around."
-Morris, 1977

Meow!

For one of my 1994 resolutions, I want to make up to that cat. I think he's the king of the cats and has somehow influenced all the other felines in the neighborhood.

He does seem to have a somewhat evangelical air about him, especially at 3:00am. I've heard him wailing that cat yodel outside my window calling to other pusses so abused and tormented by fellow humans. I seem to be paying for all their sins.

And I'm telling you, these cats are heavy-duty lobbyists.

The same piece of clip art was used and resized for a different effect.

Text indent is set with Indents and Lists (in the Format menu).

The WordArt uses a special shape for effect.

Example 7: Newsletter, Page 3

The third page gets even a little wilder. Here is some experimentation with graphics and WordArt effects.

Tip
Don't be afraid to vary column widths. This page started out with a single text box and the rest of the elements were added around it.

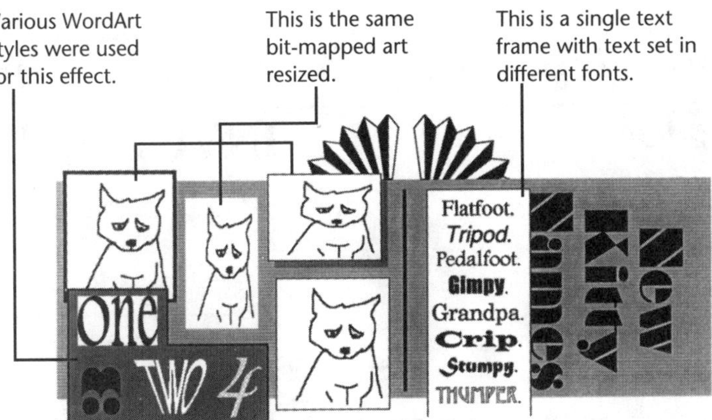

My neighbor's cat hates me. I'm not sure what I've done to cause this. When I come out in the morning, still bleary-eyed from lack of sleep and stained on both shoulders with baby-spit, I find him glaring from the tree that overhangs the drive. His eyes gleam red, even in the soft morning light. His ears lay back flat against his head in a dead giveaway of fierce hatred.
I slink down slowly into the seat of the MG (boy that leather is cold in the morning!) so that I don't startle him with any sudden moves. When I get the engine started—usually on the third try—his hiss is so deafening I can hear it over the tinny putt-putt of the MG's motor. As I back the car out of the drive, he clutches that tree limb with his three good legs and yowls at me fiercely. I don't know what he's so upset about.
I paid his vet bills a long time ago.

Solution Number	Solution	Decision
1	Give him kitty biscuits.	He'd probably take my fingers, too.
2	Take him to a kitty psychiatrist	I can't even afford my own psychiatrist, and I'm going to take my neighbor's cat?
3	Move	Well, I am kind of tired of sub-zero weather. Do they have cats in Kauai?

Possible Cat Beefs

Reason Number	Rationale	Resolution
1	I don't feed him.	Nah. His owners do.
2	I don't pet him.	Nope. He'd scratch my eyes out.
3	I ran over his foot.	Well, maybe. But cats don't *remember* things, do they?

I'm Sorry, Kitty

Here, Kitty, Kitty
Have a mousie on me
I smashed your fourth footsie
So now you have three.

The mouse is a piece of art drawn in Paintbrush and imported into Publisher.

Tip
Don't include more than you need on an invoice form. Just enough to be useful, thank you.

Example 8: Invoice

The Invoice was created as a result of the Business Forms PageWizard. You specify the column names and Publisher does the rest.

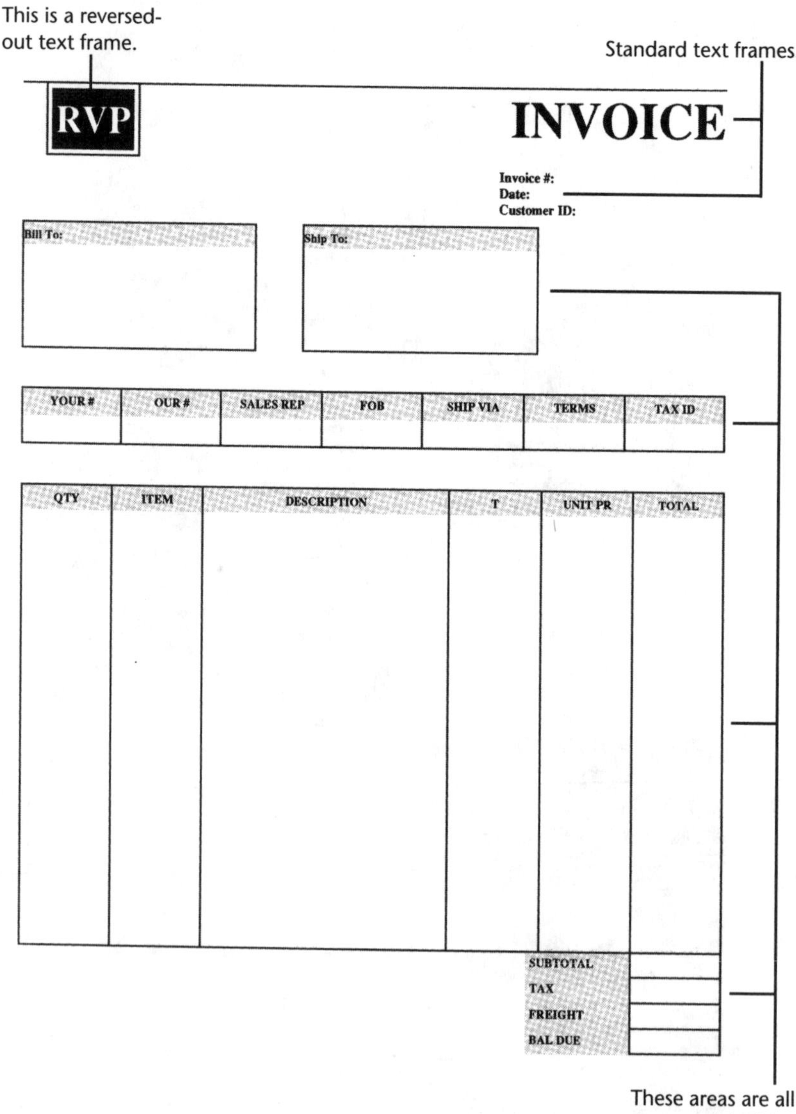

Example 9: Coupons

The coupons are based on a template file available in Publisher. The coupons are really the same small layout copied four times.

Tip
Make sure that you group all the elements in a coupon together before you try to copy it. You don't want to leave anything behind.

The publication is created in landscape mode.

The title is a standard text frame with white text.

The imported image is the one created in Paintbrush.

Small Capitals are used as the text style to call attention to the information.

Appendix A

Installing Microsoft Publisher

This appendix shows you how to install your version of Microsoft Publisher. The process is simple. Just follow these steps:

1. Turn on your computer.
2. When the DOS prompt (C:\ or D:\) appears, type **win**.
3. Press Enter. Microsoft Windows starts. Depending on how you left Windows the last time you ended a work session, the Program Manager window may open automatically. If the Program Manager appears as an icon, double-click the icon to open the window (see fig. A.1).

Fig. A.1
The Program Manager icon.

4. Insert the Publisher Setup disk into your disk drive. (You can use drive A or B, depending on the size of disks you use and the type of disk drives you have.)
5. When the Program Manager window appears on-screen, open the **F**ile menu.

6. Move the pointer to the **R**un command and click the mouse button (see fig. A.2). (You also can choose the command by pressing R, if you prefer.)

7. When the Run dialog box appears, as shown in figure A.3, type **a:setup** (if you're using drive A) or **b:setup** (if you're using drive B) and click OK. Windows then begins the Publisher installation program.

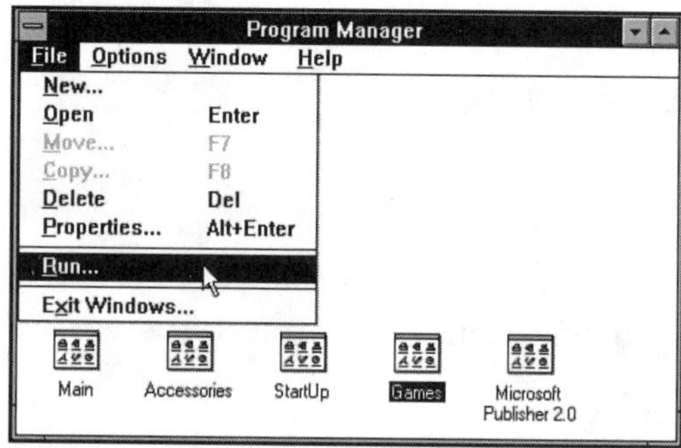

Fig. A.2
Selecting the Run command.

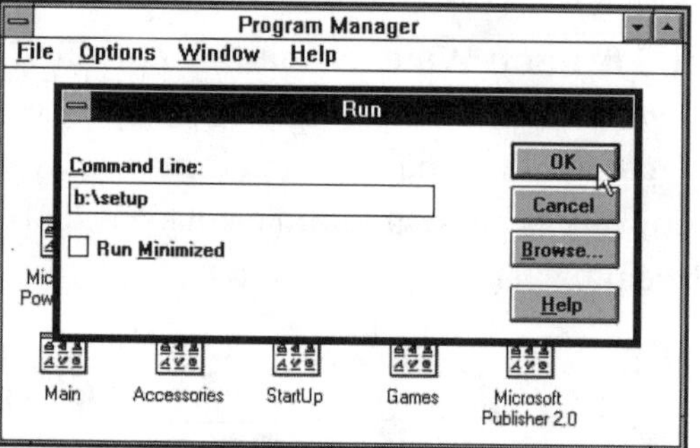

Fig. A.3
Beginning installation with the Run command.

8. When the Microsoft Publisher Setup Welcome screen appears, click the Continue button to begin installation. A pop-up dialog box tells you that Publisher will install the files to the C:\MSPUB directory by default. If you want to change that, click in the box and type a new directory for the program.

9. When the Microsoft Publisher Setup screen appears, you can choose whether you want to install Publisher in its entirety—with all clip art, template, and BorderArt files—or whether you want to select a custom installation (see fig. A.4). You can also choose a Minimum Installation, which installs only the basic files needed to run Publisher.

10. Click on the **C**omplete Installation button. The program begins copying files from the disk in drive A (or B) to your hard disk.

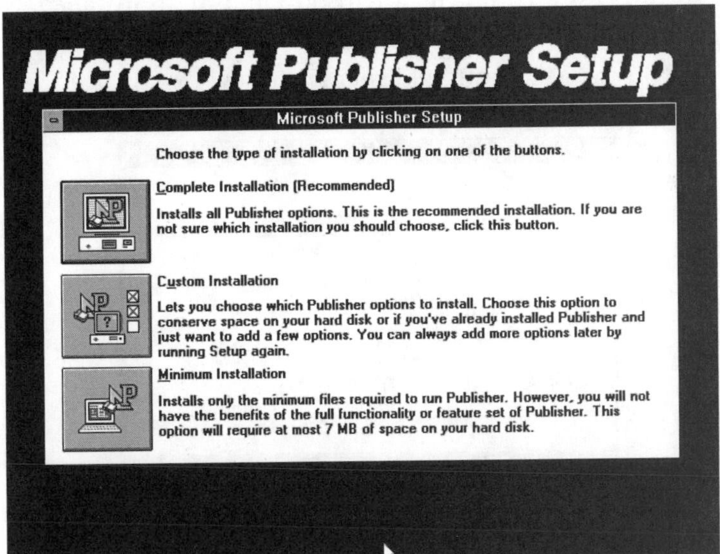

Fig. A.4
The Microsoft Publisher Setup screen.

While the installation program copies Publisher files to your hard disk, on-screen you see a small window informing you of the copy's progress; when the program is finished copying one disk, you are prompted to remove that disk and insert another. Because you have several minutes to wait while the installation process is going on, you may want to take the opportunity to fill out your registration card so that you'll be eligible for further program updates.

Note

You can use customized installation to conserve storage space on your computer by installing only the items you want to use with Publisher. Additionally, if you want to change the way you've previously installed Publisher (for example, you may have omitted the template files when you installed the program, but now you may want to add them), you can use a customized installation rather than installing the entire program again.

When the process is complete, Microsoft Publisher is installed. Now you can start the program by double-clicking on the Microsoft Publisher icon in the Microsoft Publisher 2 window (see fig. A.5).

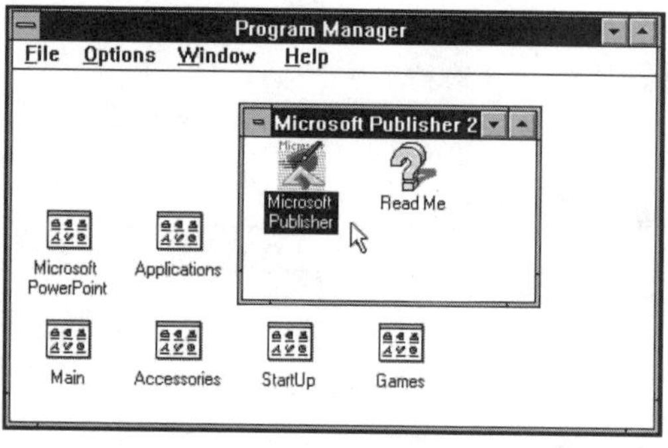

Fig. A.5
Starting Microsoft Publisher.

Glossary

Alignment. The positioning of text within a column or on a page. In Publisher, you can choose the alignment of text by clicking on an Alignment button in the Top Toolbar when the Text tool is selected, or by using the **I**ndents and Lists command in the Forma**t** menu.

ASCII. An acronym for American Standard Code for Information Interchange. This is the "common denominator" form of saving data. Most word processing programs have the capacity to save data in ASCII format, which is without formatting or font specifications of any kind. Publisher can then import the ASCII files.

Background page. Publisher provides you with a background page on which you can place items that you want to appear on every page, such as page numbers, a company logo, or the publication name.

Bad break. When a word fragment or section of a sentence is wrapped to the next line or column, giving the publication an unbalanced look.

Banner. Also called the *masthead.* It is the title of a publication.

Bit-mapped. A character or picture created from a series of dots.

Bleed. The phrase *bleed off the page* refers to a graphic element, such as a rule or box, that continues off the edge of the page.

Body text. The text of the publication that is entered in text frames.

Boot. The process of turning on the computer's power.

BorderArt. A special feature of Publisher that gives you over 100 different designer borders to work with.

Box tool. The drawing tool in the Left Toolbar used to draw boxes.

Bullets. Dots or other characters used to set off items in a list.

Callout. Text used to highlight an element in a figure or in a shadow box to summarize concepts.

Caption. The line of text used to explain a photo or figure.

Clipboard. A storage area in Publisher that stores the text block, picture, or frame most recently cut or copied.

Cold boot. Turning on the computer to initiate the startup procedure.

Column guides. The dotted lines on your Publisher screen that show you where the columns are in your publication.

Crop marks. Lines along the borders of the publication used to align and cut the pages when the document is professionally printed.

Cue Cards. Pop-up on-screen help items that allow you to read through the steps of common procedures.

Cursor. The flashing bar in a text frame where characters are inserted when you begin typing.

Default. A setting or option preset, unless you choose otherwise. The default setting for the number of columns in your Publisher document is 1, for example, until you change that setting by using the Layout Guides command in the Layout menu, a PageWizard, or a template.

Desktop publishing. A computerized method of publishing printed materials.

Dialog box. A pop-up box that provides you with additional options for your current operation.

Directory. An area on the hard disk in which a specific group of files is stored.

Dot-matrix printer. A printer that creates characters and images in patterns of dots.

Downloadable fonts. Software fonts that Publisher sends to the printer at print time.

dpi. An acronym for *dots per inch,* which refers to the quality of screen display and printed output.

Drag. A word indicating that you press and hold the mouse button, move the mouse cursor to the point you want it, then release the button.

Draw-type pictures. Also known as *object-oriented graphics*. These types of pictures are created based on extensive programming instructions. The edges are clear and sharp and the graphics can be resized, cropped, and moved without any loss of quality.

Export. The process of saving a file in a file format usable by other applications.

First time help. A demonstration screen that appears the first time you try a new task. You can opt to go through the demo, or skip it and return to the publication.

Font. One complete set of characters in a specific typeface, size, and style. For example, Tms Rmn, 12-point bold is one font.

Footers. Lines of text that appear on the bottom of every page in the publication.

Frame. Publisher keeps text in text frames and pictures in picture frames. Before you can add text, you must create a frame to store it.

Grouping. The process of combining several elements—frames, clip art objects, whatever—into a single group that you can easily move, resize, or modify.

Gutter. The amount of white space between columns.

Handles. The small rectangles that appear on a selected frame. You use handles to move or resize frames.

Headers. Lines of text that appear at the top of every page of a publication.

Highlight. Selects text so that you can cut, copy, or otherwise modify it. Before performing operations on text, you must first highlight it.

Justified text. A text alignment setting that adds space between words so that the beginning and end of each line of text are aligned.

Kerning. The process of fitting letters together for the best appearance.

Kilobyte. 1,024 bytes. It is the standard unit of measure for computer memory.

Landscape orientation. The mode in which the printer produces output along the longer horizontal axis of a page.

Laser printer. A high-resolution printer that uses laser technology to produce print that rivals electronic typesetting equipment.

Layout. The process of putting all elements together to form a publication.

Layout guides. The nonprinting guides in your publication that show you where the columns and page margins are.

Leading. Pronounced *ledding,* this is the amount of white space between lines in a paragraph or blocks of text.

Left-justified text. A text-alignment setting in which the left ends of all text lines are aligned.

Logo. A company's symbol or graphic image that is used on stationery, cards, invoices, etc.

Margin. The amount of white space reserved along the borders of a publication in which text and graphics are not printed.

Masthead. Another word for *banner,* which refers to the name and publishing information usually located at the top of a newsletter.

Megabyte. Approximately one million bytes.

Menu bar. The bar across the top of the Publisher screen in which all the menu names are displayed.

Mini-save. Saving an existing file quickly by pressing Ctrl+S.

Monospace. A term used to describe a font in which each character is given an equal amount of space.

Mouse. A small peripheral device used in Publisher to point to and select menus, commands, options, tools, and draw graphic elements.

Mouse cursor. Also called the *mouse pointer.* This is the arrow-shaped pointer or the small I-beam shaped cursor that moves in accordance with the movement of the mouse. This cursor changes shape according to your operation; when you are moving a frame, for example, the pointer looks like a moving van.

Offset printing. High-quality professional printing done on a printing press.

On-line. The printer is ready to print.

PageWizards. The new page-generating utility included in Microsoft Publisher that assembles publications such as newsletters, calendars, brochures, flyers, business forms, and so on simply by asking you a few questions.

Path. The drive, directory, and subdirectory where Publisher can find or save the file you specify.

Pixel. The smallest element in a bit-mapped graphic: a dot. Every character and image in a bit-mapped graphic is composed of a pattern of pixels.

Point. A measurement of the size of a character, as in 12-point type.

Portrait orientation. The standard mode in which the printer produces output along the longer vertical axis of a page.

Pull-down menu. A menu you can display by using the mouse to "pull it down" or by pressing specified function keys.

Quick keys. Keys displayed in the menus of Publisher; they're an alternative to using pull-down menus to select the options.

RAM. An acronym for *random-access memory*; the memory where your computer stores active programs and open files.

Resolution. Used to refer to the quality (or lack of quality) in on-screen characters or in printed output.

Rule. Line used as a graphic element to enhance the page.

Ruler. The ruler bars across the top and left side of the work area, which help you align text and picture frames.

Sans serif. Type without the small cross-lines that appear on the ends of characters in a serif font.

Scanner. A peripheral device, similar to a photocopier, that digitizes images into an electronically usable form.

Scroll. The term used to describe the action of moving the screen display.

Scroll bar. The vertical bar on the right side of the screen area that has one arrow at each end and the scroll box in the center. You use this bar to scroll through Publisher files by clicking on the gray sections of the bar or the arrows.

Scroll box. The small gray box in the scroll bar that indicates your position on-screen.

Selection tool. The tool in the Left Toolbar used to select elements on-screen.

Serif. Type with small cross-lines across the ends of the characters.

Soft font. A font packaged on disk that is copied to the printer at print time.

Template. A publication skeleton on which you build the actual publication. Use templates to save time when you create similar publications or subsequent issues of a newsletter.

Text frame tool. The tool you use to create text frames in your publication.

Tools. The on-screen buttons you select to carry out various Publisher operations.

TrueType fonts. Fonts based on a new technology that allow you to create high-quality characters in both regular text and WordArt.

Warm boot. Restarting the computer by pressing the reset button or by pressing Ctrl+Alt+Del.

White space. The unused space on a publication that helps give the reader's eye a rest and draws attention to important elements.

Widow. A very short line at the end of a paragraph.

WordArt. The special feature in Publisher that enables you to treat words like art by bending, slanting, curving, or otherwise enhancing them. You can use WordArt in headlines, banners, fancy first letters in your articles, and much more.

Wordwrap. The process in which Publisher bumps words to the next line when the words you type pass the right end of the text margin.

WYSIWYG. An acronym for *what you see is what you get,* which is used to describe programs that show on-screen what you'll see when you print.

Index

Symbols

A

B

C

D

E

F

G

H

I

J–K

L

M

Q–R

S

U

V

W

X–Y–Z